ALSO BY MARK MATHABANE

Kaffir Boy

Kaffir Boy in America: An Encounter with Apartheid

African Women: Three Generations

Love in Black and White

Ubuntu

MIRIAM'S SONG

A Memoir

BY

Miriam Mathabane

AS TOLD TO

Mark Mathabane

SIMON & SCHUSTER
NEW YORK LONDON TORONTO SYDNEY SINGAPORE

SIMON & SCHUSTER
Rockefeller Center
1230 Avenue of the Americas
New York, NY 10020

Designed by Ruth Lee

Manufactured in the United States of America

1 3 5 7 9 10 8 6 4 2

Library of Congress Cataloging-in-Publication Data
Mathabane, Miriam, date.
Miriam's song : a memoir / Miriam Mathabane as told to Mark Mathabane.
p. cm.
1. Mathabane, Miriam, date. 2. Blacks—South Africa—Alexandria—Biography. 3. Apartheid—South Africa—Alexandria. 4. Alexandria (South Africa)—Biography. I. Mathabane, Mark. II. Title.
DT2405.A44 M38 2000
968.75'3—dc21
[B] 00-026552

ISBN 0-684-83303-4

Some names have been changed to protect people's privacy.

Half title page photograph courtesy of the Mathabane family.

Acknowledgments

Miriam's Song is the result of the contributions of many wonderful people. First on the list is my sister Miriam. I would like to thank her for her capacious heart, generosity of spirit, courage, and faith in entrusting me with her life story. I hope I've done it justice.

Second, many thanks to my mother and my siblings, Linah, Diana, Florah, and George, for helping Miriam sharpen and personalize memories of her amazing life and of Alexandra, our hometown.

Third, *Miriam's Song* wouldn't have been possible without the love, understanding, and support of my wife, Gail, and our children, Bianca, Nathan, and Stanley.

Fourth, I'd like to thank Jennifer Parker for her inimitable photographs of my family and her deep love of South Africans and their unique culture.

To Dominick Anfuso, my editor, his assistant, Catherine Hurst, and all those at Simon & Schuster who worked on *Miriam's Song,* many thanks. Dominick, you believed in the story and championed it with love. I'd also like to thank my agents, Kevin McShane and Fifi Oscard, for the many years of professional service and first-class friendship.

Miriam's Song is dedicated to my friends and Comrades who came of age during the 1980s. Many died and many were detained and tortured while fighting for a better education system and for the right to be free in the land of their birth. The following song, I believe, captures the defiant spirit of this generation, whose fearlessness and sacrifices finally brought apartheid to its knees. We sang it mostly during protest marches and at night vigils. It is sung a cappella and each line is repeated four times.

Senzeni Na
What have we done
Sibozwa nje?
to be so oppressed?
Sono zethu ubu myama?
Are our crimes / sins that heinous?
Amabunu a yi zinja.
White policemen are dogs / unfeeling.
Vophu mthwala sigoduke.
Let's bear the burden of this life; we haven't far to go.

Glossary

aauww sham—how sad
amabunu—white policemen; Boers
amandla . . . ngawethu—power . . . belongs to the people
asinamali—we have no money
azikwela—we will not ride
bula—open up
bulala i nja—kill the dog
buphaki—search for lost souls
buti—brother
ditutwanes—water spirits
doek—head scarf
domba—python dance
donder—whip
donga—gully
double-up—shortcut
drop—a venereal disease
geezer—heater
hebelungu—subsidized lunch
hlasale—invasion
impimpi—informer
impis—bands of Zulu warriors
induna—chief
kaya—home
keities—slingshots
khade hafa—come here

khomba—rites-of-passage ceremony; initiated adolescent girls
kokwana—granny
kombi—minivan
kopi—a game played with three dice
ku twasa—initiation ceremony
kudyondisa vana ku ri va tiva dyondo—teaching children to value knowledge
kwela-kwela—climb-climb police truck
legwala—coward
lobola—dowry
machondo na tinhloko ta huku—cooked heads and feet of chickens
magabulela—hand-me-downs
magundwana—bald head with tufts of hair
magwinya—pudgy like a cookie
makhulu—huge
makondlo—mice
makoti—daughter-in-law
mampharacement—cement blocks
manana—mother
manchomani—singing, dancing, and drum playing
marhaku—ass
marhama—the one with fat cheeks
marhode—giant rats
marimila—mucus
marumbu—cooked chicken intestines
mbawula—brazier
mdoho—soft porridge
mealie—Indian corn
mgusha—high-jump game
midzimu—ancestors; ancestral spirits
mikwenkwes—calluses
mma mfundisi—the preacher's wife
msokobuns—sponge cakes
mucheka—traditional dress
murogo—greens
musadi—woman
mutale—type of drum
muti—bewitching potion; traditional medicine
mutlavi-tlavi—cacti
mutswala—blood brother
ndi ya livuha—thank you
ntate—old man

nyanga—one who communicates with midzimu
oompie—uncle
phahla . . . biya tiyindlu—exorcise evil spirits from homes
qha—zero
rondavel—thatch-and-cow-dung house
sangoma—diviner
sesi—sister
shebeen—speakeasy
sishimanyi—spinster
sjambok—rawhide whip
skeberesh—whore
skorop—piece job
skwiza—sister-in-law
sonjas—prickly worms
spazza—lean-to store
stands—property
stoep—stoop
swikwembu—ancestral spirits
tapeit—shiny linoleum
tatana—father
tickie—two and a half cents
tikhomba—rites-of-passage ceremony; initiated adolescent girls
tinguvu—Shangaan traditional dresses
tinjiya—grasshoppers
toyi-toyi—Comrades' dance
tsotsi—gangster
twasa—undergo an initiation ceremony
vetkoekies—fat cakes
vleis—meat
vootsek—go away
vuhlava—colorful beads and necklaces
vulongo—cow dung
vuswa—cornmeal porridge
waslap—facecloth
xithebe—reed mat
xivitanelo—dictation

Preface

When I was growing up in Alexandra, an overcrowded black ghetto about thirteen kilometers north of Johannesburg, I often heard the name of Dr. Hendrik Verwoerd. It was one of the most hated names.

I often wondered why. All I could glean was that Dr. Verwoerd was a white man who had something to do with the dismal state of black education. At the government-controlled tribal schools, we were taught nothing about what Dr. Verwoerd had done. Our government-written history books only described him as an important Afrikaner prime minister who was stabbed to death on September 6, 1966, by Dimitrio Tsafendas, a deranged parliamentary messenger. It was not until my brother Mark (known as Johannes in this book) brought me to America, in 1993, to pursue my childhood dream of becoming a nurse that I finally learned more about Dr. Verwoerd.

He thoroughly deserved to be hated. An avowed white supremacist and segregationist, Dr. Verwoerd had emigrated from Holland with his parents in 1903. Turning down a scholarship to Oxford, he studied psychology in Germany when Nazism was on the rise. Upon his return to South Africa, he quickly established himself as the intellectual force behind apartheid, South Africa's system of legalized segregation and oppression. To insure that whites, who made up only 14 percent of the population, continued to dominate blacks, who made up 74 percent, Dr. Verwoerd, as head of the Department of Native Affairs, created one of the cornerstones of apartheid: Bantu Education. More than anything else, Bantu (black) Education wreaked incalculable damage on generations of black children in order to ensure their servitude.

I can only weep at the lives and human potential Bantu Education wasted, and I marvel at how I survived its insidious poison. It wasn't easy. Upon arriving in America I found that despite having matriculated from high school after nearly eighteen years of hard work and sacrifices, I didn't know material that American eighth-graders had mastered. Under Bantu Education the government determined what subjects black children should be taught. I knew a lot about domestic science, sewing, and gardening but I knew next to nothing about world history, biology, political systems, sociology, or psychology. For instance, until I came to America I had never heard of Hitler, the Holocaust, or American slavery.

I was already twenty-three. The thought of attending class with fifteen- and sixteen-year-olds, many of whom took education for granted, was hard to swallow at first, particularly because I was already the mother of a six-year-old son. I tried taking adult education classes, but I soon realized that it would take me forever to earn a high school diploma, unless I attended school full time.

Mark and his wife, Gail, pointed out that given my desire to learn, ability to work hard, and determination to succeed, I could get a diploma in two years, despite all that I had to make up. With trepidation I took their advice. In the fall of 1993 I entered eleventh grade at East Forsyth High School in Winston-Salem, North Carolina. It was tough going back to high school. I hid the fact that I was almost twenty-four years old and a single mother. I feared that I'd be ridiculed or, worse, kicked out of school for being too old.

At first I couldn't understand the lessons. Teachers spoke English with strange accents and much of what they taught presupposed prior knowledge I didn't possess. Some students thought me weird for taking education so seriously and shunning things like parties and football games. I wished they knew the hell I'd had to endure in order to get an education. Many times I felt like quitting, convinced that I could never undo the damage done to my mind by Bantu Education.

But I persevered—in part because I'm not a quitter, and in part because I had a great deal of encouragement from Mark and Gail and from supportive teachers impressed by my thirst for learning. Among them was the late Mrs. Magdalene Watson, my English teacher. Mrs. Watson, who shared my mother's first name, taught me more than just how to communicate effectively and how to appreciate literature. As a black woman she became a powerful role model. She constantly urged me to work hard, to aim higher, and not to let my past handicap me. I graduated from East Forsyth with honors in 1995, the proudest day of my life. Shortly thereafter I received a nursing assistant degree from Forsyth Technical Community College. I'm now studying to be a registered nurse. I have acquired a new lease on life.

But for all my modest successes, I often think of how my life and the lives of the millions of black children in South Africa would have turned out had Dr. Verwoerd not taken over black education in 1954. Would our schools have been as well funded and progressive as most American schools? Would all those talented, determined, and hardworking students who dropped out of school because their parents couldn't afford the money to keep them there have achieved great things? Would all those thousands of black students who died fighting for a better education system still be alive?

How would they have contributed to South Africa? And if, under apartheid, black children had had the same educational opportunities as white children, would there be less crime, fewer murderers, carjackers, and rapists in the new South Africa, and more teachers, lawyers, writers, and nurses?

The answers to these questions may never be known, but one thing is sure: Bantu Education was nothing more than slave education. Its aim was to make blacks subservient to white people and to teach them to accept their inferior place in a South Africa ruled by apartheid. And Dr. Verwoerd minced no words about this being his ultimate goal. In a speech before Parliament in 1953 explaining the necessity of Bantu Education, he said:

> When I have control of native education, I will reform it so that natives will be taught from childhood to realize that equality with Europeans is not for them. There is no place for him [the black child] in European society above

> the level of certain forms of labour. . . . What is the use of teaching a Bantu child mathematics when it cannot use it in practice? . . . Education must train and teach people in accordance with their opportunities in life. . . . It is therefore necessary that native education should be controlled in such a way that it should be in accordance with the policy of the state.

That policy was apartheid. After Dr. Verwoerd took over black education, the number of black teachers dropped, from 8,817 in 1954 to 5,908 in 1961—in part because the government had now assumed the responsibility for training black teachers, and had reduced their pay. This led to such a chronic shortage of teachers that the 1953 pupil-teacher ratio in black schools, forty to one, by 1960 had risen to fifty to one. By the time I entered Sub–Standard A (kindergarten), in January of 1975, it was common for already overworked teachers in the lower primary classes to teach two sessions of over one hundred pupils each. It was estimated that half of black children between the ages of six and nineteen were not in school, that only one in fifty teachers had a university education, and that only one in nine teachers had completed matric (high school).

Before Bantu Education, church and mission schools, funded mainly by the provincial government, strived, despite the educational inequalities, to prepare generations of blacks for productive lives. They had produced teachers, doctors, lawyers, and political leaders such as Nelson Mandela. Taking over black education, the government accused church and mission schools of "destroying black culture" and creating "imitation Westerners" by teaching blacks mathematics, English, and the sciences.

After black schools came under Dr. Verwoerd's control, they began emphasizing tribalism, obedience to authority, and rigid discipline. The government decided how many black schools there could be, where they should be located, and who should attend them. Most insidious, the government determined what black children should be taught and at what rate. Bovet, the school in Alexandra that I attended from Sub-A to Standard Five, also came under government control. Before, it had been a mission school, founded by Swiss missionaries. Under Bantu Education, it began emphasizing tribalism and furthering the aims of apartheid—to divide blacks. For instance, only children who spoke Shangaan as their mother tongue and who lived in Alexandra could attend the school. My mother was Shangaan and I was born in Alexandra on December 18, 1969, so I was granted a permit to attend Bovet.

By the time I started school, shortly after I turned five, Bantu Education was firmly entrenched. Black schools had effectively been turned into indoctrination centers and penal colonies. Sadly, many teachers, anxious to keep their jobs, had become Bantu Education's unwitting and often brutal instruments. Our syllabus, which was designed by the government, emphasized discipline and punishment rather than understanding and nurturing. So teachers punished us daily, for wearing the wrong uniform, not doing our homework, doing it and getting it wrong, not paying our school fees on time, arriving late for assembly, returning late from lunch, making noise in the classroom, or failing the cleanliness inspection. For as long as I live, I shall never forget the pure terror I felt during cleanliness inspection . . .

MIRIAM'S SONG

Chapter 1

It is toward the end of January, the middle of summer in South Africa. It's very hot and stuffy inside the small classroom, which has few windows and no air-conditioning, and is packed with over one hundred six- and seven-year-olds. Many are bawling and sniffling after being whipped. Others are screaming and want to go home to their mothers. Still others are chanting at the top of their small lungs a song about fingernails.

My heart is thumping against my ribs and my tongue is stuck to the roof of my dry mouth. Tears prick the corners of my bulging eyes as I stare at my Sub-A instructor. She's a tall, lean woman with a harried look on her dark face. We are required to address her as Mistress. Male instructors are addressed as Teacher. The mistress is wielding a thick ruler and giving us a tongue-lashing about the importance of trimming our fingernails. It's about eight-thirty. We've just entered the classroom following morning assembly.

I long to flee the classroom, but my bare feet are stuck to the corner where I'm cowering with my friends—Cynthia, Janice, Margaret, Becky, and Dlayani. They too are terrified. Everyone in the classroom is terrified of the mistress when she's armed with the thick ruler. There's a larger group of pupils cowering in the opposite corner. We are like cattle afraid of being branded.

I anxiously watch the mistress when she barks each frightened pupil's name, and that pupil has to come forward and have his or her fingernails inspected to see if they are too long or have any dirt under them.

I pray that the mistress not call my name. Mama forgot to borrow a fingernail clipper from our neighbor last night to trim my long and dirty fingernails because she and Papa were fighting again, over money. Watching the mistress I can already feel the pain felt by the pupils I hear howling and shrieking about me, as in a madhouse, after being whipped.

After nearly half an hour the mistress finally calls my name. I'm one of the handful of pupils left to be inspected. I start to cry.

"Stop crying!" she barks. "Let me see your fingernails."

I gingerly step forward. I never take my eyes off the thick ruler in the mistress's right hand. I stop about two feet from the mistress and thrust my small hands tentatively forward. My fingers are bunched together with the fingertips facing up. I'm trembling in anticipation of the sting of the thick ruler. The mistress stoops, takes one look at my fingernails, and says sternly, "They're long and dirty. Now stop whining and sing the song."

I sing-sob the fingernails song. The mistress slowly raises the thick ruler—which seems the size of a club—high up in the air and prepares to rap my fingertips.

Nitsema minwala yikoma.
I should trim my fingernails short.
Anitwi.
I didn't listen.

Before I even finish singing "I didn't listen," the mistress whacks my fingertips hard with the edge of the thick ruler. I howl with pain. I wish Mama would come and take me away from this horrible place called school. I wish she'd come and explain to the mistress that it's not my fault that she and Papa fought and that he drove her away from the house before she could borrow the nail clipper from the neighbor to trim my fingernails.

"Didn't I tell you last week to trim your fingernails?" the mistress says sternly.

"You did, Mistress," I sob. *Marimila,* mucus, streams down my flaring nostrils and mingles with the warm tears. I'm recovering from a cold. Without a handkerchief, I use my long shirtsleeve to wipe the tears and mucus.

The mistress is furious and whacks me, on the forehead. This time the blow raises a welt and I cry even harder.

"Your shirtsleeve is not a handkerchief!" she bellows. "Where's your handkerchief?"

"I don't have one, Mistress."

Tears are soaking my raggedy black gym dress. I wish the mistress would understand that Mama can't afford to buy me a handkerchief, just as she can't afford to buy me a uniform and primers and pay my school fees on time. Papa says his hard-earned money shouldn't be wasted on school things when it's needed to keep us alive.

I wish Mama had remembered to rip a piece from her old dress as she'd promised and made me a handkerchief. But she forgot because she and Papa fought and she had to flee to Granny's place. I wish I could tell the mistress this but I don't. I'm ashamed to tell people that my parents are always fighting.

The mistress barks Cynthia's name. Cynthia is already crying as she approaches the mistress. She gets whacked for having long, dirty fingernails. Dlayani, whose Shangaan name means "Kill me," is lucky; her fingernails are neatly trimmed. So are Janice's and Becky's.

Next the mistress inspects our hair to see if it's clean and neatly combed. A lot of children have lice and dandruff. For the hair inspection the class sings the hair song:

Hikama misisi,
We should comb our hair,
Yisaseka.
so it can look beautiful.
Ahitwi.
We didn't listen.

Fortunately my nappy hair is washed and neatly combed. I escape the dual punishment of being whacked on the head with the thick ruler and then having my hair combed by the mistress, using a steel comb, which feels as though your hair is being plucked by the roots.

It is evening. I'm sitting on the kitchen floor in front of a cozy fire from a red-hot *mbawula,* a brazier, watching Mama cook dinner. I have no toys to play with, so I often watch Mama do chores. Our house, which overlooks a *donga* (gully) and a dusty street called Hofmeyer, is in yard number 47 on Thirteenth Avenue. It has two small rooms, three small windows with several broken panes, and no running water, electricity, or indoor toilet.

At night the kitchen is used as a bedroom, and I and my three sisters and two brothers sleep there. My brothers sleep on a single bed in one corner, and my sisters and I sleep on pieces of cardboard on the bare cement floor.

"Miriam," Mama turns to me and says, "take this food to your father."

She hands me a big plate to give to Papa, who is sitting impatiently at the kitchen table. As head of the household Papa gets served first, and during meals he sits alone at the table. Mama and we children sit on the bare cement floor. As I set the plate heaped with *vuswa,* our staple of porridge made from ground cornmeal, and *marumbu,* cooked chicken intestines, Papa looks at me. Something catches his eye.

"Khade hafa"—come here—he says in Venda. There is gentleness in his usually authoritarian voice, which reassures me that I've done nothing wrong and will not be chastised.

I obey.

"Let me take a look at your forehead." I lower my head and he pulls the flickering candle closer.

"What happened?" he asks as his fingers gently feel the welt on my forehead. I wince.

"The mistress beat me at school," I say in a contrite voice.

"Beat you—what for?"

"For not trimming my fingernails."

Papa glares at Mama. "Didn't I tell you not to send my children to that bloody Shangaan school?" Papa bellows. "Look at what they've done to the poor child."

"There's no school for Vendas in Alexandra to send her to," Mama says, almost apologetically. She knows that Papa is opposed to our attending a school where the medium of instruction is Shangaan, my mother's language, and not Venda, his language.

"And what kind of school is it that punishes children for not trimming their fingernails?" Papa demands.

Mama doesn't answer. When I showed her the welt on my forehead and told her what had happened, she had tears in her eyes, even as she said, "Don't worry, child. As long as you're learning something it's worth it." There was nothing Mama could do, short of withdrawing me from school. Black schools had to abide by the strict discipline rules set by the Department of Bantu Education, and corporal punishment was high on the list of those rules.

But Papa doesn't care a damn about the rules. He turns to me and says, "Tomorrow I'll accompany you to school and teach that bloody mistress a lesson. I'll *donder* her"—whip her good.

Papa must have spoken impulsively, for Mama smiles and says, "You forget that tomorrow is Friday. You can't miss work or you'll be fired. And what good will beating up the mistress do if the children can't eat and we are evicted?"

Papa scowls. He digs deep into the right pocket of his faded trousers and fishes out a two-cent coin. "Here, buy yourself some sweets."

"Ndi ya livuha"—thank you—I say gratefully, curtsying.

Papa pats me on the back of the head and tells me that I'm a good girl. I know that part of the reason he's pleased is that I always speak Venda in his presence, unlike my older siblings, who often speak Shangaan.

As Linah, Diana, and I crowd around a common plate heaped with vuswa and another one with marumbu, eating with the right hand because it is taboo to use the left to eat, I'm already dreaming of what I'm going to do with my two cents. I'm going to buy *hebelungu,* a subsidized lunch offered to schoolchildren by the Catholic church. It consists of two slices of brown bread smeared with peanut butter, and a mug of skim (powdered) milk. Next to fish and chips, there's nothing I find more delicious. And with food scarce at home because Papa only makes ten rand a week as a menial laborer, it helps to have at least one filling meal a day.

Chapter 2

Johannes is my oldest brother and the firstborn of my six siblings. He's in Form I (ninth grade) after getting a first-class pass in Standard Six. Mama is very proud of Johannes's academic accomplishments. To show her pride she often gives him a *tickie* (two and a half cents) to buy the *World,* the daily black newspaper. This despite the fact that we often don't have enough money for food.

"I want your brother to be a teacher," Mama explains, "and teachers read newspapers every day."

Johannes reads aloud various stories, mostly about violence and sports, with little about politics, as Mama cooks dinner on the mbawula. I'm sprawled on the cement floor next to the fire, half listening as I finish my homework by candlelight.

"Finally TV is coming to South Africa," Johannes says importantly. Until 1976, the ruling National Party had outlawed television broadcasting in South Africa, on the grounds that it would corrupt public morals.

"What is TV?" Mama asks with all innocence.

Johannes rolls his eyes. "You don't know what TV is?"

"No. Don't forget I never went to school, so I can't read."

I prick my ears as Johannes explains to Mama what TV is. I find the explanation way above my head. All I catch is that this amazing thing called TV is very common in a faraway place called America, where Johannes's hero, Arthur Ashe, lives and where he plans to go someday to attend university and play tennis.

"Still dreaming about America, I see," Mama says.

"I'll get there," Johannes says. "And once I do I'll become as rich and famous as Arthur Ashe. Then I'll buy you a big house with electricity and running water so you can move out of this miserable, rat-infested shack. And you'll cook on a real stove instead of a mbawula. And at night you'll sit in a plush sofa in front of a big TV in the living room, watching me win Wimbledon."

Mama smiles. "I don't know what TV and Wimbledon are, but I sure would love to live in a big nice house with electricity and running water."

"You will," Johannes says, and returns to reading the paper.

"Can you please help me with my homework, *buti* Johannes?" I ask, using the respectful term for "brother."

"Sure. What do you need help on?"

"Arithmetic. I don't know how to add numbers. And we are having a test tomorrow. And if I fail, I'll be whipped."

Johannes teaches me not only how to add but how to subtract, divide, and multiply. I'm in awe of him, he knows so much. No wonder he's always coming out number one at school. And even though he's no longer attending Bovet, teachers and mistresses are still talking about how smart a student he was. It must be from reading all those newspapers and books. They are written in English, which I do not understand, even though I already know four other languages: Venda, Shangaan, Sotho, and Zulu. I'd like to learn how to read in English too, so I can be as smart as Johannes.

Papa doesn't approve of Johannes reading all those English books and newspapers. He says Johannes is trying to be white. He also doesn't like him playing tennis or attending Tembisa High School. He says that Johannes has had enough education and should look for work so he can support the family. In tribal tradition the first-born son is supposed to take care of his parents as a means of repaying them for raising him.

Papa and Johannes fight a lot over his love for reading and playing tennis. As a result Johannes spends a lot of time at the library or at the tennis courts at the stadium on Twelfth Avenue. He has three wooden Maxply tennis rackets—next to his English books, his most prized possessions. There is a rumor floating around the neighborhood that Johannes sometimes sneaks into the white world to play tennis with white people and that white people give him old tennis rackets, shoes, clothes, and books.

I'm stunned by this. No white person has ever given me anything. I'm afraid of white people. The only ones I know are the police, who regularly invade the neighborhood, arresting people without permits to live and work in Johannesburg. Whenever I see the police I run away as fast as I can. I'm afraid they'll beat me, or eat me or something. A lot of my friends are also afraid of white people. We've seen white policemen beat up black people, and at the movies they are always shooting each other.

"Why are white people bad, Mama?" I ask.

"Not all of them are bad."

"But the police are bad."

"True, but not all white people are policemen."

"Should I run away when I see the police?"

"Yes."

"Should I run away when I see white people?"

"Not always."

"When should I run away?"

"When they want to hurt you."

"The mistress today said that white people are coming to our school."

"Is that so. Why?"

"She says they are important inspectors. She says that we should be neatly dressed and behave ourselves during their visit. If we do, she says, the inspectors may give us more benches to sit on."

"That's nice."

"I hate sitting on the floor at school."

"Why?"

"It's too cold. Especially in winter."

"Well, behave yourself and the inspectors will give you more benches."

The white inspectors—who are all Afrikaners—visit our classroom. I'm afraid of them, as are many of my classmates, but the mistress has told us not to show our fear. The white inspectors smile and nod approvingly as they listen to us fervently recite the Lord's Prayer and sing our hearts out in the hope of impressing them to give us more benches, primers, and other school things.

They don't. But my disappointment fades when at the end of the year I get promoted to Sub-B after passing the final exam. I'm very happy. Other students fail the final exam, and according to Bantu Education rules, they can't be promoted to the next class. They have to repeat Sub-A. There are pupils who are ten years old and still attending Sub-A. A lot of them eventually drop out, in part because few parents can afford to keep using their hard-earned money to pay school fees and purchase uniforms and books for a child who keeps failing.

To my horror, there are more cleanliness inspections in Sub-B, which are almost always random. I soon learn that proper hygiene is an obsession at Bovet Community School.

"Cleanliness is next to godliness" is constantly drummed into our heads—we are told that the poverty in our homes and the squalor of Alexandra is no excuse for looking and smelling like pigs—especially because one never knows when white inspectors might come to assess our progress. If students at our school are found to be slovenly, it might be held against the school, and we might not receive enough money from the Department of Bantu Education to pay for an ever-growing list of school needs: benches, desks, textbooks, chalk, salaries for teachers and mistresses, and more classroom space.

One morning after assembly the Sub-B mistress—women, who are paid less than men, always teach the overcrowded madhouses of the lower primary—announces that we are going to have our bloomers (panties) inspected. All boys are ordered outside. We girls are lined in a row and ordered to raise our gym dresses. The mistress goes around the hall sniffing our bloomers. Mine are raggedy but clean. A lot of girls have bloomers that smell of urine; some have bloomers with traces of feces from improperly wiping with pieces of newspaper because few families can afford toilet paper; and some have no bloomers at all. They all get whacked with a cane.

The mistress delivers a stern lecture on the importance of wearing clean bloomers. She says that with so many pupils packed like sardines inside the small classroom, and with little ventilation, stinking bloomers poison the stuffy air and make breathing difficult. Sub-B is like an invalid ward. It's filled with pupils with hacking coughs, asthma, bronchitis, and tuberculosis. Respiratory diseases are rampant in the ghetto. There is no sewer system, and people are crowded together in shacks, breathing air contaminated with smog from mbawulas, trash fires, and coal stoves.

A record number of pupils are enrolled in Sub-B. There isn't enough room for everyone inside the hall. During *xivitanelo,* dictation, half the class take the dictation exam outside in the dusty courtyard because being crammed together makes it easy for pupils to copy from one another. And copying is severely punished.

I'm glad I'm not among those who have to take xivitanelo outside. The last time I did I failed because I got dizzy from squatting on my haunches in the hot sun while simultaneously trying to write on my slate and listen to the mistress shouting dictation from the top of the stairs, a distance of about forty feet. Her voice kept fading in and out as she turned around to keep an eye on the dozens of pupils scattered across the courtyard, many of whom were dozing from fatigue and hunger.

Those taking xivitanelo inside have to sit on the cold cement floor because not enough benches have been supplied by the Department of Bantu Education. But I'm happy. At least I'm out of the broiling sun.

After xivitanelo the mistress goes from pupil to pupil checking the answers. Using a white chalk, she draws a big *right* (check mark) across the slates of those who got the answers correct, and a big *wrong* (cross) across the slates of those who didn't. I'm among those who get a big *right.* I'm thrilled.

As those who got *wrongs* are being whipped, I dream of lunch. I can't wait for the boy to come and jerk the huge church bell in the middle of the hall, sounding the eleven o'clock lunch break for the entire school. I'm particularly hungry this morning. I left home without eating breakfast out of fear of being punished for being late. Before I left, Mama gave me two cents to buy hebelungu. Despite the fact that it costs only two cents, hebelungu is still beyond the reach of many pupils. A lot of them go hungry, and there's a lot of stealing of one another's cents and snatching of one another's food.

I can tell that lunch is imminent. The mistress orders us to stand up and sing my favorite song, a Shangaan adaptation of the French nursery rhyme "Frère Jacques."

Hitandlala, hitandlala.
We are hungry, we are hungry.
Harila, harila.
We are crying, we are crying.
Tsimbi yi ba rini, tshibi yi ba rini
When is the bell ringing, when is the bell ringing
Hi ta dla, hi ta dla?
so we can eat, so we can eat?

A tall muscular boy named Mandleve (Big Ears) walks to the middle of the hall and grabs the thick rope attached to the bell. Mandleve is nearly eighteen but he's still in Sub-B because he always fails the exams. He's slightly retarded, and yet he loves school. He's always on time, very attentive in class, dresses neatly, and yet when the mistress asks him questions, he never knows the answer and simply grins foolishly. Whenever he writes anything, it's gibberish.

All eyes watch Mandleve intently as he jerks the rope up and down, like Quasimodo in *The Hunchback of Notre Dame,* one of Johannes's favorite books, which he's read to us at home.

"Class dismissed!" the mistress shouts.

Florah, my thirteen-year-old sister, who is in Standard Four, is waiting for me outside the school gate. She holds me by the hand and leads me to the long queue of schoolkids waiting to buy hebelungu. The queue is so long it winds like a coiled snake down the dusty street.

"You know what, Florah?" I say, staring self-consciously at my feet.

"What?"

"I wish I had a pair of shoes so I can be like other children. They're always teasing me for not having shoes. Especially because I have *mikwenkwes.*" Mikwenkwes are scalelike calluses that frequently develop on the feet of poor children without shoes during winter months, because many are afraid of bathing in cold water.

"Don't worry," Florah says reassuringly. "Mama will buy you a pair of shoes as soon as she finds a *skorop*"—a piece job.

Since I began school Mama has been unemployed, which is why she's constantly fighting with Papa over money and why I'm often punished for not having the proper uniform, slates, shoes, and primers.

"And my bloomers have holes in them," I say. "The mistress says I need new ones."

"Mama will buy you new bloomers too. If you weren't small I'd let you use my other pair until she does."

I wonder if Mama will ever find a job. She's constantly praying for one, but under Section 10 of the Influx Control Law, a cornerstone of apartheid used to decide which blacks can hold jobs in white areas, she needs a special permit to start looking for one. But to qualify for the permit she needs to already have a job.

Chapter 3

Mama buys me a pair of secondhand bloomers at a flea market, called a jumble sale. They cost five cents, a fortune. She's still not working, and Papa no longer gives her his ten-rand-a-week salary. He accuses her of wasting his hard-earned money on frivolous things, like clothes and newspapers for Johannes, when it is needed for rent, groceries, bus fare, and police bribes. Mama borrows the five cents from Granny, who works as a gardener in the nearby suburb of Rosebank. Mama knows about the bloomers inspection at school and is concerned that I'll wear out the secondhand bloomers before she can find a job and can buy me another pair. So she recommends that I not wear bloomers all the time, and that I take them off whenever I go to sleep at night because I have a tendency to wet the bed.

It's Monday morning and Cynthia is standing by the half-open kitchen door.

"Hurry up, Miriam," she says anxiously. "We'll be late for school."

Cynthia lives on Eleventh Avenue. Every morning she stops by our two-room shack on Thirteenth Avenue, and together we walk the half mile to school.

I struggle to put on my black raggedy gym dress. "I'm hurrying." I tie it with a green-and-black school belt and grab my piece of broken slate. It's ten minutes to eight. I'm so terrified that we'll be late that I don't even bother to wash my face. I merely wet my finger with saliva and wipe the sandman from my eyes and the crusty white film from the edges of my mouth.

My siblings have already left. Johannes took the six-thirty bus to Tembisa High School. My eleven-year-old brother, George, and my nine-year-old sister, Maria, left at seven because both sing in the choir at school and have morning rehearsal. Mama left about thirty minutes ago with my younger siblings, Linah, who is four, and Diana, who is two. She's taking Florah to the clinic. Florah has lately been fainting a lot at school and failed several important exams because of it. Mama has already been to the clinic twice, and both times the queue was too long and Florah couldn't be seen by one of the clinic's few overworked doctors.

Cynthia and I race down Hofmeyer Street. The narrow, unpaved, and rutted street is filled with students running in all directions, headed for their respective tribal schools.

Cynthia and I seem to be making good time. As we near Fifteenth Avenue, the bell starts ringing, summoning students to morning assembly. Barefoot and panting, I lengthen my stride. In a way it's good that I have mikwenkwes, for my feet are impervious to the sharp rocks, rusted nails, and shards of broken bottles littering the street.

"Come on, Cynthia. We can still make it. Especially if we take the *double-up,*" the shortcut.

I pull ahead of Cynthia. Suddenly I hear her shout, "Stop, Miriam, stop!"

I slow down. "What's the matter?"

"Look behind you."

"What's wrong?"

I notice that she's staring bug-eyed at my behind. I think, My bloomers must be showing.

"My God, you forgot to wear your bloomers. Your *marhaku* is showing." My ass.

I touch the bottom of my gym dress. Sure enough, in my hurry to get to school on time I'd forgotten to wear my bloomers. And the back of my gym dress is caught in the belt. My ass is exposed to the whole world.

"Oh, my God," I cry. What do I do? If I turn and go back home to put on my bloomers I'll be late. Maybe I should continue on to school without bloomers. I quickly dismiss the idea. What if we again have bloomers inspection and the mistress finds out that I'm not wearing any bloomers at all? I'd be whipped as hard with the thick ruler as that thin, sickly girl who's always without bloomers because her unemployed parents can't afford to buy her a pair.

"There's no way I can go to school without my bloomers," I tell Cynthia. "You go ahead. I'll run back home and put them on."

Cynthia hesitates, then says, "I'll go back with you."

Cynthia and I run home so I can put on my secondhand bloomers. When we get to school, assembly is already in progress. We can hear the students singing hymns. We join the group of about twenty latecomers standing forlornly outside the gate, guarded by a teacher and a mistress. Both are armed with canes. As soon as students at assembly finish reciting the Lord's Prayer, the teacher and the mistress open the gates and march the latecomers to the principal's office overlooking the lavatories, where we are whipped for being late.

The whipping hurts and raises welts on my buttocks. Ironically, there's no bloomers inspection. Instead, we spend an hour learning our vowels, which we pronounce with our mouths wide open like hippos:

AAAA!

EEEE!

IIII!

OOOO!

UUUUUUUUU!

Then we learn how to read the Shangaan words the mistress has written on the blackboard. I have to strain to read them because the blackboard is so far and the words are a bit blurry. She points with the ruler as we spell and pronounce each word.

M-A-N-A-N-A=MANANA *(mother).*
T-A-T-A-N-A=TATANA *(father).*
K-O-K-W-A-N-A=KOKWANA *(granny).*
S-E-S-I=SESI *(sister).*
B-U-T-I=BUTI *(brother).*
K-A-Y-A=KAYA *(home).*

Next we do multiplication tables, shouting the numbers with our mouths wide open:

ONE TIMES ONE IS ONE.
TWO TIMES TWO IS FOUR.
THREE TIMES THREE IS NINE.
FOUR TIMES FOUR IS SIXTEEN . . .

The shouting is exhausting and a lot of pupils like me are hungry, having not had any breakfast.

After lunch a lot of pupils fall asleep, because either their bellies are too full or they are simply too tired. We commit to memory various biblical passages and sing hymns. Those caught napping get their heads whacked. I manage to stay awake, somehow, because I love singing and listening to Bible stories.

At two o'clock Mandleve rings the bell for afterschool. I can't wait to get home and share the good news with my mother. I'm very happy because the mistress has made another big *right* across my slate and told me that I'm as smart as my brothers, Johannes and George, and my sisters Florah and Maria, all of whom she's taught. On the way home I witness a fight between two girls because one of them accidentally wiped the *right* off the slate of the other.

I'm so proud of my *right* I protect it by carrying my slate on the top of my head all the way home. Mama's very proud of me whenever I make a *right*. She tells me that every *right* I get is a contribution toward a brand-new pair of shoes. She promises to buy them for me as soon as she gets paid at the end of the month at her new skorop, her piece job as a maid in the *kitchens,* a mysterious place where white people live.

I'm as happy as a lark at the news that finally, after months of being teased by other children for not having shoes, I'll have a brand-new pair.

I can't wait for the end of the month.

"I love you very much, Mama," I say, hugging her tight.

"I love you too, my child."

Florah continues to faint about twice a week at school, but the clinic couldn't find anything wrong with her. Mama says they didn't give her a proper checkup because there were too many patients with more serious ailments and too few doctors. I'm terrified whenever Florah faints. She looks like she's dead as the big girls carry her to the huge tree next to the gate and place her under its shade. The mistress always gives her a pinch of snuff, which makes her sneeze violently and wake up.

"Why does Florah faint so much?" I ask Mama one evening after a dinner of vuswa and *machondo na tinhloko ta huku,* the cooked heads and feet of chickens.

"I don't know, my child. At the clinic they can't find anything wrong with her."

"Maybe she is possessed by *swikwembu,*" George says, meaning that Florah has been chosen by the spirits of our ancestors to become a diviner (a *sangoma*) by undergoing an initiation ceremony called *ku twasa.*

"I'm not possessed," Florah says angrily.

"You *are* possessed," he says. "Only people who are possessed by swikwembu faint as much as you do. You should twasa so you can become a sangoma and make us all rich."

"Stop teasing me," she cries.

I secretly wish Florah would become a sangoma because I love attending the twasa initiation ceremonies. My friend Becky's father is a well-known sangoma. From time to time he hosts a big weekend festival at which teams of sangomas from far and near bring their protégés, who give elaborate performances of singing, dancing, and drum playing called *manchomani.* I love watching the dancers and listening to their otherworldly music and the incantations they chant as they communicate with the spirit world. And Becky and I often imitate the drummers by playing on tins.

"Florah isn't possessed by swikwembu," Mama says, "but something *is* wrong with her. I wish I had money to take her to a specialist."

Specialists were the few white and Indian doctors permitted to practice in the ghetto. They charged more than the clinic for their services, which were considered superior to those of the mostly intern staff at the overcrowded and understaffed clinic.

"I have a friend at school who faints like Florah, Mama," I say. "And she tells me that her parents say it's because she's possessed by swikwembu."

"What's her name?"

"Janice Manganyi."

"She does have swikwembu," Mama says. "Her mother told me so the other day. She says she's waiting till she's old enough to undergo the twasa ceremony."

"You know what, Mama?"

"What?"

"I like it whenever Janice faints during cleanliness inspection."

"Why?"

"Then the mistress has to spend so much time reviving her that she forgets to punish us."

Everyone laughs.

Chapter 4

A*t the end of the month Mama, tears in her eyes, tells me she* doesn't have money to buy me the shoes I've dreamed about for almost a year. Papa lost his entire wages gambling at dice, so she had to use her wages to pay rent, or else we'd have been evicted from our shack.

She's also lost her job in the kitchens. Her madam fired her because she missed a day at work when she had to take Florah to the clinic.

I'm devastated and cry for a long time. I even refuse the two cents she gives me to buy hebelungu. She comes over to the *stoep* overlooking the street, where I'm moping, and tries to comfort me.

"Mama will get you the shoes, my child," she says. "I'm already looking for another skorop."

Mama can't afford bus fare so she walks many miles to white suburbs with names like Edenvale, Rosebank, Rivonia, Malanshof, Morningside, Parkmore, Sandhurst, but most of the madams want only sleep-in maids. Mama can't afford to sleep in because she's concerned about who'd take care of us. A lot of women send their children to faraway homelands so they can qualify for jobs as sleep-in maids. Mama vows she'll never do such a thing. Besides, we have no homeland to go to. She and Papa met in Alexandra in 1957 and have lived there all their adult lives.

At other suburbs the madams want only maids with the proper papers. Mama doesn't have any. Not having a job isn't Mama's only problem. She and Papa have to worry about the Peri-Urban Police, who regularly blitz the township to enforce the pass laws.

Pass laws—part of the influx control system—determined which blacks could stay in "white" South Africa (the land designated for whites) and for how long, and which couldn't. To stay in "white" South Africa, a black person had to fulfill three conditions under Section 10 of the Pass Laws and Black Urban Areas Act of 1945: birth, continuous employment for ten years for the same employer, or continuous residence in a township like Alexandra for more than fifteen years.

Without Section 10 qualification, blacks could stay in white areas only seventy-two hours, after which they could be arrested and deported back to one of the nine impoverished tribal reservations, called homelands.

Mama and Papa hadn't fulfilled all three conditions. Neither was born in Alexandra; Papa was born in his homeland of Venda, and Mama in Louis Trichardt. Neither had been continuously employed by the same employer for ten years—few blacks were, because with black labor cheap, whites routinely fired and hired blacks, particularly those who demanded higher wages or better working conditions.

And despite having been married for over fifteen years, Mama and Papa are not legally residents of Alexandra. They don't qualify for a permit allowing them to live together as husband and wife in Alexandra because Mama doesn't have a job and is therefore considered an illegal alien. Papa risks arrest for harboring an illegal alien.

Our yard, which is one acre in size and is home to more than a dozen families, is full of illegal aliens like Mama, and other violators of Section 10. Because of that, it is subjected to almost daily predawn raids by the Peri-Urban Police.

One morning before dawn four white policemen burst through the front door. Moments earlier I'd been sound asleep. Suddenly I hear screams and strange voices barking orders. The fingers of my left hand are crunched by a boot as the policemen step over my sisters and me while we lie on the floor by the door.

Two of the policemen shine their powerful torches—flashlights—

all over the tiny kitchen, which is crowded with sleeping bodies. The other two rush toward the bedroom, where my parents are sleeping. Diana, Linah, and I cower in the corner, screaming. A white policeman with hairy arms interrogates my brother Johannes about whether or not he is a bona fide student and barks at us to shut up.

The other two white policemen emerge from the bedroom with both my parents in handcuffs. Mama tells us to be quiet, that everything will be all right. She asks Johannes to go inform Granny that she and Papa have been arrested.

I stand by the gate with a bunch of other children and watch as our parents are loaded into a *kwela-kwela* (climb-climb) police truck and whisked away. Johannes skips school and runs all the way to Granny's, on Sixteenth Avenue.

Granny doesn't go to her gardening job that day. Instead she goes to the Peri-Urban Police Station in Wynberg and pays the two-rand fine for Mama to be freed. Mama is warned to get a job or go back to Louis Trichardt, the homeland she hardly knows. Granny doesn't have enough money to pay for Papa's release, so he spends fourteen days in jail for harboring an illegal alien and not having a permit allowing him to live with his family in Alexandra. Papa is also told to either get a permit or send his family back to Venda, a homeland he left over thirty years ago to seek work in the city. If he doesn't comply, he too risks being "endorsed out" (deported) from "white" South Africa.

I'm haunted by the image of the white policemen with their hairy arms. Every time I see a white man with hairy arms I holler. Most black children learn to fear white people from these brutal encounters with white policemen. Some have even fainted at the sight of a white person.

Jail becomes Papa's second home. He is arrested about twice or thrice a month. One evening toward Christmas Mama gathers my siblings and me around the brazier, brimming with red-hot coals, in the middle of the kitchen. She has very bad news. Papa was arrested while waiting for a bus to go to town because his employer, before he went on vacation, forgot to stamp his passbook, indicating that Papa still had a job. Papa needs the stamp every month.

"So your father threw away his pass," Mama says.

"Why?" George asks.

"Because losing one's pass is a lesser crime than not having a proper employment stamp."

I don't understand any of this but I do know that whenever Papa is thrown in jail there will be little or no food to eat. Mama will have to beg for necessities like mealie meal and sugar from the neighbors and from her relatives. She will have to go to the garbage dump called Mlothi, on the other side of the Jukskei River, to scavenge for white people's leftovers. It means I'll have to eat the prickly worms called *sonjas,* which I hate because they always give me a stomachache. It means no Christmas celebration.

During Papa's imprisonment, I take up gambling in the hope of winning enough money to help Mama buy food so we can have a semblance of a Christmas celebration. Florah and Maria also gamble, as do George and Johannes. We play mainly cards, *kopi* dice, and spinning. Mama doesn't like it one bit.

"Gambling is of the devil," she says. "Look at what it's done to your poor father."

We ignore her warnings. Nearly every child in the neighborhood gambles and some parents rely on the earnings of their gambling children. Also, when we win we can buy Kit-Kat candy, *msokobuns* (sponge cakes), *vetkoekies* (fat cakes), Eat-Sum-More biscuits, Coke, and fish and chips.

One afternoon I'm with a group of about seven girls playing a card game called boom-any-boom-jumping. I'm good at the game, which requires a player to have straight matching cards. About fifty cents is at stake, a fortune.

I'm so engrossed in the game that I do not notice one of our neighbors—a squat, jet-black man—get into his decrepit van and start the engine. He can't make a U-turn because the yard is teeming with scraps—old abandoned cars that he has stripped for parts to fix his van. He starts backing up. We gamblers are oblivious to the fact that he's headed our way. At least I am.

"Miriam, watch out!" cries Mashudu, the landlord's daughter.

"What!" I cry, startled, and look behind me.

Too late. The van is about three feet away. I try to jump out of the way but my right leg gets trapped under the van's right rear wheel.

My fellow gamblers get up and frantically signal the driver to stop. He thinks they're making fun of him and the thick tire runs completely over my leg. Miraculously, no bones are broken, but my leg is badly bruised and swells up. Because Mama has no money to take me to the clinic, she uses warm water and salt to massage my leg until the swelling goes down.

Visits to the clinic are a luxury poor families cannot afford. Consequently Mama has a host of homemade remedies. Warm water and salt is used for treating anything from wounds to sore throats. Warm pig's fat is used for earaches. Urine is used to treat burns and eye problems such as conjunctivitis. If the disease is particularly stubborn or recurrent, a sangoma is visited so the ancestors can be consulted as to the cause. Sangomas are also consulted for solutions to permit problems, lack of housing, or chronic unemployment. But Mama is a Christian. She relies more on her priest than on sangomas and visits him every week with requests for blessings so she can find solutions to the myriad of problems besetting her and our family, chief of which is finding a job.

Chapter 5

One evening I accompany Mama on a visit to her favorite priest, who lives on Sixteenth Avenue across from our school. He is a senior pastor at the Twelve Apostles Church of God, which Mama attends religiously ever since she gave up drinking. She likes Priest Mathebula because he always has time to listen to her troubles, to interpret her dreams, to confront Papa whenever he beats her, and to give her special blessings so she can find jobs. Mama is convinced that just one more blessing from him will help her find a job this time after she's been searching for one for months without any luck.

We find Priest Mathebula not at home. His wife, Linah, tells us that he's still at work. Mama says we'll wait. Linah is a kindly, matronly, bespectacled woman. She serves us tea and listens sympathetically as Mama recounts her problems. Linah is one of Mama's best friends. She's often helped the family in the past, giving Mama money, old clothes, and groceries. Mama never forgot that it was Linah who loaned her thirty rand to pay for Johannes to go to secondary (middle) school after he'd obtained one of the highest grades in Standard Six, a first-class pass. Without the money to buy books and pay school fees for Form I, Johannes would have had to drop out of school. Mama was so thankful for what Priest Mathebula's wife had done that she'd named one of my younger sisters Linah.

Priest Mathebula finally returns home. After changing from his work clothes into the dark suit he wears to every service Priest Mathebula sits across from Mama and me in the living room of his well-furnished five-room house. He leads Mama in a prayer and then patiently listens to a sad story about how she's been praying every day and tramping all over the suburbs looking for work, without any luck.

"So you still haven't found a job, Sister Mathabane?" Female members of Mama's church are addressed as Sister, and male members as Brother.

"Yes, Priest Mathebula," Mama says. "I'm at my wits' end. I have no permit to look for a job. And I can't get a permit without a job. But my children have to eat. And they need school things."

"Jobs are abundant for those who believe in the God of Israel," he says confidently, "whether or not they have permits."

"Why is there no job for me?"

"Do you believe with all your heart that God lives and can work miracles?"

"I do believe. But sometimes I think God has abandoned me. I've been praying for miracles all my life. As yet I've received none."

"He hasn't abandoned you, Sister Mathabane," Priest Mathebula says. "He's simply testing your faith."

"How long will this testing continue?"

"As long as God wishes, Sister Mathabane. He operates on his own time, according to his own laws. Remember the story of Job?"

Mama nods. "I do."

"He got so tired of waiting for God's blessing that he began cursing him. He didn't realize that God was simply testing his faith."

"I'll never curse God," Mama says emphatically, "no matter how much he makes me suffer. I'd rather chop off my right hand than curse my Creator and Savior."

"You're a woman of faith, Sister Mathabane."

"But I need help, Priest Mathebula. My children are suffering."

"Help is on the way. Remember the story of the birth of Samuel?"

"Yes, Priest Mathebula, I remember."

"How does it go, Sister?"

Mama, who has an incredibly retentive memory, recounts the Old Testament story of how Hannah, a pious and virtuous woman, longed for a child. Unable to conceive, she went daily to the temple to pray for a son. Eli the priest told her to go home and God would grant her petition.

"Do you believe that I'm God's messenger, Sister Mathabane?" Priest Mathebula asks.

"Yes, I do believe you are a direct descendant of God's apostles and that the Twelve Apostles Church of God is the only true church."

"Then go home, Sister Mathabane. Your faith is strong. The God of Israel will grant your wish for a job."

I doubt that this visit will help Mama get a job, but I'm so desperate for a pair of shoes I'm willing to believe in miracles. The next day, a Monday, she borrows ten cents from the landlord and takes the bus to the white suburb of Randburg.

At the end of the day she returns jubilant.

"God answered my prayers, children. The first street I walked along in Randburg I found a piece job. I'll be doing washing and cleaning twice a week. And I'll be paid thirty rand a month. Thirty rand! Can you believe it? I've never made that much in my life."

I'm astounded. I consider Priest Mathebula the ultimate miracle worker—especially when Mama tells us that her new employer hired her despite the fact that her passbook is not in order. I remember the countless times Mama has been refused jobs because she didn't qualify for one under Section 10.

"Will I finally get my shoes, Mama?" I ask.

"Yes, my child. I'll buy you a pair with my first paycheck."

She also promises to buy the rest of my siblings school things.

"But I must not forget to tithe," she says. "A tenth of what I earn must be given to the Lord."

"What happens if you don't, Mama?" Maria asks.

"If I don't tithe, the Lord will take away his blessing. And I'll be unemployed again."

• • •

Papa is released from jail, thin and bitter. His bitterness is worsened by the fact that in his absence his employer replaced him because he thought Papa had quit. "Discharged" is stamped on Papa's passbook, which means that he can be arrested again, this time for having been discharged.

Mama tells Papa not to worry, that the God of Israel will soon give him a job, just as he did her. Mama invites Papa to accompany her to Priest Mathebula to request a blessing for a job. Papa angrily refuses. "I don't believe in your church mumbo jumbo. I have my own gods."

"Why don't they give you a job, then?"

Mama goes to Priest Mathebula alone, and prays every night for the God of Israel to give Papa a job, saying that he's a good man who's been through hell and needs a job to provide for his family and to preserve his dignity.

Shortly after Mama begins praying for a job for Papa, he finds one at a construction company in the industrial city of Germiston. He'll be earning twenty rand a week, double what he made at his previous job. Mama is ecstatic.

"Will you finally start coming with me to church, Jackson?" Mama asks Papa one evening a week later.

"Why?"

"To thank God for leading you to a good job."

"Who said God got me this job?"

Mama smiles. "If God didn't help you, why have you been looking for a job all these months without finding one? You only found one after I asked a special blessing from Priest Mathebula."

"God had nothing to do with my finding this job, woman. So shut up. If this God of yours is such a miracle worker, why doesn't he make us rich?"

"He will if you believe in him."

"Rubbish."

Despite Papa's skepticism, Mama continues to pray to God every night. She thanks him for keeping our family together, and for providing us with food and shelter. She prays and thanks God for blessing our family. Mama's God seems all-powerful. I too begin to pray every night. In my prayer I ask for five things.

God, let Mama and Papa always have jobs.
God, let us always have food.
God, keep the horrible police away from our house.
God, let me get a new pair of shoes.
God, let the mistress stop beating me.

Chapter 6

On a Friday evening, two weeks after Papa started his new job, he brings home a big brown bag. Diana, Linah, and I congregate eagerly around the dimly lit kitchen table as he unpacks it. It contains a packet of candles, chicken heads, chicken feet, a small packet of salt, and a sheep's head, which I hate because I always have to eat the cooked eyes.

But at the bottom of the bag is a packet containing my favorite food in the world—fish and chips. Few things match the mouthwatering deliciousness of fish and chips wrapped in greasy newspapers.

"Miriam," Papa says. "Divide the fish and chips evenly among the three of you."

"Yes, Papa."

"And don't forget to give Diana the lion's share. She's the youngest."

"I will, Papa."

Papa leaves for the bedroom, followed by Mama.

I eagerly rip the greasy pieces of newspaper. My eyes pop out. Papa bought two of the most delicious items along with the fish and chips: Viennas and Russians. There's nothing more delicious than slowly nibbling a well-roasted Vienna (hot dog) or Russian (Polish sausage).

Linah and Diana get equal shares of the fish and chips, and I get the lion's share. I'm glad Maria is out playing, else she'd have had the lion's share.

Papa emerges from the bedroom.

I notice that Mama is holding a brown envelope in her hand. It means Papa has given her part of his weekly wage. I'm very happy, for it means we'll have food during the week and I'll have money for hebelungu.

"Aren't you having dinner?" Mama asks Papa in a sweet voice as he's heading for the door.

"Keep my plate warm," Papa says. "I'll eat when I get back."

Out goes Papa into the noisy night.

"Where's Papa gone?" I ask.

Mama hesitates, then says, in a crestfallen voice, "To a meeting."

Papa returns from the "meeting" around midnight. He's drunk. He heads straight for the bedroom, bypassing the covered plate of food on the table. I know why he's headed for the bedroom and I'm afraid. I know Papa lost money gambling and that he plans to demand the food and rent money he gave Mama. I know that Mama will refuse and that there will be a fight. I wish Johannes and Florah were home to protect Mama as they've done in the past. But Florah is away attending *tikhomba,* a rites-of-passage ceremony during which she's secluded for four weeks with other initiates and taught all the mysteries of being a grown woman. Johannes is away at a weekend tennis tournament and won't be back till Sunday.

"I say give me my money!" I hear Papa shouting in the bedroom.

"What money?"

"My money."

"What about the children? What will they eat all of next week if you lose every penny of your wages?"

"I won't lose. Now give me my money or I'll beat you."

"I won't let my children starve," Mama says. "Why don't you grow up, Jackson? Gambling is for boys, not for a grown man like you. You have seven children. And they starve and wear rags because of your irresponsibility."

Suddenly Mama screams. Then there's the noise of furniture being shoved aside. The bedroom door bursts open and Mama, wearing only her flimsy nightgown, runs out of the house into the dark street.

"Give me my money, you hear?" Papa screams at her from the door.

"I won't let my children starve."

"If you don't give me my money you'll sleep outside," Papa says.

"I don't mind."

Papa curses, then locks the door and pockets the key.

An hour or so later there's a faint knock on the door. George stealthily goes to the door.

"Is that you, Mama?" he asks in a whisper.

"Yes. Let me in. It's freezing cold out here."

"I can't. Papa took the key."

I can hear Mama cursing.

"I have an idea. I'll let you in through the window."

George opens the window and Mama tries wriggling in. It's too small.

"Don't worry, child," she says. "Hand me a blanket. I'll sleep by the door."

I feel like crying. Mama is sleeping outside in the bitter cold for our sake. She doesn't want Papa to take the money for rent and food and gamble it all away. I wish Papa would stop gambling and I don't understand why he can't. Even though I love Papa, I hate him when he gambles and beats up Mama. Other fathers don't gamble and beat up their wives. They give them their entire wages on Fridays, and their children always have food to eat, better clothes to wear, and pocket money to buy fish and chips during school lunch.

End-of-the-year exams are in two weeks. I study very hard. After exams the mistress reads aloud the results. I've come out number four of more than a hundred pupils. I'm going to Standard One next January.

Mama is overjoyed when I give her the sealed envelope containing the slip of paper showing that I have passed, and the marks I've received in each subject. All my siblings have passed, including Florah, despite her fainting sickness. Mama praises us for working hard, and God for keeping us in school despite our not having school things like other children. Maria is going to Standard Three, George to Standard Five, Florah to Standard Six, and Johannes to Form II, his second-to-final year of matric.

When Christmas comes, we celebrate it in grand style. Two miracles have happened, both because of Priest Mathebula. Mama has held on to her piece job in the kitchens for four months—a record. And Papa has stopped gambling after Priest Mathebula came and talked to him about the shame of starving innocent children and letting them wear rags, especially when they are so smart at school. When Papa receives his modest bonus at the end of the year from his new employer, he stuns everyone by giving it all to Mama.

"Take good care of it now," he says. "I don't want you wasting it on frivolities."

Papa then calls Maria, Florah, and me to the table, where he's sitting. He's slightly drunk.

"I hear you all passed."

We all nod.

"I knew you'd pass. You inherited my brain."

Mama smiles as she looks on from the fire, where she's cooking dinner we have only during good times: chicken and rice.

Papa digs into the pocket of his overalls with his work-gnarled hands and comes up with some gleaming coins. We all curtsy and cup our hands together to accept the money. Cupping the hands when an adult gives you something is a sign of respect. I'm stunned at the amount Papa has given us. Florah has received fifty cents, and Maria and I twenty-five cents each!

Maria and I give Mama our coins for safekeeping until the new year. I know that if Papa would let her, Mama would kiss him, and we too would kiss him. But Papa doesn't like to publicly display his emotions. Only on rare occasions does he smile or laugh. In part it's because of the way he was raised. But a part of it is that there's seldom much in his life, or in our lives, to smile or laugh about.

Deep in my heart I know that Papa is proud of what we've accomplished, especially because he boasts about our accomplishments to his drinking buddies and tells them that the Mathabanes are a very smart clan, and that we've inherited his brain. But I know that we've also inherited Mama's brain. She tells me that had women during her time been allowed the same educational opportunities as boys, she'd have gone to school and become a teacher. Instead she sacrificed the opportunity so that Uncle Cheeks, her younger brother, could go. He went as far as Standard Six, but then quit and became a gangster in order to support his struggling mother. He robbed and stabbed people, and ended up in jail.

When he got out, Mama prevailed on him to join the Twelve Apostles Church of God. He did, and he not only found a job at a Jewish bakery but also found a wife, and became a deacon and the church's choirmaster. When Uncle Cheeks hears that we've all passed, he also gives us money as Christmas presents. So do Aunt Bushy and Uncle Piet, Mama's other siblings. Uncle Piet works at a trousers factory and Aunt Bushy serves tea to white people at a firm near Alexandra, a job she's held since quitting school after she became pregnant with her first child, a daughter named Fikile.

Chapter 7

Mama has a surprise for me, Maria, and Linah. She's bought us new outfits, our first in several years. This Christmas we'll be parading in the streets like other children, displaying our outfits. Mama boils water on the brazier and Maria, Linah, and I take turns being scrubbed in the family's rusted tin bathtub, in the middle of the kitchen. After we're dried, our nappy hair combed, and our skin moisturized with Vaseline, Mama goes into the bedroom and brings back the new clothes.

After I'm dressed, my friends Cynthia and Dlayani come, spiffily dressed in their new outfits, which are gaudier and more expensive than mine. But all I care about is that this Christmas I won't have to watch the beauty parade through our window, but will be a part of it.

After mandatory church services, Cynthia, Dlayani, and I join a group of neighborhood children in the annual ritual of spending Christmas Day going from street to street visiting the homes of different people. Everyone is festive, and they give us cookies and candy in celebration of the Christmas spirit. The majority of black South Africans are Christian, despite the fact that most still cling to ancestral worship and believe in witchcraft.

But even at Christmas there's a lot of violence also. Along one street we see a man stabbed to death by a group of *tsotsis,* gangsters, who work overtime during the Christmas season robbing people of their hard-earned wages.

The family caps off the day with a huge feast. Mama has cooked chicken, rice, beetroot, and vegetables. She's even baked cookies over at our neighbors', who have a coal stove. Mama also makes plenty of Kool-Aid and custard and jelly, my favorite dessert. The food is so delicious I wish it were Christmas every day.

Christmas celebration lasts well into the night. As we prepare to go to sleep on mats on the kitchen floor, Mama wishes us good night and reminds us to be up bright and early the next day.

"Why is it called Christmas, Mama?" I ask.

"Because on this day Jesus Christ, our Lord and Savior, was born in Bethlehem."

"Where's Bethlehem?"

"It's in Judea, a faraway place."

"Is Jesus still alive?"

"Why do you ask?"

"I'd like to thank him for giving us Christmas."

"He's alive, my child."

"Where is he?"

"He's in heaven with his Father."

"You mean he's in the sky?"

"Yes."

"Does he ever fly down?"

"From time to time."

"When?"

"When you pray."

I tell Mama that at school they taught us a prayer.

"Do you want me to say it?"

"Sure, my child."

I shut my eyes tight, the way the mistress taught us, clasp my hands before me, and say fervently in Shangaan:

Tata was hina langa matilweni,
Our Father who art in heaven,

Vito ra wena ari hlawuriwe.
hallowed be thy name.
Aku ta ku fuma ka wena.
Thy kingdom come.
Ku randa ka wena aku endliswa misaveni
Thy will be done on earth
Ku ta hani hi loku ku endliwa matilweni.
as it is in heaven.
U hi nyika vuswa by hina bya masiku hinkwawo.
Give us this day our daily bread.
U hi rivaleni milandu ya hina
Forgive us our trespasses
Ku tani hi hina hi rivalela vanwani
as we forgive those
Lava nga m'landu ka hina.
who trespass against us.
Unga tsiki uhi yisa emiringwanini,
Lead us not into temptation,
Kambi uhi ponisa kolowo biha.
but deliver us from evil.
Hi kuve kufuma ikawena
For thine is the kingdom
Na matimba, na ku twala
and the power and the glory
Ni masiku ni masiku.
forever and forever.
Amen.

Mama smiles proudly. She tells me that God will bless me all the days of my life for knowing his prayer.

Mama finally fulfills a promise she made to me months ago.

"I'm taking you all to Seedat today, children," she says one Saturday morning in January of 1976, a week after school reopened for the new year. After breakfast Linah, Florah, George, and I troop to Alexandra's main shopping center, on First Avenue. Seedat is a department store that sells mostly school things. At Seedat Mama opens a layaway account.

I'm beside myself with joy when Mama buys me a pair of black school shoes, called *self-shines* because you don't need to polish them. She also buys me a pair of ankle-high socks (the more expensive knee-high socks are worn by students from well-to-do families), a long-sleeve school jersey, and school supplies for Standard One: books, primers, pencils, and a *rubber* (eraser). She also buys books, uniforms, and supplies for Maria, Florah, and George. Johannes has a piece job at a tennis ranch in Halfway House and can afford to buy his own school supplies.

When we get home Papa is drunk and very angry with Mama for buying us school supplies. He accuses her of wasting money instead of saving it for a rainy day.

"Our children need these things, Jackson. Miriam has gone all year without a pair of shoes. And she's been punished for it. Have you seen the welts on her?"

"I told you not to send them to the damn school."

"If they don't go to school, what future will they have? Just because you never went to school is no reason to deny our children the opportunity."

"Can they eat books? Tell me, can we eat books?"

"Listen, Jackson," Mama says stubbornly, "I'm tired of our children looking like orphans. As long as I'm working I'll make sure they look like the children of decent folks."

Papa simply stalks out of the house and goes to the local *shebeen* (speakeasy) for more liquor. He does that each time he loses an argument against Mama and is afraid of beating her up because of Priest Mathebula and Uncle Cheeks, Mama's brother, who's threatened to beat him up if he ever again lays a hand on Mama.

But Papa stops giving Mama his wages. Mama doesn't care, because she's now working.

"As long as I tithe," she says, "the God of Israel will shower this family with blessings."

As if to prove her point, the God of Israel leads Mama to another piece job, also in Randburg, working for an Englishwoman named

Mrs. Hunt. The two piece jobs pay her the unheard-of sum of eighty rand a month. On top of that she brings home tons of leftovers and secondhand clothes and toys from Mrs. Hunt.

Mama purchases a secondhand coal stove to replace the dangerous brazier, which almost killed us with carbon monoxide poisoning one winter. She even talks of sending Johannes to university as soon as he's passed matric, to become the first teacher in the family. Mama worships teachers. To her there's no more noble profession than *kudyondisa vana ku ri va tiva dyondo,* teaching children to value knowledge.

In this she's like most parents I know from our neighborhood, who also want their children to grow up to be teachers and mistresses. This surprises me. First, because most of our parents never went to school; and second, because I don't like teachers and mistresses that much because of all the harsh punishment they mete out to students. I want to be a nurse.

Chapter 8

L*ike me, Johannes doesn't want to be a teacher. His ambition is to* become a professional tennis player like Arthur Ashe, who's been his idol ever since he visited South Africa in 1975 to play in the South African Breweries Open. Every day after school, Johannes rushes off to the tennis courts at the stadium on Twelfth Avenue or at Halfway House.

Many times he practices alone. People think he's crazy for hitting serves, backhands, forehands, and volleys against a brick wall for hours on end. He doesn't come back until late at night. Then he reads till well past midnight. He reads everything: newspapers, books, comics. He says he wants to improve his English so as to be able to speak the language as fluently as Arthur Ashe.

I don't understand why Johannes feels he needs to improve his English, because already everyone says he speaks the language as well as a white person.

Johannes also likes listening to the radio a lot. He says it helps him improve his English pronunciation. He listens mostly to Springbok Radio and to the BBC because both stations have a lot of serialized stories. I struggle to understand the English spoken by the radio people. It is different from the English they're teaching us in Standard One, which consists mainly of simple sentences.

I'm fascinated by Johannes's love of reading. He never goes anywhere without a book in his pocket. And every night, when everyone is asleep, he's at the kitchen table, reading by candlelight. When I ask him why he reads so much he says he wants desperately to go to university in America like Arthur Ashe.

To feed his passion for reading, Johannes has more books than anyone in the neighborhood or at our school library. The white people he's worked for gave most of them and he keeps them in several boxes under the single bed he shares with George. I'm eager to read them too, but most of them have big words and few pictures. Sometimes he reads to us from his books, with names like *Treasure Island, Oliver Twist, Tom Sawyer,* Shakespeare, and *Tales from the Arabian Nights.*

Next to reading, Johannes loves reciting poetry—Shangaan poems, English poems, and Afrikaans poems. When he was still attending Bovet, he was often chosen to recite poetry to the white inspectors.

I often listen to Johannes practice reciting various poems before the mirror for presentation during exams. I'm enthralled by such poems as "The Donkey," "The Highwayman," and "The Lady of Shalott" even when I don't understand them. There's something musical in the words.

One night, as Johannes is committing to memory passages from a long poem called *In Memoriam* for presentation during final exams, Papa shouts from the bedroom, "Snuff out the candle, will you?"

"It's my candle," Johannes says. "I bought it with my own money."

To get around Papa's rules, Johannes often buys his own candles and his own food. This annoys Papa, who doesn't want anyone disputing his authority in the house.

"Then take your damn candle and get out of my house."

"Leave the child alone, Jackson," Mama pleads with Papa. "He's in matric. He has to study a lot. He'll soon graduate and find a nice job and make up for all the candles he's used up."

"He already has enough education. He's sixteen. He should be working instead of wasting his time playing that silly white man's sport."

Papa doesn't like Johannes playing tennis. One time he smashed his wooden Dunlop rackets and they had a big fight. I wonder why Johannes loves playing tennis when almost all the boys in Alexandra play soccer, and they call him a sissy for playing a "white man's sport." He doesn't seem to mind when they call him names, and he seldom gets into fights. I admire him for that because I too hate fighting.

The teachers and mistresses at my school always rave about Johannes. Even Mrs. Mabaso, my Standard One mistress, when she wants me to do well, always reminds me of Johannes: "Your brother was one of the best students I ever taught. I seldom had to punish him. He always did his homework, was attentive in class, and passed his exams."

I vow to be like my brother; I pledge to do my homework on time, to listen attentively in class, and to study hard for exams. I vow to obtain the best grades and become number one. Despite the inadequacies of Bantu Education, we students always strove to do our best, in part because our teachers and mistresses expected us to do our best, as did our parents.

Few of us openly complained about the dismal state of black education—in part because most students were not yet politicized. We weren't taught anything about Nelson Mandela, leader of the African National Congress (ANC), or about Robert Sobukwe, leader of the Pan African Congress (PAC), both of whom were imprisoned on Robben Island in 1964 for fighting for freedom and equal rights for black people. Both men had been household names in Alexandra. Nelson Mandela had actually lived in the township as a young man, and had become politicized during the bus boycott of 1943, when tens of thousands of Alexandra residents protested the raising of bus fare from four to five pence. The boycott took place shortly after Mama arrived in Alexandra from Louis Trichardt, where she was born in 1939. She vaguely remembers it, but she vividly remembers the bus boycott of 1957, in which she participated.

"I was eighteen years old at the time," she tells Johannes, who is always asking her political questions. "Again the PUTCO company"—the Public Utility Transport Corporation—"wanted to raise the fare by a penny. The people refused to pay, and the boycott began on Monday, January 3, 1957. Over fifteen thousand people took part. Similar boycotts began in other townships, including Sophiatown."

Mama stops cooking porridge to take a pinch of snuff. She puts it under her tongue.

"We were living on Ninth Avenue, number thirty-four," she continues. "My father had already left my mother, and I was helping her keep the family together."

"How?" Johannes asks.

"She was working as a gardener for various white people and I would go with her and help her. I remember, when the boycott began, she was working for an English-speaking family in Cavendish. We would get up at five in the morning and walk all the way to work, a distance of about twenty kilometers."

"Wasn't it tiring?"

"It was. Especially the first couple of weeks. But we were determined not to back down. Not even when the government threatened to make a law that would forbid people in Alexandra from having buses. Our leaders called another meeting and asked if we wanted to continue. The people of Alexandra stood together. As we walked we sang, *'Asinamali'* (we have no money), and, *'Azikwela'* (we will not ride). The boycott ended in April when the bus company backed down, and there was no fare increase."

After the boycott, government repression grew, leading up to the Sharpeville massacre in 1960, which marked a turning point in the black liberation struggle. Mama remembers the events that led to the massacre.

"I was a new bride," Mama remembers. "Your father and I had been married a little over a year and I was pregnant with Johannes. Our leaders launched a campaign to get the government to abolish the pass laws. The campaign called on all Africans to leave their passes at home and present themselves for arrest. Our leaders hoped that as the prisons filled up, the economy, which depended on cheap black labor, would grind to a halt. But that was not to be. On March 21, 1960, the police shot and killed sixty-nine men, women, and children who were protesting peacefully in Sharpeville. Many were shot in the back as they fled to safety."

After the Sharpeville massacre, black leaders concluded that stay-aways, boycotts, and nonviolence would never change apartheid. The

ANC established a military wing called Umkhonto we Sizwe (Spear of the Nation), and the PAC also formed its own military wing, which it called Poqo (Standing Alone). The government outlawed both groups, jailing most of its leaders, and forcing many more to flee into exile.

In 1976, when I began my third year at Bovet, black resistance to apartheid was largely moribund. Black people had resigned themselves to the way things were. Few had the courage, strength, or time to challenge apartheid. Like Mama and Papa, they were burdened with survival. My peers and I prepared ourselves to compete for the few decent jobs that were open to blacks under the Jobs Reservations Act, a cornerstone of apartheid that reserved the best and best-paying jobs for whites.

From time to time Papa bitterly complains about the Jobs Reservations Act. He says that it prevents him from earning more than his fellow workers who are white, even when he knows more than they do about construction and carpentry, works harder than they do, and often has to teach them the job.

My dream is to become a nurse, even though I can work only at black hospitals. I don't mind that, I'd rather serve my own people than white people. Little do I know that in a few short months a political explosion the likes of which had never been seen in the history of South Africa would radically affect that dream.

Chapter 9

*On June 16 school is dismissed early. Frantic teachers and mis*tresses order us to run straight home because rioting has broken out in Soweto and the police are shooting and killing students. Florah has Linah by the hand as she, Maria, and I race up Hofmeyer Street, headed home. There's pandemonium in the streets. Shortly after I get home Johannes returns from school in Tembisa. He has a late-afternoon edition of the *World*. The entire paper is devoted to the student massacre in Soweto, and on the front page is a photo of students carrying the body of Hector Petersen, a thirteen-year-old schoolboy who's been shot dead by the police. The photo became a world symbol of the defiance and tragedy of June 16.

The next day at assembly the principal tells us that despite the massacre, schooling must go on. There's a rumble of complaining and outrage among older students but nothing comes of it. Midway through the morning lessons the rumor reaches Bovet that students at other schools in Alexandra are out in the streets protesting and that the police have been shooting at them.

The school empties. I run home with my friends Cynthia, Becky, and Dlayani. Tear gas canisters are exploding everywhere. I cough and cry and my eyes are burning. At home Mama is helping a stricken Linah who is also sick from tear gas. With a wet rag Mama daubs our eyes and noses. Mama warns me not to go outside and prays for the safety of Johannes, George, and Florah, who are out in the streets protesting.

All afternoon long I hear the sound of gunfire. Tear gas and riot-police trucks are everywhere. George, Florah, and Johannes return home carrying bags of groceries and other looted items. They tell Mama that various government buildings, delivery trucks, beer halls, and stores have been set on fire and that the people are helping themselves. They are eager to go back outside but Mama prevents them.

"You'll get yourselves killed," she says.

Fires are burning all over Alexandra. A cloud of acrid black smoke hangs over the ghetto. When Papa comes back from work he reports that his bus couldn't enter Alexandra because several buses had been burned. He had to get off in Lombardy East and walk all the way home.

At night the police drive from street to street firing tear gas into yards in an effort to confine protesters indoors. Tear gas sips through cracks in the door and window and makes Linah and Diana puke. It's impossible to sleep.

There's no school the next day. The riot police in their armored trucks are still everywhere. Florah and Johannes are in and out of the house. Each time they return they bring back looted items: bags of mealie meal and sugar, cases of cool drinks, loaves of bread, canned goods, packets of candles. I ask Florah what's going on and she tells me that students in Soweto have started a revolution.

"What's a revolution?" I ask.

"Black power."

"What's black power?"

"It means we are going to fight white people."

"And kill them?"

"Yes. Kill them."

I don't mind killing white people. Not at all. To me all white people are like the hairy policemen who terrorize me during Peri-Urban raids.

Walking home from the communal latrine a couple of days after the riot started, I hear Mashudu's mother crying bitterly. I run home and ask Mama why.

"The police shot Mashudu. She's dead."

I feel very sad. I liked Mashudu. Ten years older than me and Florah's best friend, Mashudu let me play house with her from time to time, and she taught me how to skip rope. I hate the police. Whenever I see them I run away. For many months there's no school because of the rioting. Hundreds of people are arrested and detained without trial. One of those detained is Stephen Bantu Biko, leader of the Black Consciousness movement (BC).

The BC movement had a huge following among students and black militants, particularly those who'd once belonged to the now banned PAC. Biko, a talented political thinker, was famous for his incisive attacks on white liberal thinking. He believed that blacks had to go it alone until they had developed a sense of pride and independence, so that integration with whites would no longer be "artificial," a "one-way course, with whites doing all the talking and the blacks all the listening."

On August 18, 1977, Biko dies in police custody. The police say he'd died following a hunger strike, but the autopsy reveals that he'd died from severe blows to the head. More rioting follows Biko's death. When I finally go back to school, I find that the riot police have killed several students at our school. Others have dropped out. Others have fled the country. Still others have been sent by concerned parents to schools in their homeland. Luckily all of my school friends have survived. But things are no longer the same. We've lost our innocence.

Rioting and tear gas seem to have worsened Janice's fainting. Neither snuff nor cold water revives her. Only one thing works: manchomani.

One hot Wednesday afternoon she faints as we get ready to begin sewing class. She's carried to the huge leafy tree by the gate, where she's laid on a reed mat, called a *xithebe*. Mistress Mabaso summons me, Becky, and Cynthia to perform manchomani. We have no drums, so we grab a couple of round dented metal buckets, turn them upside down, kneel, and then begin drumming rhythmically with our hands as we attempt to communicate with the spirits possessing Janice's body.

Suddenly, at the sound of the drums, her body goes into convulsions as if she's having a seizure. We increase the speed of the drumming. Her body starts shaking violently, her mouth opens, and out come guttural sounds, followed by a strange voice that is not Janice's. The voice is speaking Nguni, the language of the spirit world.

Amadoda Bulelizwe,
People of this world,
Ngi phuma gude.
I come from afar.
Angilalanga.
I can't find any rest.
Sebekhuluma ngami.
There's a great deal of talk about me.
Sebeyangi zonda . . .
I'm hated because of it . . .

As Janice transmits this message from the spirit world, Becky, Cynthia, and I increase the pace of the drumming until it reaches a crescendo. Then the spirit inside Janice screams and leaves her. Her body becomes instantly limp. She breathes slowly and deeply. She awakes as from a deep trance. She looks about, wondering where she is. She's genuinely surprised to find herself under the tree. She asks what happened and I explain. We return to the classroom and continue with our lessons.

Mamahulu (Big Mother) is a sangoma. She's Mama's older sister. Before she became a sangoma she'd been in the habit of being possessed by swikwembu, just like Janice. She's regarded as one of the most powerful sangomas in Gazankulu, the homeland of the Shangaans in the Northern Transvaal. From time to time she visits Alexandra to *phahla* and *biya tiyindlu,* exorcise evil spirits from homes whose occupants have experienced bad luck or suffered tragedies.

Papa is convinced that he's been bewitched. He cites as reasons his repeated imprisonment on pass law offenses, the family's inability to improve our lives, and Mama's inability to get a permit. Mamahulu is summoned to our home one weekend to help exorcise the spell. To honor her visit, Papa buys a goat and slaughters it. Mama cooks up a storm. Throughout the day Mamahulu is in secret consultations with my parents over the nature and onset of our problems. She consults her divination bones and comes up with an explanation: one of our neighbors is jealous and doesn't like to see us get ahead. The only way to thwart such an evil-minded neighbor is to cleanse our home of the neighbor's harmful *muti*, or bewitching potion.

Everyone is present at the cleansing ceremony Sunday night except my brothers, George and Johannes. They don't believe in witchcraft and want no part of its ceremonies.

Mamahulu is very scary looking. She's a large unsmiling woman. Her eyes are always bloodshot. We sit in a circle in the middle of the kitchen, chanting a song as she performs the cleansing ceremony. I watch her intently. As we chant she proceeds to imitate the various forms through which witchcraft has entered our house. She imitates the sounds and gestures of an ape, a cat, a lion, and a rat.

At the end of the ceremony she orders every member of the family to take a bath in the same tub. Herbs are mixed into the warm water and the bath is supposed to cleanse us all of bad luck. After we have bathed, Mamahulu dumps the filthy water outside along a path with a lot of traffic. This is meant to return the bad luck to the evil-minded neighbor.

After the cleansing ceremony Mamahulu makes a number of small incisions on everyone's chest with the same sharp razor blade. The incisions hurt but I grit my teeth. She anoints the cuts with a special ointment and gives each of us an amulet to wear as protection against future evil. Mine is a copper bracelet.

I'm awed by Mamahulu's powers, especially because my parents believe in her implicitly, particularly Papa, who is very happy after the ceremony. When Mamahulu invites me to visit her in Giyani someday, I agree with alacrity. I imagine her as living amid fabulous wealth, like the Zulu sangoma whose story Johannes read in the *World*. The sangoma was said to have one hundred wives and over two hundred children, a string of Mercedes-Benzes, a huge mansion, and even his own helicopter. This image of Mamahulu as being rich is reinforced by the fact that her son Freddie has over a dozen wives and owns a car.

"Can Mamahulu cast spells on any bad person?" I ask Mama after Mamahulu has left.

"No," Mama says. "Her muti is only for doing good and saving lives. If she ever uses her powers to do evil, she'll lose them. Why do you ask?"

"Oh," I say with an impish smile, "I was simply curious."

I don't tell Mama that I have a couple of particularly bad persons I'd love to cast spells on: teachers and mistresses who whip students; white policemen with hairy arms; and one of the biggest bullies at my school and in my neighborhood, a girl named Amanda.

Chapter 10

"A*ttention, class!" Mistress Mabaso shouts. Her voice is like a* thunderclap. On the blackboard are samples of sentences illustrating how we should write in cursive.

My friend Dlayani is standing next to Mistress Mabaso. She is crying.

"Dlayani lost twenty rand," Mistress Mabaso says. "Has anyone picked it up?"

No reply.

Mistress Mabaso stalks up and down the aisle, her steely eyes searching for any signs of who might have the twenty rand.

"The twenty rand is rent money," she says. "If Dlayani doesn't pay the rent, you know what will happen to her family? They'll be evicted. They'll become homeless like the people you see on the streets every day. Do you want that to happen to one of your classmates?"

"No," the class cries.

"Then where's the twenty rand?"

No answer.

"Dlayani says she had the money when she came to school this morning."

Mistress Mabaso returns to the front of the classroom. Her eyes immediately rest on my desk in the front row. Dlayani sits between me and Cynthia. We are squeezed three to a desk meant for two.

I avoid Mistress Mabaso's eyes and look down. Cynthia does the same. No one in our classroom can look Mistress Mabaso in the eyes for more than a couple of seconds. She is one of the most feared mistresses at Bovet.

I start to cry because Dlayani is one of my best friends and I'm supposed to accompany her to the West Rand Administration Board to pay the rent. Her family is poorer than my own. They live in a shack smaller than ours. Her mother trudges all over the township selling bundles of spinach. Her father picks up trash.

"Miriam," Mistress Mabaso asks suddenly, "did you see the money?"

"No, Mistress."

Mistress Mabaso turns to Cynthia and asks, "Did you see the money?"

"No, Mistress."

Mistress Mabaso turns to the rest of the class. "If anyone picked it up by mistake but is afraid that I'll punish them, I promise I won't."

Minutes pass. No one confesses to taking the twenty rand.

I can tell Mistress Mabaso's patience is wearing thin. I'm convinced she's going to reach into the drawer of her table and pull out the thick hosepipe and start whipping us indiscriminately. In the past she's done that when someone has lost a pencil, a ruler, lunch money, or a book and the thief has refused to own up.

"So no one took the money, is that it? It just disappeared into thin air?"

To my surprise she doesn't reach for the thick hosepipe. Instead, she walks out the door. Immediately a babble of voices erupts as pupils argue over who could have stolen Dlayani's twenty rand. Suspicion falls on Cynthia and me as Dlayani's seat mates. If looks could lynch, my classmates would have strung us up.

The room falls quiet when we hear voices outside the door. In walks Mistress Mabaso accompanied by Mr. Tiba, who teaches Standard Five.

"All boys stand up," he demands.

"Follow me."

The rickety desks creak as all thc boys squeeze out and follow Mr. Tiba outside. Everyone knows what is about to happen. Mr. Tiba is taking the boys to the latrines to be strip-searched. Mistress Mabaso will do the same to the girls. I sigh with relief. There won't be any indiscriminate whipping. The true culprit will surely be found.

I'm so relieved that I'm one of the first students to offer to be searched. I open the palms of my hands to show I have nothing in them, then I raise my arms high above my head. Mistress Mabaso frisks me. She even searches inside my bloomers. I'm clean.

I try to console Dlayani. "Don't worry, the money will be found."

Suddenly Mistress Mabaso turns around and demands, "What's that you're saying, Miriam?"

Heart pounding, I reply, "I was telling Dlayani she shouldn't worry."

Looking at the rest of my classmates something catches my eye. I notice that one student keeps moving to the back of the line. Her name is Amanda. Short and tough, she's a bully who's fought with and trounced many a girl. She lives in the yard next to ours on Thirteenth Avenue, and we both attend the Twelve Apostles Church of God, which is located in her yard. Several times she's challenged me to a fight and I've refused.

Finally every girl has been searched and found clean. It's Amanda's turn.

"I don't want to be searched," she says.

Mistress Mabaso stares at her, dumbfounded. The rest of the girls are aghast. Amanda must be out of her mind. No one dares disobey Mistress Mabaso and lives to tell about it.

"What did you say?" Mistress Mabaso's eyes reflect both incredulity and rage.

Amanda doesn't answer.

Mistress Mabaso turns to the rest of the class and says, "Step outside. I want to talk to Amanda alone."

We promptly obey. Once outside, we jostle one another for the most advantageous spot by the window from which to witness the high drama about to unfold inside the classroom. Having been among the first to step outside, I have my face pasted against the cracked window and I can see and hear everything.

"Who are you not to be searched?" Mistress Mabaso demands fiercely.

Before Amanda can reply, Mistress Mabaso slaps her hard across the face.

I'm stunned. I've never seen a mistress or teacher slap a pupil before. Then she slaps Amanda again.

"Where's the money?" she demands.

Amanda's lips are pursed in defiance.

Mistress Mabaso slaps her again. Amanda doesn't cry. Mistress Mabaso grabs her and forcibly frisks her.

"Where is the money?"

Amanda doesn't say a word. There's a look of hatred and defiance in her eyes. I'm convinced she's being stubborn—she has a reputation for defying mistresses—and doesn't have the money. My sympathy immediately shifts to her.

"Where is the money?" Mistress Mabaso asks again.

Amanda says nothing.

Suddenly Mistress Mabaso punches her in the mouth. Amanda screams and then spits out something. It's a tooth. Blood spurts out her mouth. I'm in shock. Why is Mistress Mabaso battering an innocent student?

"Where is the money?" Mistress Mabaso demands, raising her fist, ready to strike Amanda again.

"Here it is," Amanda says, spitting out a crumpled and bloodied piece of paper. It's a twenty-rand bill. Apparently, she'd been hiding it under her tongue.

"Go wash it and give it back to Dlayani," Mistress Mabaso says.

Amanda dutifully obeys. She heads out of the classroom, her head bowed. The rest of us girls file back in and take our seats. Mistress Mabaso steps out, and she returns with the boys. Amanda comes in with the washed twenty-rand bill.

"Give it to Dlayani."

I watch Amanda walk with downcast eyes to our desk. When she reaches it, I can see hatred in her eyes. She stretches out her hand and Dlayani takes the damp twenty-rand bill.

"Say you're sorry," Mistress Mabaso says.

Amanda hesitates, then mumbles, "I'm sorry."

"Now take your books and get out of here. I don't want thieves in my class."

A humiliated Amanda slowly packs her books and walks out. Class resumes, but I can hardly concentrate on the lessons. Did Amanda deserve to be beaten like that even though she'd stolen the money? But then I realize that if Mistress Mabaso hadn't beaten her, she wouldn't have given the money back, and Dlayani and her family would have been evicted from their shack.

After school, Dlayani and I walk to the West Rand Administration Board in Wynberg to pay the rent. On the way she says to me, "I'm sorry about what happened to Amanda. I wish she'd given me the money before the mistress beat her."

"Me too."

"Do you think Amanda hates me for what happened?"

"I hope not."

"But I'm afraid she'll want to fight me."

"If she challenges you to a fight, do as I do," I say.

"What do you do?"

"I simply walk away."

That evening I tell Mama what happened.

"Like mother like daughter," she says. "Amanda learns everything from her mother. Even the fighting. I fought her mother once. But that was before I joined the church. Now that I'm God's servant, I don't fight. But Amanda's mother still provokes me from time to time. I simply walk away because I know the devil is tempting me."

"Is that why you say I should walk away from fights?" I ask.

"Yes. It's always better to turn the other cheek, my child."

Chapter 11

"*Miriam Mathabane,*" *Mistress Mabaso calls out.*

"Present," I say, raising my hand.

"James Mathebula," Mistress Mabaso calls out.

James raises his hand and replies, "Present."

Mistress Mabaso goes down the alphabetical list and after each "Present" places a check mark alongside the student's name in the attendance record. She performs the ritual like clockwork each morning before class begins. Absenteeism is severely punished, except when one has a legitimate excuse, like a death in the family. Sickness is seldom accepted as an excuse, unless one has a letter from a doctor.

One person is absent: Amanda. I look out the window and there she is with her mother. They're defiantly making their way across the courtyard. They are headed for the principal's office at the back of the school. I wonder if Amanda's combative mother has come to beat up Mistress Mabaso.

Minutes later there's a knock at the door.

In walks a tall, gangly boy in a neat school uniform and a blazer. "Mistress Mabaso," he says respectfully, "the principal wants to see you in his office."

"Tell him I'll be there in a minute," Mistress Mabaso says. There's no trace of anxiety in her voice. Mistress Mabaso tells us to review our arithmetic tables for a pop quiz. She tells the class prefect to write down the names of all noisemakers and then goes out. Seconds later Cynthia goes to the class prefect, a boy who sits at the back of the room, and asks for permission to go to the toilet. I know that Cynthia is using the excuse of going to the latrine in order to eavesdrop on what is about to happen in the principal's office.

Cynthia returns about ten minutes later. "You won't believe what happened," she whispers.

But before Cynthia can answer, the door opens. To everyone's surprise, Amanda enters, followed by Mistress Mabaso. I look out the window and I see Amanda's mother going out the gate. For some reason, given Amanda's mother's reputation as a brawler, I expect to see blood on Mistress Mabaso's dress or marks on her face to suggest a fight. There's none.

"Take your seat," Mistress Mabaso says to Amanda.

"Yes, Mistress," Amanda says in a contrite voice and sits down.

Lunch arrives.

Cynthia, Dlayani, Margaret, and I share a sumptuous lunch consisting of fish and chips, Viennas, Russians, and Fanta paid for with the two rand I won playing cards the day before.

"Mistress Mabaso stared straight into Amanda's mother's face," Cynthia reports, "and she said, 'Your child was caught stealing. It's wrong to steal. Then she compounded her crime by denying it. Do you know that she can be expelled for such behavior?' "

Cynthia pauses to munch her Russian, then says, "Amanda's mother said to Mistress Mabaso, 'I'm sorry for what Amanda did. I want to thank you for disciplining her.' "

"She said that?" I ask in an incredulous voice.

"Yes."

"What happened next?" Dlayani asks between nibbling her greasy chips.

"Amanda's mother then asked Amanda to apologize to Mistress Mabaso."

"Did she?" I ask.

"She did."

I wasn't surprised. Few parents dared dispute the authority of a teacher or a mistress in the classroom. Teachers and mistresses were considered an extension of parental authority and had permission to punish students for wrongdoing. And few teachers and mistresses wanted to lose respect by not punishing students, for it meant losing control over the classroom, which undermined their ability to teach. So even the gentle teachers and mistresses—and they were quite a few—felt compelled to punish students in order to maintain control over the classroom.

Despite being punished, Amanda never stops getting in trouble. One day she steals Dlayani's pencil. And not having a pencil during note taking or an exam meant a whipping. To insure that one always had a pencil, we would break a single pencil into three or four smaller pieces, sharpened them, and stored them under the desk.

Margaret sees Amanda filching Dlayani's pencil minutes before an exam and tells Dlayani. Now Dlayani, like myself, has been labeled as a coward for refusing to be drawn into fights. But the dread of being punished by Mistress Mabaso makes her say to Amanda, "Give me back the pencil, you thief, or I'll beat you after school."

Amanda apparently can't believe that Dlayani has dared her to a fight instead of threatening to report her to the mistress.

"Okay," Amanda says. "After school, then. I've been longing to teach you a lesson, you bloody Shangaan."

Amanda doesn't give Dlayani her pencil back. Luckily I have a spare one, which I loan her. But for the rest of the day she's distracted.

"What's the matter?" I ask her just before the bell rings for afterschool.

"I'm scared of fighting Amanda," she says.

"Then why did you dare her to a fight?"

"I wasn't thinking clearly. I was angry."

"You can still back out, you know."

"I can't."

"Why not?"

"Everyone will think I'm a coward."

After school arrives. A contingent follows the two combatants. The fight can't take place near the school lest a teacher or mistress catch sight of the fighters and whip both of them.

I'm carrying Dlayani's books. I'm very concerned because I know she's not a fighter and that Amanda has a reputation as the meanest brawler around. We reach Fourteenth Avenue, a street the group considers far enough away from school for the fight to take place without fear of being detected. We form a ring around Dlayani and Amanda, on a grassy patch of ground. Both tuck the sides of their gym dresses into their bloomers, a move signaling that no quarter will be given or any asked for during the fight.

Dlayani's face shows absolutely no sign of fear. Amanda's face has a grin. She's almost salivating. She wastes no time pouncing on Dlayani, grabbing her by the shoulders. They grapple. Amanda tries to wrestle Dlayani down, trying to pin her to the ground so she can apply "the Amanda treatment": pummeling her opponent with fists and clawing her face with her long fingernails until she begs for mercy.

But Amanda has miscalculated. Dlayani refuses to go down. On the contrary, the "coward" surprises everyone by landing more blows on Amanda than Amanda does on her. And Dlayani's blows are more telling, for Amanda is bleeding from a torn lower lip and one of her eyes is starting to get puffy.

Realizing that she might lose the fight, Amanda resorts to a favorite desperation tactic: biting. She sinks her sharp, protruding teeth into Dlayani's firm and ripening breast.

I've never heard anyone scream in pain as hard as Dlayani screamed. Amanda, traces of blood on her yellow teeth, lets go of her and grins.

"I told you I'd teach you a lesson," Amanda says as Dlayani sinks to her knees, clutching her bleeding right breast. She's in deep pain. Amanda picks up her books and calmly walks home. Cynthia and I come to Dlayani's aid. Her white school shirt is soaked with blood. She can't stop crying. Cynthia and I gingerly unfasten her shirt to check on the extent of her wound. I'm shocked. Her right breast has now swollen to about twice its normal size.

"We must take her to the clinic or she'll die," a panicky Cynthia says.

"I've no money," I say. "Have you?"

"No. Does anyone have money?" Cynthia asks the group of spectactors who've been witnessing the fight. No one does. We spent it all during the sumptuous lunch.

I suggest to Cynthia that we take Dlayani to my house, which is a block away. There I boil some water on the Primus stove and mix it with some salt. I dip a piece of rag in the mix and carefully dab the wound. Dlayani grimaces but doesn't cry. I can't believe the size of the holes in her breast made by Amanda's fangs.

I give Dlayani something to drink, she rests, and then Cynthia and I walk her home. Her mother comes back from selling spinach. We relate what's happened. She can't afford to send Dlayani to the clinic, so she continues with the home remedy. New to Alexandra, and a meek woman by nature, she has no inclination to confront Amanda's mother over the incident.

Despite her wounds, Dlayani is back in school the next day. She dare not stay home to recuperate without a valid reason. And Mistress Mabaso would have punished her and Amanda had she found out that they'd fought.

Chapter 12

A*manda, Becky, a group of other children from the neighborhood,* and I are treasure hunting by rummaging through a mound of business envelopes near the communal latrines overlooking the Twelve Apostles Church of God. The envelopes are dumped regularly by the squat, jet black man with the decrepit van who picks them up at a factory in Wynberg.

I open one and find ten crisp one-rand notes.

"I've found money!" I cry with delight, brandishing the notes.

"How much did you find?" everyone asks.

"Ten rand."

"It's mine," Amanda says, picking up the empty envelope.

"No it's not, I found it."

"It's mine, I say," Amanda says. "Give it to me or I'll hit you."

I run home.

"Mama, I found money."

"Money? Where is it?" she asks eagerly. There's not a cent in the house. Papa lost his entire wages again gambling. We can't even afford to buy a loaf of bread. Mama had to borrow a cup of Omo laundry detergent from a neighbor.

I show Mama the ten rand.

"Did you steal it, child?" she asks suspiciously.

"No, Mama. I picked it up when we were playing by the envelopes."

"Which envelopes?"

"You know that mound of rubbish near the latrines? I found the money there."

Mama is overjoyed. The money is a gift from God, she says. He doesn't want us to starve. He wants Mama to have bus fare to go to work. He wants me and my siblings to have lunch money for school.

Mama is about to put the ten rand in her purse when Amanda and her mother come marching toward us.

"Musadi"—woman—Amanda's mother says in a huff, "your daughter is a thief. She stole my money."

"It's your money?"

"Yes. I gave ten rand to Amanda to go pay rent. It was in this envelope," Amanda's mother says, brandishing the brown envelope.

Mama gives me a severe look. "Did you steal the money, child?"

"No, I picked it up at the rubbish dump."

"She's lying, musadi," Amanda's mother says. "She stole it."

"I didn't steal it," I cry indignantly. "You can ask my friends."

"She stole it, musadi. Whom do you believe? Your lying child, or me?"

"I'm sorry," Mama says, handing the ten rand over to Amanda's mother. "You know how children are."

"I know," Amanda's mother says, accepting the money. She and Amanda leave.

Mama turns to me. "Miriam, I'm ashamed of you. How dare you embarrass me like that!"

"I swear I didn't steal the money, Mama," I say, crying. "I picked it up at the rubbish dump."

Several weeks later there's another treasure hunt with Amanda, Becky, and a group of other kids from the neighborhood. Again I find a brown envelope with money.

"I found some money," I blurt out and then instantly check myself, remembering how Amanda and her mother had cunningly robbed me of my find the last time.

"How much?" everyone says, crowding around me.

I don't say. I simply walk home.

"I found money again, Mama," I say hesitantly.

"Were you playing with Amanda again?"

"Yes," I say, "but it's not her money."

"How much did you find?" she asks.

"I didn't count it," I say, handing her the envelope.

She counts the money. There's twenty-five rand. Mama is about to head into the house when, to my horror, Amanda and her mother come marching toward us.

"Musadi," Amanda's mother says, "your daughter's done it again."

"You mean she stole your money again?" Mama asks.

"Yes."

"How much was it, musadi?" Mama asks.

Amanda's mother is tongue-tied. Apparently she hadn't expected the question. I'm glad I didn't count the money in Amanda's presence.

Amanda's mother looks at Amanda.

"It was ten rand," Amanda says.

"Are you sure it was ten rand, musadi?"

"I'm sure, musadi."

"I'm sorry," Mama says, "but my daughter found twenty-five rand."

Ashamed at having been caught in a lie, Amanda's mother grabs Amanda by the hand and they walk away.

Mama turns to me and says, "I'm sorry for not believing you the first time, child."

"What's my real name, Mama," I ask one day. "Miriam, or Luambo?"

"Both are your real names, child. But Luambo is the more important."

"Why?"

"Because it's the name your *midzimu*"—my ancestors—"know you as," Mama says.

She then proceeds to explain the complicated process of how I came to be named. Seven days after I was born she took me to Mtumbu, the family traditional doctor. Mtumbu, a wizened Venda woman who lived on Eleventh Avenue, conducted an elaborate baptism ceremony to connect me to my ancestors and to protect me from harm in my vulnerable years of infancy. She first bathed me in water mixed with special herbs and roots, then nicked every part of my body with a sharp razor, including the fontanel. Next she trimmed my fingernails and toenails, burned and ground the clippings to fine ash, and mixed them with special muti, traditional medicine.

She then anointed the cuts and my soft spot with the muti. The remaining muti she gave to Mama with instructions to keep anointing my fontanel, using the pinkie of her right hand, once a day, until the bones in my skull closed. Also, she told Mama to add dashes of the muti to the *mdoho,* the soft porridge that is to be my only food, along with Mama's breast milk, for the first few months of infancy.

"After the baptism ceremony she then gave you your ancestral name, Luambo," Mama says.

"What does it mean?"

Mama smiles. "Just before you were born, your father and I used to argue a lot."

"About money?"

"What else? Mtumbu knew about this, for I told her everything. So she named you Luambo, which means 'Too Much Argument' in Venda."

"Where did I get the name Miriam?"

"I gave it to you," Mama says. "When I took you for your ten-day checkup, I had to have one. The clinic had a rule that a child had to have a Christian name. So I fished one out of my head. I named you Miriam, after the sister of Moses."

"You mean the one who cared for the baby in the bulrushes?"

"Yes. How do you know the story?"

"We read it at school. We also saw the movie. It's called *The Ten Commandments.*"

Mama proceeds to tell me the origins of the names of my six siblings.

"Your brother Johannes was my first child. And if the child is a son, the father gets to name him, for a son is considered heir to his father's name and fortune. So your father named your brother Johannes, after his youngest brother. Johannes also happens to be the name of Hahani's"—my father's sister's—"husband."

"What's Johannes's ancestral name?"

"Thanyani. It means 'Be wise.' When he was born I was eighteen. People were constantly taking advantage of me because I was young and a new wife. Your father's sister named your brother Thanyani to remind me to be wise. The name also means 'The Wise One.' "

"What about Florah?"

"Florah is the name of my aunt," Mama says, "and your sister's ancestral name is Mkondeleli, which is Venda for 'Endurance.' When Florah was born I was very unhappy because your father had begun drinking a lot. So Mtumbu told me to hang in there."

"What about George?"

"George is the name of one of my uncles. When your brother was born your father and I were constantly fighting. So Mtumbu named him Ndwakhulu, which means 'Big Wars.' "

"What about Maria?"

"I named her after the mother of Jesus," Mama says. "She was my second girl and fourth child. I thought two boys and two girls enough children, so Mtumbu named her Azwidhovi, which means, 'No More Children.' "

"What about Linah?"

"I named her after Priest Mathebula's wife because she helped me a lot. When Linah was born I was going through a very hard time with your father. He was constantly drinking and gambling. Priest Mathebula's wife was always there to help. Mtumbu knew of my hardships and frustrations also, so she called Linah Ndicheni, which means 'Leave me alone.' "

"And what about Diana?"

"When she was born your father's drinking and gambling had worsened. Again members of the church stepped in to help. The wife of Priest Khosa helped me find a piece job. With the money I was able to pay the clinic so I could be attended by nurses during delivery. So I named Diana after Priest Khosa's wife. Mtumbu named your youngest sister Khangweni, which means 'Forsaken.' Mtumbu thought that my ancestors had forsaken me because I was suffering so much in my marriage to your father."

Chapter 13

The only person who's never forsaken Mama is Granny. She never hesitates to spend whatever little money she earns as a gardener to help Mama. Whenever Mama and Papa fight—which is often—Mama always finds refuge at Granny's two-room shack on Seventeenth Avenue. It's Granny who brings her back and pleads with Papa to stop abusing her child.

Granny herself was abandoned by her husband when Mama was six years old. She never remarried but had two more children, Aunt Bushy and Uncle Piet. She lives with them and Aunt Bushy's daughters, Nkensani (Thank you) and Fikile (She's arrived).

Fikile and Nkensani are illegitimate. Fikile, whose father is Venda and a former bus driver, is two years younger than I and very smart. After enrolling in Sub-A she was promoted to Standard One, skipping Sub-B, but despite her intelligence, she hates school. More precisely, she hates being whipped, so she's constantly truant.

Teachers and mistresses constantly yank me out of class to go looking for her whenever she's absent. I'm often accompanied by a posse of four or six big boys, but each time we find Fikile, she outruns us. She takes after Aunt Bushy, who was also an excellent runner at Bovet but had to drop out in Standard Five because she didn't have money for books, school fees, and a uniform. Aunt Bushy now serves tea at an office building in Wynberg, and has held the same job for over ten years.

The Mathabane family also has excellent runners. Maria and George anchor the track team at Bovet, which is considered one of the best in Alexandra. Linah is also a fine runner. I'm slightly overweight and do not run, but I love attending track meets at the Alexandra stadium and cheering George, Maria, Fikile, and Linah to victory. All four run barefoot, and they are so good that songs are sung in their honor whenever they run.

But the best athlete in my family is Johannes. Ever since he picked up tennis at age thirteen, after receiving a wooden racket from one of Granny's employers and adopting Arthur Ashe as a role model, Johannes has been obsessed with the game. Now he's so good his name is constantly in the newspapers. He's the best tennis player in Alexandra and has won a couple of tournaments. Having finished matric, he spends his time playing tennis at the Barretts Tennis Ranch in Halfway House. My parents want him to get a job, but he insists that tennis is his only hope of ever realizing his dream of attending university in America.

No one except Mama takes this dream seriously. A lot of people laugh at him and say that Mama wasted her money sending him to school when all he wants to do is to play a sissy sport instead of looking for work. Papa is especially hard on Johannes. The two are constantly fighting over the fact that Johannes is not working. That's why Johannes stays away from home all day, returning only at night when Papa is asleep.

One night Johannes arrives home very excited.

"I've finally found a way of getting to America, Mama," he says.

"You have?" Mama asks.

"Yes."

"How are you going to get there?"

"Through a scholarship."

"From whom?"

"Today I met a white couple who've promised to help me apply for it."

Mama is dubious of Johannes's white friends, especially because they've gotten him in trouble before with people who consider anyone associating with whites a sellout.

"Are these whites from South Africa?"

"No. They're from America."

"What are their names?"

"Stan and Marjorie Smith. Stan is one of the best players in the world. He won Wimbledon and the U.S. Open and is good friends with Arthur Ashe."

"Where did you meet them?"

"At a tennis tournament in Johannesburg."

"Are you sure they'll help you get to America?" Mama asks.

"They promised."

"Don't you think you have a better chance of finding a job than of going to America, son?"

"I must get to America, Mama," Johannes says. "I must."

I wonder why Johannes is so determined to get to America. I ask Mama one day and she replies, "Your brother tells me that black people in America are free. They have good jobs and live in nice houses. Also, their children attend the same schools as whites."

"Are there police raids in America?"

"No. And black people there don't have to carry passes."

I like America and pray that Johannes makes it over there. Maybe someday he'll be able to get us all to America, away from the pain and suffering, away from the violence and death, away from the constant and terrifying police raids.

I'm sleeping on pieces of cardboard on the kitchen floor with Florah, Linah, and Diana. Because of the cramped condition of the kitchen, we are huddled together near the door. My head is directly facing the door. Maria is curled up next to me. Florah and Diana are sleeping facing the opposite way. George and Johannes are asleep on the twin bed with the sagging mattress.

Dawn is breaking outside. Its light is filtering through the small kitchen window overlooking the street. I've been awake since Papa inadvertently stepped on my right hand as he was trying to negotiate his way to the door across sleeping bodies. The crushed hand still hurts. Suddenly I hear a loud knocking on the door of the shack next to ours, where my friend Becky lives. The knocking is followed by shouts of "Open up! Open up or we'll break down the door!" I freeze. It's the Peri-Urban Police. They've again invaded our neighborhood.

I suddenly realize that Mama is still in the house. And her papers aren't in order. I grope under the pillow for my dress just as Florah is creeping toward the bedroom door.

"Mama," she whispers. "Peri-Urban is here."

Suddenly there's a loud banging on the front door. *"Bula! Bula!"*—open up!—a male voice shouts in Sotho. I fumble to put on my dress and then open the door. A large black policeman storms in and immediately blinds me with his torch. Diana and Linah are awake and screaming. Maria is standing next to Florah; both are trying hard to stop shaking. George and Johannes are also awake.

The large black policeman goes over to where Johannes is standing.

"Where's your pass?" he demands in Sotho.

"I don't have one."

"Are you still in school?"

"No."

"Why not?"

"I've completed matric and I'm looking for a job."

"You better get yourself a pass soon, you hear? You are old enough to carry one."

The large black policeman heads for the bedroom door. Will Mama be arrested like the last time? I hear voices in the bedroom but I can't make out what is being said. Finally the policeman emerges, followed by Mama.

"Leave your door open, musadi," the large black policeman says to Mama. "That way no one will come."

"I will. And thank you very much for understanding."

"You're welcome."

The large black policeman heads out the door.

"Do you know that black policeman, Mama?" Johannes asks.

"Why do you ask?"

"He didn't arrest me. And he didn't arrest you either. Did you bribe him or something?"

"No."

"Then why didn't he arrest us?"

"He gave me a break. His wife goes to our church."

Suddenly I realized who the large black policeman was. "Is he Lerato's father, Mama?" I ask.

"Yes."

"Lerato's father is a very nice man," I say. "He gave Dlayani, Cynthia, and me a lift the other day in his big American car."

"Did he?"

"Yes. We were on our way from the Indian place."

"He's a nice man, indeed," Mama says. Mama turns to Johannes. "He told me that it's high time you got a pass."

"You know why I can't get one. I don't have a job."

"Why don't you look for a job?"

"I'm looking."

"No you're not," Mama says. "All you're doing is playing tennis and dreaming about going to America."

In pursuit of his dream to get to America, Johannes asks me to watch out for letters from America. He promises to give me three cents for each letter. Every afterschool I stand by the gate with a group of neighborhood kids. We watch out for the mailman as he comes riding down the street on his bicycle. There are no letters from America for months.

Johannes finds a job at Barclays Bank in downtown Johannesburg through one of his white tennis friends. The job instantly transforms our lives. Having passed matric, Johannes makes about ten times what my parents earn together. With his salary he pays rent, buys groceries for the family and school things for my siblings and me.

Mama is very happy. She says that the God of Israel has finally answered her prayers and that Johannes will be our savior from poverty.

Chapter 14

One day a letter arrives for Johannes from the United States. That evening, my siblings and I huddle around the kitchen table and listen to Johannes tell us about the letter's incredible contents. He's been offered a full tennis scholarship by Limestone College in South Carolina. He'll be leaving in August, two months away.

Mama falls on her knees and thanks God for the miracle. Johannes admonishes us not to tell anyone, for fear that jealous people or the government might prevent him from leaving.

I'm very sad. Johannes left for America this morning. We hugged and kissed him farewell from inside the shack. We waved good-bye as the car disappeared in the morning mist. Before leaving, Johannes told me and my siblings to study hard, stay out of trouble, and that someday he'd help us attend university in America.

I don't know where America is, but it must be an important place because when I got to school the principal makes an announcement during assembly. "Johannes Mathabane," he says proudly, "a former brilliant pupil at Bovet Community School, left this morning for the United States of America." Teachers and mistresses and students clap their hands. "He is the first member of our school to do so," the principal goes on, "but I certainly hope he won't be the last."

During class my Standard Two mistress shows us a copy of yesterday's *World,* which has the following banner headline:

TENNIS STAR

JETS

TO AMERICA

The mistress explains that the tennis star in the story is the brother of "Miriam Mathabane, a member of our class." The mistress asks me to stand up, which I shyly do. Everyone looks at me with envious eyes. The mistress points to the desk where Johannes used to sit and says to the class, "If you too study as hard as Johannes Mathabane did, you'll achieve your dreams. You may even follow him to America. Who wants to go to America?"

Everyone raises their hands. The mistress asks us if we know anything about America. A lot of students have seen movies about America, and they mention cowboys, Indians, fast cars, spaceships, rich and beautifully dressed people.

Lunch hour comes and students crowd around me. They ask me all sorts of questions about my brother. Some ask me if I too will soon be going to America. I tell them yes, as soon as my brother gets to America he's going to send for me and the rest of the family.

"You mean you're going to fly in an airplane?" someone asks, bug-eyed.

"Yes," I reply.

Everyone wants to be my friend. People offer to buy me lunch. I feel very proud to have a brother like Johannes. But when I get home that afternoon, I become sad because Papa is very angry with Mama for allowing Johannes to go to America.

"Now we'll be as poor as church mice again," Papa says. "And mark my word, he'll never come back. He'll forget about us."

Papa was right. With Johannes gone, we're poor and miserable again. Mama lost her job when her employer moved. Papa has resumed drinking and gambling. Florah, whom Johannes had sent to secretarial school, quit for lack of money and is now hunting for jobs like Mama.

As always, Mama prays every night and every morning. She asks me to read her the Bible every night because none of my older siblings want to. She says God will bless me for reading the Bible to her. She says also that God will provide for us now that Johannes is gone, and will protect us against all evil, including the police. Following the crushing of the student rebellion, the police have resumed their pass raids with a vengeance.

"How can Christ protect us from the police?" I ask one night. Six-year-old Diana is snuggling against Mama's lap.

"If we believe that he's the living God," Mama says, "he'll solve our permit problem. And if we get a permit, I won't be arrested anymore."

"If I believe in Christ will I have food every day, Mama?" Diana asks. "I hate eating sonjas and *tinjiya*"—grasshoppers.

"Yes, my child, you'll have food every day. There's nothing beyond the power of the living God."

"Stop misleading those poor children with nonsense," Papa says from the bedroom. He's drunk. Things are so bad that he now drinks even during the week.

"What nonsense?" Mama asks with an impish smile.

"You've been going to that damn church for more than ten years now. The police raids haven't stopped one bit. No God can stop Peri-Urban from coming."

"The God of Israel can," Mama says. "He broke down the walls of Jericho and he drowned Pharaoh's chariots in the Red Sea."

"Bah."

"Why have you hardened your heart against the living God?" Mama asks. "You're just like Pharaoh, you know that?"

"At least he had plenty to eat."

"We too can have plenty to eat. The minute you accept Christ as your Lord and Savior, manna will flow from heaven. All our troubles will be over. You'd stop drinking and gambling. You'd find a better job. Our children would have food and clothes and books and toys."

"Look at it this way, woman," Papa says. "I do in a way believe in the Christian God. After all, it was I who gave you permission to go attend his church. And I can withdraw that permission anytime I bloody well please."

"I know you're the boss, Mr. Mathabane," Mama says. Whenever she is attempting to humor Papa, Mama always calls him boss.

"I'm glad you remember that," Papa says.

"But doesn't it look strange when the boss isn't at church with his wife and children? Especially when other bosses accompany their wives and children every Sunday?"

"They're fools. I'll never prostrate myself before a white man's God in a million years. I have my own gods."

"And what have they done for you lately?" Mama asks. "Why don't they make you win at dice?"

"Stop blabbering, woman," Papa says angrily. "You are the reason I don't win at dice. Your heart is set against my playing."

"Why shouldn't it be when you're gambling away money our children need?"

"Shut up, will you!" Papa says. "And snuff out that damn candle before it burns out. It costs money, you know. And I haven't seen the white man's God giving you any candles. I have to sweat for them."

Mama is stark raving mad. One minute she was fine and the next she was a raving lunatic. Papa says it's because of too much religion. Granny thinks that Mama is possessed by swikwembu and needs to twasa so she can become a sangoma. Other people say Mama is crazy because she's overwhelmed by responsibility. Still others say she misses Johannes, who left for America five years ago but has sent us only a handful of letters and no money. Florah suspects witchcraft and blames the neighbor fingered by Mamahulu. Doctors at the clinic and at General Hospital are baffled.

Whatever the cause, Mama is very sick. She refuses to eat. She calls food shit and accuses the family of trying to poison her. She's as thin as a matchstick. Her eyes bulge and her cheeks are hollow. She shits and urinates in her panties. She has violent streaks. Sometimes I'm afraid of her. Each afternoon when I get back from school I find her sitting by the entrance to the yard, her legs folded, singing her favorite church song:

Rock of Ages, cleft for me,
Let me hide myself in Thee.
Let the water and the blood
From thy wounded side which flowed
Be of sin the double cure,
Save from wrath and make me pure.

Could my tears forever flow,
Could my zeal no languor know,
These for sin could not atone,
Thou must save, and Thou alone.
In my hand no price I bring.
Simply to Thy cross I cling.

I cry whenever I hear Mama sing the song. I cry even harder when strangers laugh at her. Sometimes she wanders off by herself. George and Florah, fearing for her safety, finally agree to have her committed to a mental ward at Tembisa Hospital. She is confined for three months but that doesn't help. In desperation Granny takes Mama to Mamahulu in Gazankulu. Granny believes that only Mamahulu, by consulting our ancestral spirits through her divination bones, can determine if Mama has swikwembu or if she's been bewitched.

During Mama's absence, Papa drinks even more. There's often nothing to eat. Luckily one of Florah's friends helps her find a job refurbishing old pianos and we are able to pay the rent and avoid eviction. Collin, Florah's boyfriend, helps with the groceries. But there isn't any money to pay school fees or buy books, and Linah, Diana, and I are continually whipped. I consider dropping out and going to work, but Florah urges me to stay on.

"You're only thirteen," she says.

Eight weeks before Christmas Mama comes back. She's been gone almost a year. Everyone is overjoyed. I'm even more overjoyed because she's finally cured. She's still thin and hollow cheeked, but she's no longer mad. She tells us that she'd indeed been bewitched and that Mamahulu had pinpointed our neighbor as the wizard. But typical of Mama, she wants no revenge. She simply wants to go on with her life.

"Only God has a right to punish," Mama says. "My duty as his servant is to forgive even my enemies."

Mama continues to sing her favorite song, "Rock of Ages." But this time I'm not afraid of her. My sisters and I sing along, holding hands, as we cry tears of joy.

Chapter 15

Johannes's success as a student at Bovet has put a lot of pressure on me and my siblings. Teachers are constantly reminding us of how he was a model student, how he always came out number one, how well he spoke English, and how well-read he was. George feels so much pressure he starts imitating Johannes. Despite being an excellent runner and soccer player, he starts playing tennis. He also starts speaking English, reading avidly, and purchasing newspapers every day, as Johannes used to do.

He reads the newspaper sitting at the kitchen table, as Johannes used to do. And like Johannes, he adopts the habit of reading aloud various stories to the rest of the family.

One evening in February of 1982 he reads us a front-page story in the *Johannesburg Star,* the largest English daily. It's about the death, in police detention at the notorious John Vorster Square, of the secretary of the African Food and Canning Workers Union, Neil Aggett. The police maintain that Aggett committed suicide by hanging himself, but few people believe the explanation. There are rumors that his suicide was caused by ill treatment. He'd been kept naked in his cell, made to stand for hours, and severely beaten by the police. The story reminds me of the death of Stephen Biko, five years earlier, except that Neil Aggett is white.

"Why would they kill a white person?" Florah asks George. Mama is away with members of her church visiting the sick, and Florah is cooking dinner.

"Anyone who challenges apartheid," George says, "whether he or she is black or white, is seen as a threat."

"Does that mean that Johannes too is considered a threat?" Florah asks. In America Johannes has begun speaking out against apartheid. He recently sent us a letter in which he mentioned that he'd begun speaking to various groups, including churches and schools, about the evils of apartheid, and what it meant to grow up in Alexandra. There is a great deal of concern in the family that speaking out might endanger his life, but we seldom discuss the subject.

"Yes," George says. "His life is in danger."

"What kind of danger?"

"If he came back they'd detain him."

Part of me wishes for Johannes to come back so he can help the family. Another part wishes for him to stay away so he can escape detention.

"Johannes called me at work today," Florah says as we are sitting at the table having dinner. It's a Friday and Papa, as usual, is out drinking.

"What did he say?" Mama asks.

"He asked if we'd received any of the letters he's sent us."

"We haven't received any letter since the last one he sent us in March," George says. It's November.

"He says that he's written us five letters since then," Florah says.

"I wonder what could have happened to them," Mama asks.

"The police probably took them," George says.

"Took them?" Mama says, perplexed. "Why?"

"As a way of harassing us," George says. "They don't like Johannes speaking out against apartheid. So by intercepting the letters they hope to make him stop."

"He shouldn't stop," Mama says without hesitation. "He must tell the world the truth about what is happening to us black people. It's the right thing to do."

I'm surprised to hear Mama say this, as is everyone else.

"What if he's killed?" Florah asks.

"Then God would have willed it," Mama says. "Nothing happens without God's permission."

At the end of 1982 I sit for final exams. Ever since Mama went crazy I haven't been able to concentrate on school. Even though I do well on the final exam, my cumulative marks for the year—we have four exams each year, and they all count toward the end-of-the-year grade—are low. I drop out of the top ten class rankings for the first time since I began school.

Mama says that I did my best and should be proud, especially because I've been chosen class prefect by my classmates, who say I have a good personality and always go out of my way to make new students feel welcome.

"But marks are important, Mama," I say. "Johannes was always number one."

"Marks are important, child," Mama says. "But remember, you are not Johannes. You are Miriam. You did the best under the most difficult circumstances. Had I been around and well, I have no doubt you'd have come out number one."

Florah is pregnant. Mama rejoices. Since Collin paid *lobola* (dowry) for Florah, Mama has been concerned that Florah was barren. Children are very important in a tribal marriage, and Mama was afraid that Collin, whom she adores for helping the family when she was ill, would leave Florah for another woman.

While Florah's pregnancy delights Mama, the news of Maria's devastates her.

"Why did you ruin your future?" Mama asks Maria one afternoon after Maria tells her that she is pregnant. Unlike Florah, who is twenty-one, working, and married, Maria is only sixteen and still in Standard Four.

Maria doesn't answer. She's too ashamed.

"Who is the father?"

"Collin."

"Florah's husband?"

"No, it's a different Collin. He goes to my school. He's Cynthia's cousin."

I know Collin. He and Maria are on the track team at Bovet. I wonder what will happen to my sister now. Will she drop out of school like all the other girls her age and younger who became pregnant during the riots?

"You know you'll have to leave school, don't you?" Mama says.

"Yes," Maria says, on the verge of tears.

"But it's not the end of the world, my child," Mama says. "Once you have the baby I want you to return to school. I want you to get your matric so you can get a good job and become a somebody. I'll take care of the baby for you."

"Thank you, Mama," Maria says, wiping tears from her eyes.

Mama hugs her.

That night Mama tells Papa that Maria is pregnant. Papa is so angry he threatens to kill Maria. He calls her a *skeberesh,* a whore, and chases her out of the house. Maria goes and stays with Granny for about a week until Papa has calmed down.

"Please do not become pregnant, Miriam," Mama says to me one evening after I've read her the Bible. "If you do, it would kill me."

We kneel down together on the cement floor and she prays to God to protect me from becoming a teenage mother. I'm confident that I'll be able to resist the pressure to become sexually active early because of my faith in God and my steadfast belief that people should have sex only after they're married. When other sexually active girls make fun of me for being a virgin I don't care, because I know that in being a virgin I'm pleasing Mama, the most important authority figure in my life.

Chapter 16

M*ama's zeal for Christ has increased since her bout with insanity* even though people already called her the most devout woman in our neighborhood, if not in the whole of Alexandra. Not content only to go to church on Sundays, she attends what is called the "Monday-to-Monday" church, where every day of the week she takes part in some church-related activity. This on top of hunting for jobs and taking care of the household.

On Mondays she accompanies church members on what is called *buphaki,* which involves trudging around Alexandra in search of lost souls. It doesn't matter whether it is raining, very hot, or whether vicious disease-ridden dogs are on the prowl in the dusty streets. The Twelve Apostles are glad to suffer any trial or tribulation for the glory of the living God of Israel.

On Tuesday evenings she attends choir practice for about two hours. It doesn't matter that her voice isn't the greatest and she has a tendency to sing the loudest and off-key. On Wednesday she attends the Progress and Meeting hour, during which church members "break" (share) the Word and assess the state of the church.

Thursday is another day for buphaki, and Friday is youth choir, when she has a break. She needs it because it's payday for Papa and she has to devise all kinds of stratagems to prevent him from drinking and gambling his entire wages. She prays a lot after Papa gives her some money and then goes out to a shebeen or a gambling den. She asks God to protect the money for the sake of us children. But God seldom protects the money for our sakes, for Papa always comes back and demands "his money" so he can go gamble again.

Saturday is often the gloomiest day of the week for the family. Papa is usually broke and we face the prospect of a week filled with hardships and hunger. I usually accompany Mama to Priest Mathebula's, where she's supposed to give a detailed report on her family life, on how many souls she's saved during the week, and on how the God of Israel is working miracles in her life. But Mama's report is always a litany of problems, and she ends up borrowing money from Priest Mathebula's wife.

Incredibly, come Sunday, Mama's spirits are always high. She's the first to get up, usually at about six. I hear her singing hymns and praising the Lord as she goes about getting ready. Believing that a bride of Christ must always be handsomely dressed, she irons her white, frilly Sunday dress and dusts her white broad-brimmed hat and white gloves, and polishes her white shoes. She then wakes us up to start getting ready for church. Since we have only one small rusted tin tub and bathing water has to be boiled in a kettle over a Primus stove, it takes us several hours to bathe. Diana, Linah, and I dress in our best rags and then eat breakfast, if we are lucky to have anything in the cupboard.

George doesn't attend church. Like Johannes he calls it a waste of time. Maria and Florah often spend weekends with their boyfriends. I'm indifferent to church but I go in order to please Mama. Linah, who is eleven years old and already a rebel, also is indifferent, in large part because she can't stand Diana, her biggest rival for our parents' affections.

Nine-year-old Diana is the most devout person in the family, after Mama. Every Sunday morning while the rest of us are sleeping, she's up and ready to go, uttering her all-too-familiar singsong, "Hurry up, hurry up, or we'll be late for Sunday school."

Mama is constantly begging me to accompany her and Diana to Sunday school.

"I'm not a little child like Diana," I say. "Sunday school is for children. I'm thirteen years old. Besides, I have chores to do. Now that Maria is pregnant I have to clean the house, wash laundry, and do my homework."

"Sunday school is not just for little children," she says. "In fact, it's mostly adults."

"If Sunday school is for adults, what's Diana doing there?"

"Come and see. She's like a young Jesus."

Intrigued, I decide to go. The class is packed with spiffily dressed men and women. As far as I can tell, Diana is the only child under ten. The teacher, a tall man in a neatly pressed black suit and tie, warmly welcomes everyone. With a broad smile he asks for newcomers to stand and introduce themselves. I'm reluctant to stand but Mama urges me to.

The Bible study class begins.

"Can anyone tell me what Genesis one, verse one, says?" asks the teacher.

Several adults, most of them illiterate, shake their heads. Diana, who is sitting next to Mama and is dressed in her favorite frilly skirt, astonishes me by standing up. "I know," she says in her tiny voice.

"Okay, Miss Mathabane," the teacher says indulgently. "Please tell us what it says."

"In the beginning God created the heaven and earth." Diana recites the verse from memory in Zulu. *"And the earth was without form, and void, and darkness was upon the face of the deep. And the spirit of God moved upon the face of the waters."*

"And what's the Twelve Apostles' interpretation of the verse, anyone?"

"I know," Diana says.

Everyone stares at her in astonishment.

"Okay, Miss Mathabane," the teacher says. "Illumine us."

"The darkness is the ignorance of the people to the Word of God. The Twelve Apostles have a mission to go out and confront this darkness with God's light. That's why Mama always goes to buphaki."

Diana pauses, then continues.

"When the Twelve Apostles preach to those who haven't been

saved, they are like the voice of God bringing light to darkness. In other words, the verse means that no one can be saved without being filled with the spirit of the living God. And we, the Twelve Apostles, have a mission to save the world."

There's stunned silence. Finally the teacher says, "That's so true, Miss Mathabane, that's so true. Praise the lord for speaking to us through you this morning for our illumination."

I can't believe what I've just witnessed. My own nine-year-old sister uttering such biblical profundities. Mama beams with pride.

"Thank you, Miss Mathabane," the teacher says.

I expect Diana to take the compliment and sit down. But no, she's not finished grandstanding. I remember that she loves attention.

"And John one says the same thing," she says. "Do you want me to recite the verse?"

"Certainly, Miss Mathabane," the teacher says indulgently. "That's exactly the verse I was going to connect with Genesis. Please go ahead."

"John one says, *In the beginning was the Word, and the Word was with God, and the Word was God. The same was in the beginning with God. And all things were made by him; and without him was not anything made that was made; in him was life; and the life was the light of men.*"

The teacher looks at Mama and says, "Your daughter is truly a child of God, musadi."

"I know," Mama says.

"I bet she'll be prophesying soon," the teacher says.

"I hope so."

I burn with envy. What galls me the most is that I know that I can do what she's done, too, even better. I know more Bible verses and hymns by heart than she does. She learns everything by listening to Mama. On the other hand, I can read. Why can't I also be the darling of all these nicely dressed men and women? Maybe one of them might even offer to adopt me so I can live in a nice house with plenty of food and toys, and maybe have a bed of my own.

I decide then and there to turn a new leaf. I too will start attending Sunday school religiously, even if I feel bored. Within a few months I become, next to Mama, the most churchgoing member in my family. I even surpass Diana in my devotion to the living God of Israel. She's begun to lapse, and is more attracted to street life, and has even picked up gambling.

On the other hand, I join the choir and acquire a different set of friends, who love the Lord. One of them is a girl named Latisha. She sings soprano and I sing alto. Like me she's studious and comes from a family of seven. Her father is an underdeacon in the church. While our peers are out having fun, we are either reading the Bible or practicing hymns. I'm so happy I even begin the laborious process of teaching Mama to realize her dream of learning how to read the Bible in Shangaan.

Chapter 17

I *tutor Mama only when Papa is away from home. He's against* Mama learning how to read and write. He says that she has more important things to do with her time than make a fool of herself at such an old age. But Mama tells me that it's never too late to learn, that her dream is to know how to read and write so she can read things like signs on the road and instructions on medicine bottles, instead of guessing all the time. Also, Mama wants to learn how to read her favorite book, the Bible, and how to write her own letters to Johannes in America.

"I've made it this far without knowing how to read or write," Papa argues.

"You'd have made it even further if you knew how," Mama says. "You're the smartest man I know, Jackson Mathabane, but you're also the most stubborn. You won't do something that's good for you because your wife tells you to."

"It's because I wear the pants in this house," Papa says, "not you."

School is out for the winter holidays. It's a weekday afternoon and I'm teaching Mama how to read the Bible. I ask her to identify and spell letters and words. I'm surprised Mama knows her ABCs and vowels.

"I thought you never went to school," I say.

"I didn't," she says, "but I wanted to very much. Your granny took me to school for two weeks and then yanked me out. She had no money. My father had just abandoned her for another woman."

"You mean the grandpa who lives in Diepkloof abandoned Granny for another woman?"

"Yes. And your uncles Piet and Cheeks and your aunt Bushy and I suffered a great deal because of it."

"Do you hate him for it?"

"No."

"Why not?"

"Because no good can come out of hating him. Besides, I have better things to do with my time than hate people."

It's typical of Mama. She always forgives and never holds grudges.

"After I dropped out of school, your uncle Cheeks tried to teach me," Mama says. Uncle Cheeks is a former tsotsi who's spent time in jail for armed robbery. After his release, Mama convinced him to accept Christ as his personal savior. He did. Afterward he stopped drinking, stabbing and robbing people, found a job at a Jewish bakery, married a fellow church member, and became choir director. Mama ascribed all this to Christ.

"Why did you marry Papa, Mama?"

"I had no choice. Your granny forced me to marry him. The family needed money. I was sixteen years old at the time. I didn't want to get married yet. I wanted to go to school."

"Do you love him?"

"Back in my days it didn't matter whether a woman loved a man or not. A girl had to marry the man her parents chose for her."

"I won't get married young," I say.

"That's very wise."

"And when I marry, I'll marry someone who doesn't drink or gamble like Papa."

"That's even wiser."

"Do you hate Papa for drinking and gambling and beating you up, Mama?"

"He didn't always do that. At first he was hardworking and gave me his wages every Friday. Then you children were born, one after the other. Suddenly there wasn't enough money for diapers, rent, bus fare, food, and clothes. Your father only made five rands a week so he started gambling to earn more. He'd lose and then drink in order to forget his losses. Then he kept losing his job and getting arrested for being unemployed. That's when he changed."

"Is that why he's sometimes a different Papa when he's sober?"

"Yes. He even feels ashamed for the bad things he does when he's drunk."

"Why doesn't he stop drinking?"

"He can't help it."

There's an insistent knock on the door. It's Papa. He bellows that we should open the door or he'll break it down. He's drunk. Mama and I abruptly end the lesson. We remove the books from the table and hide them. I'm afraid that Papa, if he finds out I was teaching Mama to read, will burn my books the way he burned George's books after Mama purchased them with food money without telling him. I open the door.

Papa staggers in and demands his dinner. As I watch him eat, I wonder if he's ever had any dreams like Mama. Why didn't he go to school? What was his childhood like? Why is he such an angry and bitter person? Will he ever change? Why do I love him in spite of the bad things he does?

"My dream is to have you grow up to be a teacher, my child," Mama says after another reading lesson at the kitchen table. She's making remarkable progress. She's now able to read simple sentences from the Bible, which she chants like a mantra all day.

"I hate teachers," I say, closing the well-worn Shangaan Bible Johannes won as a prize after being voted the best student in Standard Six.

"Why?"

"Because they beat us all the time."

"They want you to learn."

"Not when they beat us for things we have no control over."

"Such as?"

"Not having the proper uniform and not paying our school fees on time."

Mama looks at me sympathetically.

"And all this beating doesn't work," I say. "Fikile gets beaten all the time. Yet she keeps cutting school and misbehaving."

"Then become a teacher who doesn't beat children," Mama says.

"I don't want to be a teacher," I insist.

"Then what do you want to become?"

"A nurse," I say readily.

"Why a nurse?"

"Because I want to be like Mrs. Kobi."

Mrs. Kobi is a staff nurse at the clinic. She lives across the street, in the same yard as Lerato's father. Mrs. Kobi has a daughter named Thabiso (Joy), about my age, with whom I often play.

"I like the way Mrs. Kobi dresses. She's always neat in her blue-and-white nursing uniform."

"So you mean you don't like me because I wear *magabulela?*" Hand-me-downs.

"No," I say quickly. "I love you too."

"Then what's so special about Mrs. Kobi?"

I decide to tell the truth. "I love how Mrs. Kobi lives," I say.

"Have you been inside her house?"

"Yes. Thabiso has invited me a couple of times. It's the most beautiful house I've ever seen, Mama," I say exuberantly. "It's not a shack like ours. It has four big rooms. The floor is all *tapeit*"—shiny linoleum—"not cement like ours. There's a black-and-white kitchen unit and a refrigerator. There's even a sink with a faucet, so they don't have to queue at the communal tap. And there's a big shiny enamel stove on which Mrs. Kobi cooks all kinds of delicious food: vegetables, mashed potatoes, squash rice, curried chicken."

Mama looks at me a long time. "You know what, my child?" she says.

"What?"

"Someday you'll be like Mrs. Kobi. You have what it takes. You're kind, gentle, and loving. Good nurses should have those qualities."

I'm disappointed. I thought Mama would say I'm smart, like Johannes. I'm tired of being called a nice person, especially because my friends think I'm a fool for being kind, gentle, and loving. I want to be street smart so I can belong to their group.

"How can loving people make me like Mrs. Kobi?" I ask.

"Because love can accomplish anything, child," Mama says. "It's more powerful than all the knowledge in the world. The Bible says Jesus is love. He commands us to love one another. If you have love in your heart you can be anything you want to be. You can even move mountains. Remember First Corinthians thirteen?"

"Yes." The verse is Mama's favorite.

"Can you teach me how to read it?"

Mama knows the verse by heart. I teach her how to read it.

> I may speak with the tongues of men and angels, but if I'm without love, I'm as a sounding gong or a clanging cymbal. I may have the gift of prophecy, and know every hidden truth; I may have faith strong enough to move mountains; but if I have no love, I'm nothing. I may dole out all my possessions, or even give my body to be burnt, but if I have no love, I'm none the better.
>
> Love is patient; love is kind and envies no one. Love is never boastful, nor conceited; nor rude; never selfish, not quick to take offense. Love keeps no scores of wrongs; does not gloat over other men's sins, but delights in truth. There is nothing love cannot face; there is no limit to its faith, its hope, its endurance.
>
> Love will never come to an end. . . . There are three things that last forever: faith, hope and love; but the greatest of them all is love.

Chapter 18

I *hate many of my teachers and mistresses. A lot of them are nice* people overall, and I know they're doing their best to make us learn, but I hate the fact that they are constantly punishing us, especially because the punishment is often so harsh and arbitrary. It's as if they're taking out their frustrations on us.

One day I arrive at school without having eaten breakfast because there's nothing to eat at home. I'm so hungry I feel dizzy. Teacher Nyoko is busy writing math problems on the blackboard. We are having one of our weekly math quizzes. I know if I don't eat something I won't be able to concentrate. And if I can't concentrate I'll fail the quiz and be punished. Luckily, Cynthia has an orange she's brought for lunch.

"Can I have a piece?" I whisper to Cynthia.

"But we aren't supposed to eat in class," Cynthia says.

"I know. But I'm very hungry."

While Teacher Nyoko is not looking, Cynthia peels the orange and gives me a piece. Apparently I'm not the only hungry student, for about four other girls ask for pieces. Cynthia has no choice but to give them, else they'll rat.

Suddenly Teacher Nyoko stops writing on the blackboard and turns. His face is livid.

"Who's eating in class?" he demands.

No one answers.

"I smell an orange," he says, sniffing. He puts down the math textbook and chalk. "Now tell me who's eating an orange. If you don't I'll whip the lot of you."

I stand up. I'm willing to take responsibility since I'm the one who insisted Cynthia peel the orange.

"Who else was eating with you?"

"I was eating alone."

"Don't lie to me," Teacher Nyoko says, heading back to the table. He picks up the thick piece of hosepipe. I know that if he discovers that I'm lying he'll beat the shit out of me.

"Where are the peels?" he asks.

I reach under Cynthia's side of the desk and remove the orange peels.

"Stand up!" Teacher Nyoko says to Cynthia.

Shaking, Cynthia stands up.

"Who else was eating the orange with you?" Teacher Nyoko asks Cynthia. A terrified Cynthia points to the four other girls who shared the orange with us.

Teacher Nyoko summons us to the front of the classroom. He then picks two strong boys and asks them to come to the front of the class too.

"Miriam," he bellows, "you're the ringleader. You get whipped first."

Teacher Nyoko orders the two boys to stretch me facedown across a bench and pinion me. One boy grips both my hands, and the other my legs. Teacher Nyoko proceeds to lash me across the buttocks and upper thighs with the hosepipe.

I've never been so severely whipped before. I scream in pain but he doesn't stop. Finally, when I think I'm going to faint, he stops. Cynthia is next, and then the four girls.

My buttocks and upper thighs are so swollen that sitting down is torture. For over a week I experience excruciating pain whenever I try sitting down. All because I dared eat a piece of orange in class when I felt hungry and was afraid that I'd fail a test.

• • •

Teacher Nyoko has other unusual means of punishing us. One Friday the entire class fails a particularly tough math quiz.

"I told you to study hard," he says as he's handing out the dismal quiz scores. "Should I whip the lot of you?"

"No!" the class says unanimously.

"Then tell me what kind of punishment is most appropriate."

No student ventures to suggest any other form of punishment.

"I'm in a particularly forgiving mood today," Teacher Nyoko says mysteriously. "It's the end of the week."

There's a collective sigh of relief.

"But you must do me a small favor in return for my not whipping you for failing the math test."

There are bewildered looks across the classroom. What favor could we possibly do for the almighty Teacher Nyoko?

"I'm broke," he blurts out. "I don't get paid till the end of the month. I badly need cigarettes and some money to buy beer over the weekend. Do you think you can help me out?"

Of course we'll do anything to avoid being whipped. Teacher Nyoko, hat in hand, walks up and down the aisle extorting money from impoverished students. I don't have any, but I borrow five cents from Cynthia to make a contribution. The extortion over, Teacher Nyoko counts the money. He then sends one of the big boys to the corner grocery store to buy him a packet of Rothmans cigarettes. The rest of the money he pockets.

Over the weekend I run into Teacher Nyoko. Drunk, he's reeling along one of the dusty streets. I'm shocked at the sight, even though it's common knowledge that many teachers are heavy drinkers.

"Hullo, Teacher Nyoko," I say.

"Hi, Mathabane. How are you?" Teacher Nyoko says between hiccups.

"I'm fine."

"Have you done your math homework?"

"I have."

"Good. You must always do your homework," Teacher Nyoko says drunkenly.

"Yes, Teacher Nyoko."

As I walk home, I wonder if Teacher Nyoko is any bit aware of the example he's setting. Is he in the least ashamed to be seen drunk, not only by his students but by their parents also? Apparently he's not. There are frequent sightings of him from time to time in various shebeens. But to his credit, Teacher Nyoko never misses class because of a hangover. He simply whips us harder.

Teacher Mkhari, another heavy drinker and occasional extortionist, is supposed to instruct us on how to write formal letters. Instead he decides to test us on poetry. Memorizing poems is a requirement in the various language classes. Teacher Mkhari wants us to recite an English poem we read about three days ago. Students are quaking. He never told us that he'd quiz us on it. He's again ambushed us.

"I remember, I remember." Teacher Mkhari utters the opening lines of Thomas Hood's famous poem. He randomly points his cane at a tall boy who sits near the window. The boy stands up.

"Complete the poem for me," Teacher Mkhari orders.

The tall boy is unable to recite the rest of the poem.

"Your hand, sir," Teacher Mkhari says.

He gives him five lashes, but the boy doesn't flinch. "Know the poem by tomorrow," Teacher Mkhari says, "or there's some more in store for you."

Around the classroom a babble of murmurs has arisen. Students are frantically attempting to remember the poem's lines. Cynthia, Dlayani, and I sit in the front desk, near the door, so we'll be among the last called.

Over half the class has been whipped. Teacher Mkhari is headed our way.

"I don't know the poem," Cynthia whispers to Dlayani and me. "Do you?"

Dlayani shakes her head. I nod.

"You do?" Dlayani and Cynthia whisper simultaneously. "How does it go?"

I glance in Teacher Mkhari's direction. His broad back is facing me as he whips a girl, who keeps writhing and blowing on her hand after each lash. Good, that will delay his reaching us. I begin whispering the poem to Cynthia and Dlayani. They screw their faces as they attempt to memorize the four-stanza poem.

Only one very smart boy named Etienne recites the poem without missing a line and he escapes being whipped. The classroom is like a hospital ward as students groan and writhe as they nurse their painful palms.

Finally Teacher Mkhari reaches our desk. Voice shaking, Cynthia manages to recite the first stanza but doesn't remember how the second one begins. She screams "Ouch!" and writhes with each blow.

"If you're so afraid of being caned, Cynthia," Teacher Mkhari says with a smile, "then remember to do your work."

It's Dlayani's turn.

"I remember, I remember," Teacher Mkhari says, pointing the cane at her. Dlayani recites the first and second stanza perfectly and then stops. Her mind has gone blank, probably from watching the cane in Teacher Mkhari's hand. I root for her to remember. She screws up her forehead.

"I know it, Teacher Mkhari," she says plaintively. "I swear I know it."

"If you know it, my dear," Teacher Mkhari says, "please recite it."

He waits for about thirty seconds.

"I remember, I remember," Dlayani keeps saying, like a broken record.

"You've said, 'I remember, I remember,' ten times already, my dear," Teacher Mkhari says with an ironic smile. "Don't you remember?"

Several students laugh. Dlayani too can't help laughing.

"Maybe this will jog your memory," Teacher Mkhari says. "Your hand, please, my dear."

Dlayani tentatively extends her left hand, and Teacher Mkhari raises the cane high into the air. Teacher Mkhari brings the cane down, but at the last minute Dlayani retracts her hand in terror. The cane swishes through the empty air.

"You've just added one more lash to your total, my dear," Teacher Mkhari says.

Finally it's my turn.

"You know," Teacher Mkhari says before I start reciting the poem, "I taught your brothers, Johannes and George, and your sisters Florah and Maria. They all knew their poems. I hope you won't break the family tradition."

I'm confident I can recite the poem. I love poetry. Even though Teacher Mkhari hadn't told us to memorize Thomas Hood's poem, I'd done so. I'd fallen in love with the poem. I had memorized its lines as I went about doing chores.

The entire class is watching me.

> I remember, I remember,
> The house where I was born,
> The little window where the sun
> Came peeping in at morn;
> He never came a wink too soon,
> Nor brought too long a day,
> But now, I often wish the night
> Had borne my breath away!

I pause to clear my throat and then continue.

> I remember, I remember,
> The roses, red and white,
> The violets, and the lily-cups,
> Those flowers made of light!
> The lilacs where the robin built,
> And where my brother set
> The laburnum on his birthday,—
> The tree is living yet!
>
> I remember, I remember,
> Where I was used to swing,
> And thought the air must rush as fresh
> To swallows on the wing;
> My spirit flew in feathers then,

That is so heavy now,
And summer pools could hardly cool
The fever on my brow!

I remember, I remember,
The fir tree dark and high;
I used to think their slender tops
Were close against the sky:
It was childish ignorance,
But now 'tis little joy
To know I'm farther off from heaven
Than when I was a boy.

I was never prouder of myself than when I uttered that last line and Teacher Mkhari said, "Well done, Miriam."

Chapter 19

Our two-room shack is plagued by marhode, *giant rats. They* breed in the mounds of trash scattered about the yard. Since the riots of 1976 there's been no regular trash pickup in the township because many a trash truck was commandeered and burned. The authorities are apparently in no hurry to restore the service.

During the night, while we are sleeping on the floor, the giant rats mount their invasions and fight their vicious battles for morsels of food. Their squeaks and snarls are bloodcurdling. Often Diana, Linah, and I cower in terror and fight for enough blanket to cover our feet, the favorite target for the rats.

One night they chew the entire skin off the bottom of my feet. I feel nothing during the night when this is happening. I realize something is wrong only when I wake up in the morning and try to walk. I instantly collapse from the unbearable pain.

"What's wrong?" Mama says.

"It's my feet," I cry, writhing on the floor.

She inspects the soles of my feet, and lets out a scream of horror and cups her mouth.

There's no money to take me to the clinic, so Mama proceeds to apply the usual remedy: washing the soles of my feet with warm water mixed with salt. The mixture stings. She bandages my feet with pieces of rags she's torn from old dresses. It takes almost two weeks for the soles of my feet to generate new skin.

The rats attack Diana, then Linah. Anyone who sleeps on the floor is a target. Mama embarks on a crusade to exterminate them. First she tries a potent rat poison called Ratex. She doubles and triples the dose, but it has little effect. The only thing it does is almost poison a two-year-old cousin, who one morning crawls toward the saucer with rat poison pellets, thinking they are candy. Only Mama's quick thinking saves him.

After the rat poison Mama tries the rat traps. I accompany her to the Indian marketplace on First Avenue in search of the best rat traps.

The Indian shopkeeper gladly sells us three giant rattraps. We take them home. Their steel snap is so huge that Mama dare not set it, for fear of chopping off a finger. Papa sets them. He baits them with pieces of meat and puts them in strategic locations around the kitchen and bedroom. The first night I listen attentively for the steel snaps to come crushing down, indicating that the giant rats have finally met their match. No sound. In the morning Mama inspects the rattraps. The pieces of meat are gone, but the rattraps didn't snap.

"These rats are witches," Mama says. "How could they have taken the bait without getting their heads chopped off?"

"Why don't you get a cat, Mama?" I suggest.

Mama's eyes light up. "Good idea," she says. "Why didn't I think of that before?"

"And there are lots of cats around the neighborhood that belong to no one. I can bring one home."

"Please do."

I find a stray black cat wandering about the trash. I pick it up and bring it home.

"Not that one," Mama says uneasily.

"How come?"

"It's black. We have enough bad luck as it is."

• • •

One Saturday Papa returns from a shebeen cradling a huge gray cat.

"If this cat doesn't kill the rats," George says, "then we'll have to leave this haunted house."

For the next couple of days there is constant clamor throughout the night. In the morning we find the huge gray cat sleeping contentedly near the cabinet. His belly is stuffed with rats. Everyone is impressed. George nicknames him Gladiator.

As long as Gladiator is around, the giant rats never come near our house. But one day Mamahulu comes to conduct yet another exorcism of the bad luck preventing the family from getting a residential permit and Mama from finding a steady job. She takes one look at Gladiator and immediately summons Mama.

"Get rid of that thing immediately," Mamahulu says.

"Why? He's a mere cat. He keeps rats away."

"No ordinary cat can be that big. He's deformed."

"It's because he's always stuffed with rats."

"I don't care if he is stuffed with pudding," Mamahulu says. "If you don't get rid of him, witchcraft will gain a footing in this house. Witches love to disguise themselves as fat cats."

My parents apparently dread witchcraft more than they do giant rats, so reluctantly, we part with Gladiator. Curiously, the rats never bother us anymore.

Stray dogs are everywhere. They are constantly sniffing around the mounds of trash, but most are so scrawny I can count their ribs.

One time I see a scrawny dog licking the bottom of a naked potbellied little boy of about four who's just finished having bloody diarrhea in the middle of the yard. I shoo the dog away and go fetch the boy's mother from a nearby shebeen. She's drinking and I can tell she doesn't want to be bothered, but she comes anyway. She drags the little boy to the communal tap, shoves him under the tap, and opens the cold water full blast. When he cries, she slaps him and tells him to be quiet. I feel sorry for the little boy, and I shudder at the thought that my family and other families get their drinking water from the same tap.

Another time I shoo away a dog that is sniffing around the carcass of another dog that's just been run over by a truck. The dead dog stays in the hot sun for several days and huge maggots appear. Barefoot little boys play soccer in the street near the dead dog. Their raggedy ball occasionally lands on the carcass; one of the boys fetches it, doesn't wash his hands, and later on uses those same hands to eat.

I always shoo dogs from a safe distance because they are my mortal enemies. Many of them are said to carry strange diseases that make people mad. I saw them bite and almost kill a woman taking a double-up. There's a particularly vicious black dog called Danger in our neighborhood. It's a stray dog, and has been adopted by a cripple who enjoys setting it on kids who make fun of his deformed foot.

I have to walk past the cripple's shack each time I go to the store. One day, as I'm hurrying home with a loaf of brown bread and a bottle of paraffin, I hear a snarling sound behind me. I turn around and I see Danger coming toward me. I freeze. My heart is pounding.

"*Vootsek,* Danger!" Go away! I attempt to shoo the dog away.

Danger keeps coming.

I drop the bread and paraffin and bolt for home. People scatter in all directions as they see Danger chasing me. Before I've gone five yards, I feel Danger's fangs digging into my right buttock. The pain is searing. I scream, "Let me go! Let me go!" Danger won't let go. I trip and fall. Danger is all over me. I'm flailing with my hands. Suddenly I hear a voice shout, "Stop it, Danger!"

Danger stops and retreats to the voice. Tongue lolling and tail wagging, he circles around the cripple. I'm howling with pain but the cripple doesn't come to my aid. No one does. I slowly get up and brush dust from my dress. I pick up the loaf of bread from the dust. The paraffin has all spilled. My buttock is on fire. Blood is oozing down the back of my right leg.

I gingerly limp home, about two hundred yards away. Mama rushes to me as she sees me stagger through the door, crying. She helps me remove my dress and bloomers. We have no money for the clinic, so she has to apply the usual remedy: bathing the wound with warm water mixed with salt.

"I told you not to provoke that dog. It could've killed you."

"I didn't provoke it, Mama. It just pounced on me."

The wound takes several weeks to completely heal. It's most uncomfortable when I sit down, especially for long periods of time. Sitting in class is torture, but I never miss a day of school, for fear of being punished.

I consider myself cursed. Danger bites me two more times when I'm walking home from the store in exactly the same spot. I develop a phobia for dogs, which has lasted to this day.

Chapter 20

I*'m known as the neighborhood coward because I always walk* away from fights when provoked, but all of my four sisters, including little Diana, are veterans of many a street brawl. They have the battle scars to prove it: broken teeth, scratches, torn dresses. I've never fought anyone in my life, which is extremely unusual for someone living in a violent ghetto like Alexandra where adults fight all the time—with knives, fists, clubs, boiling water, bricks—and children do their best to emulate them.

Because I don't like fighting, kids constantly pick on me, calling me all sorts of names: *legwala,* coward, *marhama,* the one with fat cheeks, and *magwinya,* pudgy like a cookie. Others call me a nun because of my diligent attendance at church. Still others call me Mrs. Pimples because my face is covered with pimples, and *sishimanyi,* spinster, because I don't have a boyfriend.

All these names hurt. If they were hurled at any of my sisters, they'd fight. My response is to swallow the insult and stoically walk away, muttering a comforting Bible verse, like "Blessed are the meek, for they shall inherit the earth" or "Forgive them, Lord, for they know not what they do" or "Whosoever shall smite thee on the right cheek, turn to him the other also."

Mama raves about my pacifism. She calls me a true child of God. But sometimes I wonder if being a child of God also means being the butt of endless and mean-spirited jokes. It's not that I'm afraid to fight, it's just that Mama tells me that God doesn't sanction fighting. I search the Bible for instances where even the children of God were forced to fight. I find plenty of such instances in the Old Testament, where Jews were constantly defending themselves. The New Testament, which is considered inviolable truth by the Twelve Apostles, frowns even upon self-defense. Christ is the quintessential pacifist.

My friends and I see various movies based on Bible stories at the King's Cinema, which reinforce this pacifist image of Christians. One of them is called *The Robe.* I thoroughly enjoy the movie, but at the same time it depresses me, for in it Christians are at their meekest. The Roman emperor Caligula butchers them and throws them to the lions and they even sing hymns as they are being burned at the stake.

One day I have an epiphany. I recall the miraculous transformation of my uncle Cheeks from a notorious tsotsi to a devout Christian. Yet even though he's a Christian, no one messes with him, least of all Papa, who is scared of him and stopped physically abusing Mama when Uncle Cheeks threatened to beat the daylights out of him.

I decide to consult Uncle Cheeks on whether it's virtuous or foolish to be a coward for Christ.

"Uncle Cheeks," I say one evening, "I have a problem. People call me a coward because I don't like fighting."

"Are you one?"

"No."

"Then it doesn't matter what people call you."

"It does matter, Uncle Cheeks. I hate it when they call me names because I walk away from fights."

"Why don't you fight back?"

"Fighting is stupid. It accomplishes nothing."

"You're right. I've fought most of my life and was almost killed several times. Yet all I have to show for it are scars."

"But I don't like being called a coward."

"So you're concerned about your reputation."

"Yes."

"Well, my dear, a person's reputation is important. Particularly in the ghetto."

"So what do I do to protect my reputation?"

"Fight when provoked."

"Fight? But Christ says we should turn the other cheek."

Uncle Cheeks stops in the middle of the street to make the point, "Turning the other cheek is bullshit. There's something called self-defense. If someone cuts you, you cut them back. That way they won't walk all over you."

I recall that during his heyday as a tsotsi Uncle Cheeks was notorious for being "an artist with a knife" in a ghetto well known for such artists.

"But Christ says we should—"

"Christ didn't live in Alexandra, my dear. Here, if you turn the other cheek you're dead."

"Do you still fight, Uncle?"

"Only when it's necessary."

"When do you know if it's necessary?"

"When my reputation is on the line." He laughs. His laugh is as hearty as Mama's.

"Have you ever seen the movie *The Godfather*?" he asks suddenly.

"Is it a Bible story?" I ask, thinking he means God the Father.

Uncle Cheeks laughs. "No. It's a gangster movie. I know the church says you shouldn't watch violent movies, but you should see this one. Pay special attention to a man everyone calls the Godfather. He's generally a kind, loving, giving, and forgiving person, just like you, my dear. He goes the extra mile to avoid a fight and to reason with people. But when his reputation is on the line and he has to fight, he's the most ruthless killer alive."

We are now standing under the faint yellow light of the street lamp around which moths are hovering. I can tell from his excited voice and the determined expression on his face that the former gangster and jailbird is speaking now. His instincts—born of having had to fend for himself in a ghetto that, when he was growing up, was known as Hell's Kitchen and Slaagpaal (Slaughterhouse)—have taken over.

"My dear Miriam," Uncle Cheeks says. "I know what I'm telling you is not what the Bible says. And it's not what I should be telling you as an adult, least of all as a church elder. But I care deeply about you. I want you to know about survival, especially survival in a jungle like Alexandra. Be like Christ in most things—but never never allow people to walk over you. When your reputation is on the line, fight. Once bullies know you can fight, they'll leave you alone."

It's late afternoon. Alexandra is shrouded with its usual blanket of smog from a thousand braziers and coal stoves. I'm playing *mgusha* in the dusty street. Mgusha is a kind of high-jump game played by two teams. After each successful jump the rope is raised incrementally. The winning team often sings the following song, taunting the losers:

One game *mapondo-pondo—qha* (zero)
Two games *mapondo-pondo—qha*
Three games *mapondo-pondo—qha* . . .

My team, which consists of my friends Becky, Lulu, and Susan, is winning, so we keep on singing the song. The song provokes Amanda, who is the leader of the opposing team.

"Stop singing that song," Amanda demands.

Everyone fears Amanda, so silence reigns. We stand by awkwardly, not knowing whether to end the game or to continue playing. But I've been enjoying myself, so I say to Amanda, "It's unfair for you to say we should stop singing the song. You always sing it when you're winning."

Amanda glares at me. "When I don't like a song, I don't like it. You hear me, marhama?"

Sensing that she's itching for a fight, I make no reply. I know she's furious. She hates to lose. And whenever she loses, she fights.

"I'm afraid of no one. Least of all you three cowards. I can beat the shit out of the three of you together. Especially you, *tallie,*" Amanda says, pointing at the tall and gangly Becky.

Suddenly she slaps Becky thrice across the face in rapid succession. Though only fourteen, Becky is almost six feet tall yet she's more of a pacifist than myself.

"Anyone wanna fight?" Amanda casts about for takers. The meek expressions on the faces of Susan and Lulu make it clear that they aren't about to risk being mauled by Amanda.

I'm eager to leave the tension-filled scene. "The meek shall inherit the earth," I mumble to myself as I head for home.

"Where are you going, legwala?" Amanda asks.

"Home."

"Who said you could go?"

"Do I need permission to go to my home?"

"You're cheeky, aren't you?"

"No."

I know that Amanda hasn't forgiven me for the humiliation her mother suffered during that twenty-five-rand incident. I also know that Mama, a teetotaler, has taken issue with Amanda's mother operating a shebeen because selling liquor is against Christ's teachings and reflects badly on the church.

Knowing all this, I'm eager to avoid a fight with Amanda. The Bible verse about the meek inheriting the earth comes to mind again. But then I remember Uncle Cheeks's advice: "Once bullies know you can fight, they'll leave you alone."

I say softly, "I don't want to fight, Amanda. I have no quarrel with you. Tell me how have I wronged you."

"I said you're cheeky."

"I'm not cheeky."

"Are you calling me a liar?"

"I'm not a coward," I say angrily. "If you want to fight, I'll fight you."

My friends stare at me, aghast. They must think I am out of my mind. At first my response rattles Amanda. Then she flashes her trademark triumphant grin, revealing her buck teeth.

"I've long wanted to teach you a lesson, marhama," she says. "Let's go to the battlefield."

Chapter 21

The battlefield is a small, bumpy patch of grass about twenty-five feet away from the street, next to the rectangular zinc building of the Twelve Apostles Church of God. We have to cross a gully called a donga, which is reeking with raw sewage. Amanda's two-room shack is near the battlefield, and her mother, father, and siblings often witness her gladiatorial triumphs and cheer her on.

I suddenly remember why Amanda loves fighting opponents near her home and why she never loses, no matter how formidable her opponent. Her family is always close at hand, either to intimidate her opponents with their boisterous shouting or to come to her aid should the necessity arise. With a tinge of misgiving, I realize that my own family is in the next yard, separated from me by a high fence of *mutlavi-tlavi*, cacti. Should I ask Becky to run home and alert my family to the possibility that I might need their help if the going gets tough?

That'll be a sure sign of cowardice, I think. Instead, I mutter a prayer: "Dear God, I don't want to fight, but I feel I must. So please give me strength."

As often happened during fights involving Amanda, word quickly spreads that another lamb is being led to the slaughter. The fact that

I'm considered a hopeless underdog, given my reputation as a legwala, leads to an unusually high turnout of eager spectators.

There's no sign of any member of my family. I wonder if I've made the right decision, but it's too late to back out now without losing face and forever confirming my reputation as a legwala. Having never fought anyone before, least of a brawler like Amanda, I frantically try to recall some of the best strategies for fighting such an opponent. I think of the movies I've seen, but they always show men fighting with guns and swords. I have neither. Besides, I'll be fighting a woman, and women in the ghetto have a special way of fighting.

Luckily, a couple of days before, I'd witnessed a fight between two girls who had been fighting over a boy. Such fights are often the most ferocious. The girls, about sixteen, one large and the other thin, had used a variety of tactics. I'd been most impressed by the thin one who compensated for her small size by using tactics I thought particularly suitable for fighting a brawler like Amanda.

About three or so feet from the donga, Amanda suddenly turns and slaps me hard across the face. This does wonders to my confidence. I realize that she's afraid, that the slap is designed to induce me to fight right then and there, where her family can see her, and come to her rescue, should the need arise.

I grab her by her shoulders and lower her head, as I saw the thin girl do. Simultaneously I raise my right knee and ram it smack into her face. She howls with pain and clutches her bleeding nose. I again ram her face with my knee. Like a wounded tiger she attempts to wrench loose from my grip. She claws at my face but can't reach it because of the way I'm holding her down by the shoulders. I again administer the battering ram. As she screams in pain I hear the crowd yell, "That's it, Miriam. That's it! Beat her! Trash her. Thrash her good! Teach her a lesson!"

The cheering inspires me. I fight like a person possessed. Somehow Amanda manages to wrench loose from my grip. She punches me in the face. I punch her back. We fall on the ground and roll in the dust. I somehow manage to grab her by her long hair. She digs her sharp fingernails into my arms but I refuse to let her go. Realizing that we've rolled close to the donga, I grab her head and plunge it into the reeking mud.

She screams. The frenzied crowd keeps yelling, "Do it again, Miriam! Do it again! Let her taste the shit!" It's clear that I have the upper hand now. I'm sitting atop Amanda, and being slightly overweight is a plus.

Suddenly I feel a blow to the back of my head. I turn and see Amanda's youngest brother, about eight, wielding a poker. He's with Amanda's four other siblings, who are carrying clubs and iron bars. I let go of Amanda and spring to my feet. Amanda, her face caked with stinking mud and her dress soiled, staggers to her feet and joins her siblings. I'm outnumbered six to one. One of them gives her an empty Coke bottle and she smashes it against a stone, retaining a jagged piece. She brandishes the crude knife in front of me.

"I'm going to slit your throat, you Shangaan," she says menacingly.

I know I'm outnumbered and unarmed and I know that her siblings are waiting for her to give word for them to rush me.

Suddenly I hear a shrill familiar voice.

"Leave my sister alone or I'll kill you, you bloody bastards!"

Florah! I turn my head. I see her jostling her way through the crowd. Amanda and her siblings run home. Their mother is standing by the door of her shack. From the look of things she's the one who'd dispatched the rescue party. She calls our family all sorts of names and Florah responds in kind. As Florah escorts me home, people cheer. I should be elated, but somehow I feel guilty for having fought. At home, I tell Mama what happened.

"The devil tempted you, my child, but it's okay to yield to temptation once in a while. I bet you Amanda won't bully you again."

She never did. And I was never again tempted into a fight with anyone.

Our shack collapses while I'm at school. Maria, who is now eight months pregnant, barely escapes with her life. She'd been washing dishes when she heard a rumbling noise outside and went out to investigate. As soon as she was out the door the wall collapsed. Had she remained by the sink she'd have been buried under a ton of bricks.

Vacant shacks are scarce in the already overcrowded ghetto. There's been a large influx of people from the homelands searching for work. Luckily for Mama, Peri-Urban gives our family priority because Mama now has a permit, thanks to Mamahulu's exorcism of the bad luck in the family. Within three weeks we find a two-room shack on Sixteenth Avenue, number thirty-five.

Mama finds a job as a maid in Randburg shortly after we move. Her new employer is a kindly English-speaking woman who has children of her own and gives Mama old clothes and allows her to take home leftover food. She pays Mama 150 rand a month, a queenly sum.

The job is timely, for shortly thereafter, on August 13, 1983, Florah gives birth to her first and only child. She names the baby girl Angeline Nonceba. She's been trying to conceive for a very long time but has had difficulty because her uterus was ripped by a badly inserted IUD. It was inserted by overworked staffers at the overcrowded family planning clinic at the women's hostel. But she's very happy. She tells Mama, "I don't care if I never have another baby because of what the IUD did to me. At least I have my Angie."

Two months later, Maria delivers a baby boy. Because she is unmarried, Mama names the baby. She calls him *Nyiko* (A Gift). Maria translates that to Given. Mama urges her to return to school as she'd promised.

"Now that I'm working I'll help you take care of the baby," Mama says.

"I've changed my mind," Maria says. "I don't want to go back."

"Why?"

"I'm too old."

"But you're only seventeen."

"That's too old. If I go back I'll be in Standard Five, the same class as Miriam."

"What's wrong with that?"

"She's my younger sister."

"So?"

"They'll make fun of me for being in the same class with her."

"Who'll make fun of you?"

"My classmates."

"Why should it matter? Are you going to school to please your classmates, or to build a future for yourself and that child you just brought into the world?"

"I'd rather go to work, Mama," Maria says.

"What kind of work will you do without even a high school certificate?"

"I'm good at sewing. I'll go to designer school and then start my own business."

I'm saddened that Maria is ashamed to go back to school because she has a baby, but I can understand her fears of peer pressure. I wonder if I'd have the courage to go back to school after having a baby. I'm glad I'm not sexually active. I vow not to be until I'm finished with school and married. I don't care if my friends call me names. I don't want to be like Maria.

Bovet has a rule meant to discourage teen pregnancy. The school prohibits any dating whatsoever. Those discovered dating are punished. One day shortly after lunch, I'm summoned to the Sub-B hall. I find the place filled with students accused of violating the antidating rule. They are being interrogated by a group of teachers and mistresses.

Why was I brought here? I wonder. I have no boyfriend.

"Miriam, are you ready to confess?" asks one of the mistresses.

"Confess what, Mistress?"

"Confess your relationship with Michael."

I'm stunned. For several moments I can't speak. Finally I manage to stammer.

"Which Michael?"

"Michael Baloyi."

I feel like laughing, but this is no laughing matter.

"Michael is not my boyfriend."

"Don't lie!" the mistress says, brandishing a cane in my face.

I look wildly about the hall. The other teachers and mistresses are busy interrogating suspected couples.

"I swear I'm not Michael's girlfriend," I say.

Michael is called forward. He is shaking. He's a soft-spoken, bookish boy. His sister Margaret is one of my friends.

"Michael," the mistress asks, "are you ready to confess?"

"Confess what, Mistress?" Michael asks, bewildered.

"Your relationship with Miriam."

Michael is as stunned as I was when the outrageous statement about our alleged relationship was first made to me.

"I'm not her boyfriend, Mistress."

"Don't lie," the mistress says, brandishing the cane at Michael.

Michael is as dumbfounded as I am. What do you say when an authority figure is adamant that you're lying about a fictitious relationship?

Michael has a brilliant idea. He asks for witnesses.

"Who says that Miriam and I are dating?"

"Other students have seen you together several times."

"Seen us together—where, when?"

I realize the awful mistake the mistress has made.

"Excuse me, Mistress," I say. "I think I can explain."

The mistress looks at me triumphantly, apparently assuming that I'm about to finally confess.

"Go ahead."

"I sometimes stay after school to study because it's difficult for me to study at home," I say. "There are too many people in our house, including infant children. Michael occasionally does the same. And from time to time we walk home together since we are neighbors."

"What do you talk about on the way home?"

"We mostly talk about homework."

I can tell from the dubious look on the mistress's face that she doesn't believe me. I'm in despair. What can I do?

All those accused of violating the antidating rule are whipped.

Chapter 22

At *Sixteenth Avenue Papa finds a bosom buddy named Mr.* Nyathi. Mr. Nyathi has a fifteen-year-old daughter named Gertrude, who quickly becomes my best friend. Gertrude's mother also becomes Mama's best friend. The two women love joking about their husbands, who are so much alike. Both are heavy drinkers, and both love fighting with their wives. Papa and Mr. Nyathi are so fond of each other that they call each other *mutswala* (blood brother). Loners by nature, both spend hours talking and drinking beer. Gertrude's father is from Zimbabwe, which is north of where Papa grew up. Both are very proud of their cultures and tribes, which are related.

Papa's friendship with Gertrude's father leads to unusual changes in his personality. One evening Diana and Papa are sitting across from each other at the kitchen table. Diana is doing her homework. I'm cooking supper. Mama is away doing buphaki.

Diana gets up to go pee at the communal latrine. As soon as she's out of the house, Papa reaches across the table and grabs one of her primers. He flips through it, admiring the pictures. I've never seen Papa with a book in his hands before. I watch the expression on his face. His prominent brow has corrugated lines, like one who's reading with concentration. I notice that his lips are moving silently, as if he's mouthing words.

I'm astounded. I know Papa can't read. Shortly thereafter, Diana appears by the doorway. Papa quickly closes the book and puts it back. I serve him dinner of pap and chicken feet, all the time trying to picture him as a child. Did he ever have an opportunity to go to school when he was growing up in Venda? What does it feel like not to be able to read? Does he want to learn to read and write as Mama does but is too proud?

Papa is a complex man. I know he loves us in his own way. I also know that he's afraid, especially of change. That's why he clings to the past. He insists that we speak only Venda in his presence. He feels that if we speak Shangaan, our mother tongue, we'll grow up Shangaans instead of Vendas. And a man's children are formed in his image. He's very proud to be a Venda. He thinks that the Vendas, who are the smallest of South Africa's eleven tribes and are often looked down upon as uncouth, are the greatest tribe in the world, better even than the Zulus, who are the largest tribe and have the most illustrious history.

One change in Papa's personality endears him to me. Sometimes, when he's drunk and in a particularly good mood, he'll gather us around the fire and tell us stories about the Vendas. I'm fascinated by the matriarchal Venda culture, and his descriptions of the Venda homeland, traditions, and legends have me enthralled. He tells us that the Bavendas are an ancient people who originally migrated from central Africa in the seventeenth century. They settled in the lush Soutpansberg area under their great chief Dimbanyika. They called the area Venda, which means "pleasant land."

Under the leadership of great warriors such as Makhado, the Lion of the North, they fiercely resisted being conquered by the Boers and various black tribes who invaded their land. For a long time they also refused to admit missionaries into their territories. They're deeply superstitious and believe in witches, witchcraft, and water spirits called *ditutwanes,* which are supposed to be half human, with one leg, one arm, and one eye. The most sacred places of the Bavendas are the Thathe Vondo Forest, the burial ground of Venda chiefs, and Lake Fundudzi, home of the white python god of fertility.

Their traditional houses are called *rondavels,* which are built of thatch and cow dung and have a sharp metal spike protruding from the highest point of the roof to insure that witches do not enter at night and whisk away the spirits of sleepers. Their most famous ritual is the *domba,* or python dance, during which bare-breasted Venda maidens, arms linked in conga formation, writhe like a python to the throbbing beat of the *mutale* drums. The domba is performed by Venda maidens during fertility rites preparing them for womanhood.

Papa sometimes whirls about the kitchen and sings a song about a young man who feared being bewitched and flees from Venda to the city:

Ndoloyiwa, Ndoloyiwa
Tsini ndi shabela kule Hamagandani
Tsini ndi shabela kule
I've been bewitched, I've been bewitched
That's why I'm running far away
That's why I'm running far away

Mugari gari, Mugari gari ya komba
Tsini ndi shabela kule Hamagandani
Tsini ndi shabela kule
I'm not kidding, I'm not kidding
When I say I'm running far away,
Running far away.

At other times, Papa gathers Given and Angie on his lap and teaches them Venda:

Dzina lawo ndinyi?—What's your name?
U dzula gayi?—Where do you live?
U na minwala migayi?—How old are you?
miyanga—mother
khotsiyanga—father
khaladzi—sister
murathu—brother
makhadzi aunt

khotsi munene—uncle
makhulu—grandpa/grandma
matsheloni—dawn
madekwana—evening
masiyani—noon

"Venda is the most beautiful place in the world," Papa says with a touch of nostalgia. "It's a land full of lakes, mighty rivers, mountains, caves, and forests. In these places live midzimu, the spirits of our ancestors. We give offerings to our ancestors for the blessings they bestow upon us. And whenever we are sick or experiencing trouble, we know it's because our ancestors are displeased. We then visit a *nyanga,* who communicates with our midzimu to find out what is causing their displeasure."

Papa distrusts what he calls "white medicine." Whenever he's sick, he always consults a nyanga first so he can find out what he's done to earn the wrath of his ancestors, who are punishing him with illness.

"If Venda is so beautiful, Papa," I ask, "why are we stuck in this horrible place?"

"This is where the jobs are, my child," Papa says. "But someday we'll all return to Venda. When I've saved enough money to buy us a big farm, we'll grow mangoes, papayas, bananas, corn, oranges, and avocados as big as your head."

We all laugh. I desperately wish Papa would be this accessible, this playful, this human every day, instead of only when he's drunk.

At school Teacher Mguni, who directs the intermediate choir, tells us that for our annual singing competition we'll be performing a Venda song called "Shango Lasho Venda" (Venda, Our Beloved Country). Papa promises to help me with pronunciation of Venda words. Except for Teacher Mguni, no one in the choir can read music, so we memorize the song, which is very long.

The choir practices from two in the afternoon till five for two months. We also have morning practices, which begin at 6 A.M. and end when assembly begins. We practice this hard because we are the singing champions in Alexandra and face tough competition from the other schools. All the practice pays off. We win a huge silver trophy as first prize and are chosen to represent Alexandra at the regional competition in Soweto. There also we win first prize, and a trip to the national contest in Bloemfontein, the capital of the Orange Free State province. We come in second, losing to a team from Venda. But we hold our heads up high, for it took a team from Venda to beat a choir from one of the smallest schools in Alexandra.

Even though I enjoyed singing "Shango Lasho Venda," I'm stunned when Teacher Mguni, another proud Venda like Papa, recommends that I switch from Shangaan to Venda for my vernacular. "Your father is a Venda," he says.

"But I have only one more year of school to go. Shangaan has been my vernacular since I began school."

"You are your father's child, not your mother's. Besides, I've already spoken to your father about it, and he's agreed."

Switching vernaculars in my second-to-last year in primary school is very risky. Under Bantu Education, vernacular is the most important subject of the curriculum. If I fail vernacular I'll fail the whole exam, even if I have perfect scores in all the other subjects. And that will mean I won't get to go to Alexandra High. Teacher Mguni also insists that Diana and Linah switch from Shangaan to Venda. Papa tells Mr. Nyathi and his other drinking buddies that his daughters are now full-fledged Vendas because they're learning his language at school.

Chapter 23

Papa *isn't thrilled that I've decided to go visit Mamahulu in* Giyani for the Christmas holidays. I plead with him to let me go. I tell him that, unlike many of my friends, I've never gone on a vacation in my life. Also, I remind him of the promise I made to Mamahulu when she came to exorcise bad luck and evil spirits from our home—that I'd visit her. Mamahulu is the only one of Mama's relatives that Papa likes, maybe because she gives him discounts for exorcisms and lucky charms. He relents and gives me permission to visit her. Fikile offers to come along with me.

Mamahulu's son Freddie, the one of the thirteen wives, operates a taxi service between Johannesburg and Giyani. He gives Fikile and me a ride in his van. We leave on a Friday evening, a week after final exams. We are packed tightly into the van with nearly a dozen other passengers and a variety of goods and furniture. After a six-hour drive along N1 we reach Giyani shortly before midnight. I welcome sleep, especially on a soft sponge on the cow-dung floor inside a cool rondavel, one of five that make up Mamahulu's kraal.

At dawn, Fikile and I go out for a walk to check out the area. When we get back Fikile says, "I wonder what they eat for breakfast here."

"Probably the same bread and tea we always have for breakfast in Alexandra."

"What about eggs?" Fikile asks. "Mamahulu has tons of chickens."

We ask about eggs and are told that women don't eat eggs. Why? We are told that eggs will damage our ovaries and prevent us from bearing children. We are told that we'll breakfast on bread and tea as soon as Willie, Mamahulu's grandson, returns from buying bread at the store. Several hours pass and there's no Willie, no bread, and no breakfast. Fikile, who becomes dizzy and cranky if she doesn't eat breakfast on time, goes to Mamahulu and asks, "When are we having breakfast?"

"As soon as Willie gets back with the bread," Mamahulu says.

"But he's been gone nearly three hours."

"The store is very far."

Willie returns at about one in the afternoon.

"Is the store you went to in Alexandra, or what?" I ask Willie as we're eating the coarse brown bread with sugared black tea without milk.

He laughs, revealing his teeth, brown from drinking well water. "No, it's just over the mountain."

"Next time we'll go buy the bread," Fikile says. "I'm a runner. It'll take me less time than it took you."

"Okay," Willie says, grinning.

Giyani is extremely hot and the people are dirt poor. They live far from one another. There are hardly any businesses. The main work is field work, which is done mostly by women with babies strapped to their backs. Mamahulu is considered rich mainly because she has lots of chickens and goats. She usually gets paid in livestock for her exorcisms and muti-potions.

"Maybe we've only seen the bad part," Fikile says hopefully. "Tomorrow when we go to the store we'll see the better part, on the other side of the mountain."

"I hope you're right," I say. "I'd hate for us to spend three whole weeks, including Christmas, in this desert."

"At least we'll get to relax," Fikile says. "If we were back home we'd be working all the time."

But our relief is premature. No woman at Mamahulu's sleeps beyond six in the morning. After having the leftover bread and tea without milk for breakfast, we join Freddie's wives at chores: cleaning the huts, washing laundry at the river, tilling the fields, and cooking pap and *murogo* (greens) in huge three-legged black pots in an open fire in the middle of the courtyard.

Our anticipation of eating chicken is dashed when we learn that none of the chickens are ever eaten except on very special occasions. Instead, we have pap and murogo for lunch. After lunch we join Freddie's wives on a trek of several miles to the river to do laundry. On the way the women joke and sing, but the journey is made unbearable for Fikile and me by the intense heat, to which we are unaccustomed. When we get to the Shingwedzi River, however, we take a delicious swim in its soothingly cold and clear water.

I'm surprised by how young Uncle Freddie's wives are. Lisa, the oldest, is in her twenties and has four children. Ruth, the youngest, is thirteen but has no children. I'm drawn to her because she's the most educated of the wives, having finished primary school. Apparently she's also Uncle Freddie's favorite. She is scorned by the other wives for not having borne any children, and is accused of monopolizing Uncle Freddie's affections.

One day I ask her why she married so young. She's surprised by the question.

"Women always get married young here."

"Don't you go to school?"

"We do, but not for long. As soon as a man comes with lobola, our fathers insist we leave school and get married."

It turns out that Uncle Freddie has many wives largely because the women's fathers think him rich, since he owns a taxi and works in the city. The highlight of the Christmas holidays for the women is when he brings each a colorful *mucheka,* traditional dress, and gives his brood of children oversized khakis.

I find it strange that the women seem content to be left at home to work and raise children while Uncle Freddie most of the time is away in the city enjoying himself.

After washing laundry on smooth rocks we head back home, toward evening. Some of the women carry huge buckets of water on their heads, and they show Fikile and me how to do the same. It's quite tricky balancing a heavy bucket full of water for miles on one's head, but I find it challenging.

Dinner is more pap and murogo.

Fikile says, "I'm not eating."

"You'll starve," I say.

"I'll wait for breakfast," she says.

"But there's no bread."

"We'll go buy it."

The next morning we wake up early to go to the store on the other side of the mountain. I've never walked so far to buy a loaf of bread. Fikile and I leave at about eight, hoping we'll be back in thirty minutes at the most. We are gone four hours, longer than Willie, because we are unfamiliar with the rugged terrain. The sun becomes scorchingly hot.

"Do you think we've lost our way?" Fikile asks.

"No," I say. "Willie said to follow this path and we'll eventually get to the store."

"But we've been walking for hours. I feel dizzy already."

"Me too. And my feet are killing me."

When we finally reached the store, what a disappointment. It is nothing but a *spazza* (lean-to store) with mostly empty shelves. But we do find stale bread, plenty of it.

"This is the last time I come to Giyani," Fikile vows on our way home. "It's better to starve in Alexandra."

There's nothing to do in Giyani but work, if you are a woman. And Fikile isn't fond of working. By the end of the week she's ready to go home. "I'm sick of drinking brown water. I'm sick of shitting in a hole deep in the woods. I'm sick of walking all the way to the river to wash laundry."

I'm more diplomatic when I talk to Mamahulu. I tell her that we've enjoyed our stay but that we need to go back because my church choir is giving several performances over Christmas and I'm an invaluable member.

"No problem," Mamahulu says. "If Freddie has room in his van, he'll drive you back."

We pray that Uncle Freddie will have room but we are out of luck. He's overbooked with people visiting relatives in Johannesburg for the holidays. Since we aren't paying passengers, we are bumped off.

Fikile is distraught at the prospect of spending Christmas in Giyani.

"I've never gone without eating chicken during Christmas," Fikile says, "and I'm not about to."

"You heard what Willie said. None of those chickens are ever eaten except on very special occasions. And he says Christmas is not one of them."

"I'll have chicken," Fikile says determinedly.

Christmas eve, while I'm busy sweeping the huge courtyard, Fikile lures one of the chickens into a nearby clump of trees. Once out of sight, she bashes its head with a rock. She emerges and says grimly, "It's dead, Miriam."

I'm aghast. "What do you intend to do with it?"

"I'm going to tell Mamahulu. I'm sure she'll let us cook a dead chicken for Christmas."

I marvel at Fikile's brilliant scheme. Mamahulu will surely let us eat the dead chicken.

But not Mamahulu. When Fikile tells her that she found a dead chicken behind a clump of trees and asks if we should go ahead and pluck its white feathers and cook it for Christmas dinner, Mamahulu says, "Bring me the chicken."

Fikile and I run and get the dead chicken.

Mamahulu inspects it, then says, "Follow me."

We follow her outside into the courtyard. She orders Willie to dig a hole.

"This is where the dead chicken belongs," Mamahulu says as she buries it. "Not in your stomachs."

Fikile and I are too shocked to say anything.

Christmas day we are up at dawn, working. There are no preparations for an elaborate Christmas dinner. Instead we cook the usual pap and murogo. When Fikile complains that she's tired of eating pap and murogo, Mamahulu offers her Kool-Aid with brown bread for Christmas dinner.

"I want to go home," Fikile says despondently.

"You'll have to wait until Freddie comes back," Mamahulu says.

"When is he coming back?"

"After the holidays."

"After the holidays!" Fikile can't believe it. "That's in two weeks."

"Yes."

By now I've become a stoic. I've resigned myself to whatever. But not Fikile. She inquires whether there are any relatives in the area where we might find decent food to eat until Uncle Freddie comes. Nkateko, Mamahulu's youngest daughter, offers us some hope. "Grace, my older sister, lives nearby."

"What do you mean by 'nearby'?" I ask, mindful of the walk to the store.

Nkateko laughs. "I forgot that you're not used to walking like we are. Her place is several miles from here."

"I'll go to the end of the world for a taste of decent food," Fikile declares.

After enduring pap and murogo for several more days, Fikile and I set out for Grace's place. We trudge through the bleak landscape for several hours until we arrive at a cluster of huts on the other side of yet another mountain. It's around early afternoon. Grace is very glad to see us, but all she can offer us is more pap and murogo. Fikile is in despair. "You mean we've walked all this way for more pap and murogo? No meat?"

"People only eat meat when their husbands are visiting from the city."

Our miseries know no end. One night while I'm out in the woods relieving myself in the hole, a hyena comes prowling by and I flee without wiping myself. One of the goats dies of some illness and Fikile finally has her meat. I hate the smell of goat meat so I eat the murogo.

Luckily for us, the second week of our stay coincides with the coming out of tikhomba. Tikhomba are adolescent girls who've undergone initiation into the mysteries of womanhood, in preparation for marriage. The ceremony is held at Mamahulu's place. I find out that this is where Uncle Freddie usually gets his young brides.

The ceremony is very beautiful and everyone is happy. The tikhomba are handsomely dressed in *tinguvu,* Shangaan traditional dresses, and *vuhlava,* colorful beads and necklaces. They perform elaborate Shangaan dances while singing to the beat of drums and ululating. The mothers of the tikhomba bring tons of food to the ceremony, including sheep, rice, vegetables, fruit. Fikile and I can't believe our luck. We stuff our bellies full so we can endure the coming days of pap and murogo.

Uncle Freddie comes a couple of days after the ceremonies, and tells us that he has room to take us back. The eve of our departure, Fikile can't sleep.

"I want to make sure he doesn't leave without us," she says.

While I sleep she packs and unpacks and keeps vigil over the van. At the crack of dawn she's ready to go.

"Please come and visit us again," Nkateko says.

"We will," Fikile says, waving from inside the van.

She and I never set foot in Giyani again.

Chapter 24

L*isa, Uncle Freddie's first wife and the mother of four of his* twenty children, comes to visit Mama shortly after I return from Giyani. Lisa is distraught. She complains that she's finally had it with Uncle Freddie. "He's constantly marrying new wives," she says. "He no longer has time for me. I want you to talk to him. If he won't start paying more attention to me, I'm gone."

"What about the children?" Mama says, aware that a tribal wife leaves her children behind if she divorces her husband.

Lisa starts to cry. "That's what hurts, Mamahulu. I know I have to leave them behind if I leave Freddie. But I need a life. I can't take it anymore."

When Uncle Freddie comes, Mama tells him about Lisa's frustrations and needs.

"What should I do, Mamahulu?"

"You can stop robbing cradles," Mama says. "Most of those little girls you've taken as wives should still be in school."

"But I can't help it if they throw themselves at me, Mamahulu."

"So you want to end up like your father, is that it?" Mama says.

Uncle Freddie's father was a famous sangoma who had many wives. When some of his patients couldn't pay him, they'd give him their young daughters as payment. Rumor had it that one of his wives poisoned him to death.

"I take good care of them, Mamahulu," Uncle Freddie says. "They have a home and plenty to eat."

"And you buy each of them one mucheka a year," Mama says sarcastically. "Is that taking care of them?"

"I'm not a rich man."

"The more reason to have no more than one wife."

But Uncle Freddie can't stop. Few men can resist the temptation of getting more than one wife when wives are so easy to acquire. Lisa finally leaves Uncle Freddie but has to leave her four children behind.

One day Ruth, Uncle Freddie's youngest wife, comes to visit. Mama is surprised by how young she is and by the fact that she dropped out of Standard Five in order to marry Uncle Freddie, when she had the brains to go much further.

"What's a smart girl like you doing with an old man like him?" Mama asks.

"I love him."

" 'Love him,' " Mama says. "Don't you see that he's already married? Don't you realize that with so many other wives he has little love left for you?"

"But he told me I'm his favorite," Ruth says.

"Yes. And he told all his other wives that too while they were still young. Do you know why Lisa left him?"

"No."

"Because she was tired of competing for his affection with younger wives. Wait until you have a couple of children and see if you're still his favorite. I bet you he'll marry someone younger than you."

I've never seen Mama this impassioned before about the prevalent issue of polygamy. After Ruth leaves to return to Giyani, I ask Mama why she's so concerned about men having multiple wives.

"Because everything my mother suffered was the result of her father taking a younger woman for a second wife," Mama says. "The younger wife couldn't stand having a rival. She tried to bewitch her but she failed. Then she murdered my grandpa to prevent him from making Shibalu, my mother's brother, his heir. My grandpa was a wealthy man. He had *stands*"—property—"and shops. After his death everything went to his second wife, and we were left destitute."

Mama pauses to collect herself.

"And then my own father," Mama continues, "left my mother after marrying a second wife. The second wife didn't want a rival. So she told my father that it was either my mother or her. Since she was younger, he chose her."

"But a lot of women are second and third wives," I say. "Even Papa's father had many wives. It's the way things have always been."

"I know," Mama says, "but that doesn't make it right. Christ says that a man must marry one woman and be faithful to that woman, and she to him. When you grow up, child, never agree to share your husband with other women. It's the quickest way to old age, to misery, and to an early grave."

Uncle Freddie is very angry. "Mamahulu, why are you bent on wrecking my home?" he says one weekend during a visit.

"What do you mean, child?"

"Lisa came to stay with you and then she left me. Then Ruth comes to stay with you and you tell her she should leave me because I'm an old man."

"I didn't tell her to leave you."

"Didn't you tell her that I'm an old man?"

"Aren't you?" Mama says. "You're almost three times her age."

"But I'm still strong. I can still make children."

"Is that how you measure strength? By making children?"

"Why do you hate me, heh, Mamahulu?"

"I don't hate you, child," Mama says. "I just don't want to see other women's children suffering because of you."

"I provide them with a home and with food, don't I? And my children don't go begging."

"Tell me, child," Mama says. "Do you think it's right for a man to have many wives?"

"If he can afford them, yes."

Mama laughs. "So it's a matter of affordability, is that it? What if a woman can afford to have many husbands, would it be okay for her to have more than one?"

"Of course not. Custom doesn't allow it."

"Do you believe that Christ is the Son of God, child?"

"I do."

"Do you know that he says that he came into the world to do away with the old customs and to institute new laws for those who believe in him?"

"What laws are those?"

"One of them is that you can't serve two masters at the same time."

"What does that have to do with my having many wives?"

"It means you can't love more than one woman at the same time."

"No it doesn't. I have no problem loving more than one woman at a time."

"You may think you can," Mama says, "but you're bound to favor, however subtly, one over the other."

There's no way Uncle Freddie can win an argument against Mama, especially one concerning the Bible. But he never permits any of his wives to visit Mama again, on the grounds that Mama is "corrupting" them.

Mama is not only against polygamy, she's also against divorce. When Florah tells her that she's thinking of leaving Collin, she won't hear of it.

"I don't understand you women of today," Mama says. "At the slightest problem you think of leaving. Whatever happened to loyalty to your husband? Collin is a very good man. He doesn't beat you. He supports Angie. And look at me and your papa. I thought of leaving him many times, but each time I'd think of you children."

"I'm not like you, Mama," Florah says. "I can't stay with a man who cheats on me and who doesn't support me in disputes with his stepmother."

"Collin says you disrespect his stepmother."

"She doesn't deserve respect," Florah says angrily. "She's constantly meddling in my marriage. She wants Collin to give his wages to her instead of to me. She doesn't appreciate the fact that I clean the whole damn house by myself and do laundry and cook. I want out."

But Mama tries everything to get Florah and Collin to patch up their marriage for Angie's sake. She prays, she talks to Collin, she goes to Priest Mathebula. I also want their marriage to last. I like Collin very much. Of all the men Florah has known, he respects her the most and never beats her. I especially like him because during Mama's insanity, when Papa was drinking heavily and not giving us any money, Collin always bought us groceries. Also he's the most educated of Florah's boyfriends, having completed matric, and works as a manager at a factory.

Nothing Mama tries works.

"I think I know the solution to Florah's marriage problems," I say one evening after Mama and I have finished reading the Bible.

Mama looks at me. Because of my regular reading and study of the Bible, Mama now considers me a font of wisdom.

"They don't have a place of their own. You know how much Florah hates living with Collin's stepmother."

"But a *makoti*"—a daughter-in-law—"must get along with her stepmother."

"But don't you see?" I say. "Florah can't get along with her stepmother if she's constantly under her scrutiny. She says Collin's stepmother criticizes everything she does. Even when Collin agrees with Florah, he seldom has the courage to rebuke his stepmother because they'll get kicked out. And where will they go?"

"I see what you mean," Mama says, nodding.

I smile.

"How did you get so wise?"

"I may not talk much, Mama, but I see a lot and I think a lot."

Mama asks Florah to stay with Collin and promises to help them find a place of their own. Florah agrees.

Chapter 25

At *fourteen, I've become very self-conscious about my looks. A lot* of my friends are starting to use creams to lighten their skin and to stretch (straighten) their kinky hair. They make fun of my homely appearance, particularly because I have large cheeks and am slightly overweight. But the butt of their jokes is my pimples. My face is full of them. They're large and ugly and I'm desperate to get rid of them.

"How did you get rid of your pimples?" I ask a girl in our yard whose face used to be teeming with them. Now it's smooth and unblemished.

"Do you really want to know?" the girl asks.

She flashes a half-embarrassed smile, then says, "I got me a boyfriend."

"What do boyfriends have to do with pimples?"

The girl laughs. "You attend church too much, Miriam. You should become street smart. Boyfriends have everything to do with pimples."

I'm bewildered. "I don't know what you mean."

"Once a girl with pimples starts having sex, they go away."

"You're joking."

"I'm not."

"But I don't want to have sex."

"Then you'll be stuck with those hideous pimples the rest of your life. Pimples are a sign that you're starved for sex."

Now I understand why some boys have been making advances toward me. They must be taking one look at my pimples and concluding that I'm starved for sex. I never follow up on the girl's suggestion, which apparently a lot of girls believe, just as some AIDS-stricken men in the township believe that having sex with a virgin cures the disease.

I'm mortified of becoming sexually active, in part because I haven't the foggiest notion of what sex is all about. All I know about sex is what I read about in the Bible, that it is something sacred, to be saved for marriage. Also I remember what happened to Maria, and the promise I've made to Mama that I'll finish school and become a nurse.

Pimples are an obsession, but not my hair. I'm happy with it being nappy because I always wash it thoroughly and comb it. Then along comes Florah. Tired of working for white people who pay her little, she is eager to start her own business to be financially independent of Collin, who still gives his stepmother his wages. She recently completed a course at a beauty school in downtown Johannesburg. There she studied how to perm hair "the American way." She suggests that I be one of her first customers. She's purchased all kinds of TCB and Black Like Me chemicals—neutralizers, shampoos, moisturizers, and perms. And she shows me pictures of black American women with their long straightened hair, which many of my friends adore as glamorous.

But still I have doubts. "You aren't going to ruin my hair, are you?"

"Of course not," Florah says. "That's why I took the course. It was taught by people who've studied in America."

"It's just that some of my friends have ruined their hair by trying to make it look American."

"It's because they used primitive methods."

I know what primitive methods Florah is talking about. Many of my friends who can't afford expensive chemicals use them. One method involves lathering your hair with a foamy white chemical that burns like hell. Then you rush off to the communal tap to rinse the stuff off. Sometimes there's a long line and nobody wants to let you cut in even when you scream that your head is on fire, so most of your hair falls off, leaving you with *magundwana,* a bald head with tufts of hair.

Those who can't afford the lathering chemical or consider it too risky resort to an even more primitive method. They bake a smooth stone hot on top of a brazier or stove. They then stretch the hair with a comb, as one would do with a curler, and then use the hot stone to delicately singe the hair till it straightens. You need very thick hair and careful hands because with short hair and careless hands you can easily end up singeing your scalp.

Florah turns out to be a pretty good hairdresser. My permed hair becomes the envy of my friends. For a time it even overshadows the ugly pimples. But then Florah and Collin fight and she moves to Soweto to stay with friends. I find myself in a dilemma. My hair is now addicted to chemicals, and only Florah has them and knows how to apply them just right. My hair starts looking like porcupine quills. Then on top of pimples I develop dandruff.

I'm utterly wretched. My schoolwork suffers. Finally a friend of Florah's who's studied her methods in the hope of starting her own business comes to the rescue. She only makes matters worse. My hair starts changing color. It curls into all sorts of funny shapes by itself. I long for my nappy hair, which was so easy to manage with its soft texture and natural sheen. I finally decide to get a crew cut, in the desperate hope of having my hair, in time, regrow to its original appearance and beauty. It never quite does.

But I'm one of the lucky ones. Nkateko, Mamahulu's youngest daughter, comes to live with us for several months after suffering the worst humiliation for a tribal bride: the parents of her new husband returned her to her home for failing to bear children. She has become a fanatical follower of the ZCC—Zion Christian Church—the largest Christian denomination in South Africa, which blends Christianity with traditional African beliefs and rituals. ZCC members dress in green and white and pray constantly.

Nkateko prays three times a day, with such fervor that Angie and Given make fun of her. Mama gets her a job in the suburbs working for a friend of Mrs. Hunt, in the hope of helping Nkateko rebuild her shattered self-esteem and her life.

One day Nkateko returns home in tears. Her small head is covered with a *doek,* a head scarf.

"What's the matter?" Mama asks.

At first Nkateko is reluctant to talk. Then she gathers enough courage to remove her doek. Everyone shrinks back in horror. All her thick, lovely, nappy hair is gone. She's as bald as an ivory tusk. And the small shape of her head makes her look comical, like Jojo, a cartoon character in the *World.*

"What happened?" Mama asks.

Nkateko doesn't speak. She simply produces a bottle. I look at the label. It has a picture of a white woman with cascading black hair.

"I wanted my hair to look like hers," she says.

"And you used this?" I ask.

"Yes. I found it while cleaning Madam's bathroom," Nkateko says.

As she's speaking I read the label.

"I sat down on Madam's hairdressing chair and liberally applied the stuff on my hair," Nkateko says. "I can read, but not that well. So when I saw the word 'hair,' I thought it was one of those chemicals Florah uses. Then when I tried combing my hair, it started falling off. I was panic-stricken. I thought Madam had booby-trapped her cosmetics because a lot of maids use their madams' products."

Mama starts laughing. I don't know whether to laugh or cry.

"The reason your hair fell off," I say, "is because this is a hair remover. White women use it to take the hair off their legs and armpits."

Nkateko laughs even louder. She has the rare ability to laugh at her own mistakes.

"I saw only the word 'hair' and said, Hallelujah, I'm in business. Now I can finally get that perm I've long wanted, without the expense."

Fortunately for Nkateko, her hair eventually grows back.

Mama has a philosophical view of the hair-stretching mania infecting her daughters. It's a philosophy derived, as always, from the Bible.

"My children," she'd say, "if God wanted you to have stretched hair, you'd have been born with such hair. And if God wanted you to have white skin, he'd have given you white parents. There's a reason he gave you nappy hair and black skin. That reason is because both are the best and most beautiful for you. They are his precious gift to you. Always remember that whatever the texture of your hair, the color of your skin, the shape of your nose, lips, and face, you are beautiful and divine, because God has made everyone in his image, which is beautiful and divine."

Chapter 26

People are fond of saying to Mama about me, "The man who marries your daughter, musadi, will be most fortunate. He'll have married the perfect wife."

"I know," Mama says. "I'm very proud of her. She's the apple of my eye."

I find this praise somewhat disconcerting, mainly because the traits for which I'm praised are submissiveness, obedience, and hard work. Of all the seven siblings I'm the one who submits most readily to whatever rules my parents have laid out for us. Johannes, Florah, George, Maria, and even Linah and Diana have from time to time rebelled against parental authority. I never have. As for obedience, everything my teachers, parents, and other adults ask me to do, I do without as much as a murmur, even when I have some misgivings. I have an inordinate respect for authority and desire to please.

But both submissiveness and obedience are nothing compared to my mania for doing chores. When I'm not at choir practice, at church, or at school, I'm always doing chores. On Saturday, while my friends go window-shopping at the Indian marketplace or in downtown Johannesburg, or when they accompany their boyfriends to the local stadium to watch a soccer match, or to King's cinema for a movie, I'm at home cleaning, cooking, and doing laundry.

I expressly wake up very early in the morning in order to have a full day of chores. I scrub the floor, polish it, sort laundry, wash it in the tub, dry it on the clothesline, then iron it. I prepare all the meals—breakfast, lunch, and dinner—for everybody.

My submissiveness, obedience, and addiction to working endear me to Papa. He's constantly boasting about me to his drinking buddies, one of them a gray-haired old man who owns a grocery store. I'm surprised when the old man starts giving me free groceries whenever I go to the store. I attribute it to his kindness and to his friendship with Papa. I take it as a joke when Florah and Maria tell me that the old man is being kind to me because he's eager to have me for a second wife.

"He's old enough to be my grandpa," I say.

"The more reason for him to want a young woman," Florah says.

"It's time you attended tikhomba," Mama says to me one day. "You're old enough."

I thought the day would never come. Ever since I went to Giyani and saw the tikhomba ceremony, I'd been itching to go. Only tikhomba would certify me as a mature woman. Florah, the only one of my sisters who's gone, tries to discourage me.

"It's not what it's trumped up to be," she says.

"But you were very proud to have gone," I say. "And when you came back you were treated with respect."

"Yes. But I wouldn't recommend it for you."

"Why?"

Florah won't tell. It's taboo to reveal to the uninitiated what goes on during the tikhomba ceremony. Anyone who breaks the taboo runs the risk of going mad.

"Believe me, Miriam, it's not worth it," Florah says.

My curiosity gets the better of me. I tell Mama that I want to enter tikhomba over the June school holidays. Mama is delighted.

"You'll love it," she says.

"But Florah says I won't," I say.

"Your sister doesn't know what she's talking about."

I don't know what to say about the experience of being a *tikhomba*. On the one hand I hated it, and on the other I liked it. What I hated was the constant beating for disobeying our "mothers," the women who had the task of teaching us everything about being a complete woman. We are taught that a mature woman is self-denying and self-sacrificing, that she takes care of her children, that she stoically bears pain, that she defers to her husband, who is the head of the household, and that she bears as many children as possible to prove her womanhood. To enforce these lessons our "mothers" would constantly beat us. We'd be beaten for not eating the mounds of porridge doled out to us every day to fatten us; we'd be beaten for getting the lyrics to licentious songs wrong; and we'd be beaten for any small act of disobedience.

There were some things about tikhomba that I liked. I liked the solidarity it created among women. I also liked how the ordeal strengthened my character and my ability to endure hardship and pain, qualities I feel a woman must have to survive in a patriarchal culture.

When I graduated from tikhomba after four weeks' confinement in a house on Seventeenth Avenue, a huge feast was held in my honor. I was given many gifts. A sheep was slaughtered to celebrate the death of the girl Miriam and the birth of the woman Sayina, my tikhomba name.

In October of 1984, Alexandra—which has been on death row for many years—is reprieved. The Botha government passes a law that spares the ghetto from demolition as a "black spot." Alexandra is very lucky. Across the country, entire black communities are bulldozed as part of the government's attempts to remove blacks from "white" South Africa and deport them to various tribal reserves. One bulldozed black community in Johannesburg was later renamed Triomf (Triumph) by the whites who moved there.

The government promises to transform the festering one-square-mile ghetto into a livable community. There's great expectation and rejoicing at the news among the residents. My family has high hopes of finally being able to move out of the shack and into one of the new houses that are expected to be built. And Florah and Collin, who are reconciled, also plan to apply for a loan to purchase one of these new houses.

But like so many other schemes to improve Alexandra, this latest one results only in modest improvements. Sewers are finally installed in parts of the ghetto, a handful of nice houses are built in an area called Phase One, but the only persons who can afford them are black professionals, most of them from Soweto.

Florah and Collin continue to live with his stepmother on Ninth Avenue. Tensions between her and Collin mount and bring about yet another separation. She moves back home, but Papa chases her away, telling her to return to her husband and not disgrace the family. Mama says that the reason Papa keeps demanding that Florah go back to Collin is partly because Papa doesn't have the money to repay Collin's lobola. In desperation, Florah moves in with a tsotsi boyfriend who lives on Fourteenth Avenue.

While Florah is separated from Collin, his stepmother kidnaps Angie and takes her to a remote village in Zululand. Florah is distraught. She doesn't know where Angie is being kept. She isn't allowed to communicate with her. She goes to the Peri-Urban Police but they aren't any help. They say that their task is to combat crime and not to get involved in domestic disputes, especially those involving lobola. She confronts Collin and he says there's nothing he can do, that the only way Angie can come back is if he and Florah get back together again.

The blackmailing attempt backfires. Florah is adamant that she'll never get back together with him and tells him that she's already in love with someone else. Collin, devastated, vows to keep Angie.

George rushes through the door waving a copy of the *World*. I'm busy cooking dinner and Mama is undressing, having just returned from work.

"Bishop Tutu has been awarded the Nobel Peace Prize."

"What's a Nobel Peace Prize?" I ask.

"It's an award given to a leader who's worked for peace and justice. Bishop Tutu received it in behalf of the freedom struggle. He's the second black South African to receive it."

"Who was the first?"

"Chief Albert Luthuli. He got one in nineteen sixty."

"Does the prize mean we'll soon be free?" Mama asks.

George laughs. "No."

"Then why are you so excited?"

"It means that the world knows about the struggle, Mama," George says. "And if the world knows, then apartheid's days are numbered."

Chapter 27

Despite Bishop Tutu's 1984 Nobel Peace Prize, repression by the government continues. So does resistance, which for the first time was led by the powerful trade union movement. Black trade unions, which had previously been banned, were now flexing their new muscles, thanks to a 1977 commission that convinced the government to abolish the Jobs Reservations Act and to let black unions register and take part in collective bargaining. The resistance was led by three powerful unions, the nonracial Federation of South African Trade Unions (FOSATU), the exclusively black Council of Unions of South African Trade Unions, and the National Mineworkers' Union (NUM). The three, which later merged into the powerful Congress of South African Trades Unions (COSATU), joined the United Democratic Front.

The UDF, launched in 1983 to oppose the new constitution—which granted a limited franchise to Coloreds and Indians but not to blacks—now had over 3 million members. It was an unprecedented multiracial organization that brought together over five hundred trade-union, community, religious, sports, and other grassroots organizations. Several churches and students', labor, and women's groups in Alexandra belonged to the UDF.

The new weapon of the resistance against apartheid is strikes and stayaways, meant to cripple the South African economy, forcing the government to give in to black demands. The demands are the immediate release of all political detainees, the abolition of the hated pass laws, the halting of forced removals, the resignation of black township officials who are seen as collaborators with apartheid, and the scrapping of plans to increase rent, bus fare, and the sales tax. In Alexandra, as in other townships, the strikes and stayaways lead to violence. The government detains strike leaders and deploys troops in the townships.

Though Alexandra is under military occupation, students are allowed to return to school for final exams. I'm anxious to do my best in my last year so I can go to Alexandra High School for Standard Six. Most of my friends will be going there. The school has a new and very lovely building and an excellent choir and track team.

The most important reason I want to attend Alexandra High is that I've received a letter from Johannes in America. He's writing a book called *Kaffir Boy,* and several publishers are very interested in his story of growing up under apartheid. With some of the money he hopes to earn, he promises to pay for anyone in the family who wants to go to university.

My dream is to go to Venda University. It's one I've had ever since our school choir won that big trophy singing "Shango Lasho Venda" and ever since hearing Papa's stories about the beauty of the land, its culture and people.

Uncle Pietrus, my father's older brother's son, is delighted about my plans. He was our neighbor at Thirteenth Avenue for many years. Recently, having grown tired of the hardships of living in the city, he'd returned to Venda, where he'd bought a farm, on which he was growing avocados, mangoes, papayas, and oranges. He also operated a taxi service between Johannesburg and Venda.

"You'll love it there," Uncle Pietrus says. "There's no place like Venda."

"Everyone tells me that," I say. "But why do people leave and come to live in a place like Alexandra, which is so filthy and where life is hard?"

"There's no work in Venda. It's one of the poorest areas in the country. But things are beginning to change. Venda now has its independence. The new government is doing a lot to improve things. They're even building a casino and a hotel in Thohoyandou."

Thohoyandou (Head of the Elephant) was the capital of the Venda homeland, which was granted its "independence" in 1979, an independence recognized only by Pretoria.

"One thing good about Venda is that there are no riots there," Uncle Pietrus says. "You'll be able to complete your education in peace. The police clamped down. They are very good. Better than the police here."

I didn't know that by "very good" Uncle Pietrus meant that the Venda police often tortured activists and students and that the South African security forces were deeply involved in training the Venda security police.

"I'd like to visit Venda one of these days," I say.

"What about coming along with me this Christmas?"

Before I can go to Venda I have to sit for final exams. In preparation for finals, teachers and mistresses often give us a series of quizzes that count toward our end-of-the-year marks. The toughest quizzes are in my science class, which is taught by none other than Teacher Mguni, the choir director, who is also one of the most feared teachers at Bovet.

A girl in the class named Rosemary so dreads being whipped, especially by Teacher Mguni, that whenever he gives us quizzes she completely blanks out. In the past Cynthia and I tried our best to shore up her confidence. Two days before the first science quiz we invite Rosemary to study with us. During our review she does very well, knows most of the answers, and is bubbling with confidence. But when she takes the quiz, she can't remember a thing. She fails miserably and is whipped.

A couple of days later Teacher Mguni says we are going to have another quiz. Rosemary comes to us quaking. "Please help me."

"There's nothing else we can do, Rosemary," I say. "There's nothing mysterious about how we prepare for tests. We simply study hard. We have no muti to help you."

I say this not facetiously. There are some students who are so afraid of failing exams that they take muti potions from sangomas before sitting for an exam in order to increase their chances of getting high marks.

"There's something you can do," Rosemary says tentatively.

"What?"

"You can let me sit next to you during the quiz."

I can't believe that Rosemary wants us to be party to cheating on exams, one of the worst crimes a student can commit. Teachers at Bovet punished cheating on exams by severely whipping all the students involved and tossing out their grades. I'm not about to run the risk, especially with finals looming around the corner.

"I'll give you anything you want," Rosemary says with a piteous, pleading look.

"Anything we want?" we say simultaneously.

"Yes."

Rosemary's family is well-to-do and owns a well-stocked grocery store on Fifteenth Avenue. It is full of items Cynthia and I can't afford but intensely covet: Eat-Sum-More biscuits, Cokes, Kit-Kat chocolate, and sardines, not to mention household staples like mealie meal, paraffin, sugar, milk, laundry detergent.

"Is it okay if we came to your store and bought a few things?" Cynthia asks.

"Sure," Rosemary says. "Anytime."

"No. I mean is it okay for us to come when *you* are behind the counter? We'd like to buy things from *you*."

Rosemary understands what Cynthia means. She hesitates a moment before saying, "I can arrange to be behind the counter."

"Good," Cynthia says. "Then Miriam and I will arrange for you to see our answers during the quiz."

"Thanks a lot," Cynthia says with relief.

I listen to this exchange between Rosemary and Cynthia with mixed emotions. On the one hand I'm eager for the opportunity to get free groceries. On the other hand I feel it's wrong to engage in extortion and cheating. But Cynthia is persuasive and I agree to take the risk.

Cynthia and I are at Rosemary's store almost every day. We wait for her to man the counter and then we go in and order up a storm.

The day before the quiz, I ask Cynthia: "Do you think we'll be able to keep our end of the bargain?"

"Of course, why not?"

"You've forgotten something."

"What?"

"If Teacher Mguni catches us letting Rosemary copy our answers during exams, we'll be whipped and given zeros."

"Let's pray for Teacher Mguni to leave the classroom during the quiz."

Chapter 28

On quiz day, not only does Teacher Mguni not leave the classroom, he walks up and down the aisle, keeping a careful eye on students to make sure no one cheats. As a result Rosemary dare not crane her neck to look at the answers in our books, despite our attempt to expose them.

"I'm sorry, Rosemary," I say after the quiz, "but there was no way to help you."

"I failed," Rosemary says despondently, "and I'm going to be whipped."

"Don't be so pessimistic," Cynthia says. "You're smart. You didn't need our help. You studied harder than we did. I bet you passed."

"I know I failed. The strange thing is that I know the answers. I just can't remember them during a quiz."

The next day Teacher Mguni returns our quiz papers. Rosemary has indeed failed. I feel awful as I watch her on the verge of tears. He asks all those who've failed to stand up. He has a thick hosepipe in his hand. About a third of the class stands up. To Rosemary's relief, he starts the whipping from the other end of the classroom. It's almost time for the next period. Maybe she'll be saved by the bell.

Apparently Teacher Mguni realizes this, for he delivers the lashes with unusual speed. There's no way Rosemary can be saved by the bell because Teacher Mguni has already whipped most of the students and there's about fifteen minutes left before the end of the period.

But something else saves Rosemary. Teacher Mguni comes to two boys who sit at the back of the classroom. Their names are Markos and Khatuchera. They are friends and the biggest boys in class. Markos has spent time in prison for rape.

"Extend your hand," Teacher Mguni demands of Markos.

Markos refuses.

To the amazement of the class, Markos gives Teacher Mguni a defiant look.

"Are you deaf? I said extend your hand and be punished."

"If you dare lay your hand on me, you bloody Venda," Markos says in Zulu, "I'll teach you a lesson."

There's stunned silence in the classroom. I can't believe Markos is threatening a teacher. Recalling how Amanda was beaten up by Mrs. Mabaso, I expect Teacher Mguni to order us all outside so he can beat up Markos.

But he handles the situation differently. "Remain standing," he says to Markos. "I'll deal with you later."

I guess that Teacher Mguni plans to whip the remaining students and then get back to Markos.

"Extend your hand," Teacher Mguni says to Khatuchera.

Khatuchera refuses.

"Didn't you hear me?" Teacher Mguni says angrily. "I said extend your hand."

"What makes you think you can punish me if you didn't punish him?" Khatuchera points a finger at Markos.

Khatuchera is a Venda like Teacher Mguni, who knows his parents.

"Is that how your parents raised you, to disrespect teachers? Now extend your hand before I beat you up."

"Try."

There's a collective gasp. Khatuchera has dared Teacher Mguni to whip him. If Teacher Mguni backs down, he'll lose respect, the sole basis of his authority.

I whisper to Cynthia, "If Teacher Mguni doesn't whip Markos and Khatuchera, there's no way he can whip Rosemary."

We both look at Rosemary. She too must have reached the same conclusion, for her face has become more relaxed.

"So you want me to beat you up?" Teacher Mguni says. There's a hint of desperation in his voice.

"I said, 'Try,' " Khatuchera says, his mouth set. He clenches his fists.

Teacher Mguni raises the hosepipe and strikes Khatuchera on the shoulder. Khatuchera immediately punches Teacher Mguni in the face. The class gasps. Enraged, Teacher Mguni raises the hosepipe and is about to strike Khatuchera again when Markos grabs him from behind. The two students rain blows on Teacher Mguni. He tries in vain to parry them and to land his own. Bodies crash against desks as the three combatants go at it amid screams and shouts from students. There's no doubt that if we'd had the courage to express how we felt, we'd have cheered Markos and Khatuchera on.

Teacher Mguni manages to wrench loose and bolt for the door. Students are hysterical with laughter.

"He'll never beat us again after this," Cynthia says.

Minutes later, Teacher Mguni returns with the principal.

"What happened?" the principal asks Markos and Khatuchera. I can tell from his tone that he too is afraid of the two students. They relate their version of events.

I expect Markos and Khatuchera to be expelled on the spot. Nothing of the kind happens. I guess the principal didn't want to be assaulted by Markos and Khatuchera, too. The two students remain in class, but with one big difference: Teacher Mguni never whips them again. Rosemary was never whipped for failing the quiz. And she never fails any more quizzes given by Teacher Mguni, including the final exam.

I'm in a very happy mood when I leave for Venda, three days before Christmas. I've passed Standard Five, and come January I'll be attending Standard Six at Alexandra High. The trip takes about seven hours and we arrive before dawn.

I find Venda more beautiful than the image conjured up by the winning song "Shango Lasho Venda." Compared to Alexandra, with its smog, filth, overcrowding, and shacks, Venda is like Eden. The air is fresh; the traditional thatched-roof huts are some of the loveliest and most colorful I've ever seen; the soil is a rich red and yields a cornucopia of fruits and vegetables. There are rivers and streams and lakes and thick forests and mountains.

I stay at the home of Papa's brother. His wife, Aunt Lydia, is a sangoma and she and her husband have one child, a son about my age named Dankies. I can't help comparing where I'm staying with Giyani. I sleep on a bed instead of on a sponge. Every night during my two weeks' stay we eat meat—chicken, steak, lamb chops. Murogo is only eaten by choice. Rice is eaten as often as pap, rather than on special occasions.

I immediately impress Aunt Lydia by always getting up very early in the morning to help her clean, cook, and do laundry.

"You're unusual for a girl born and raised in the city," Aunt Lydia says. "City girls usually come here expecting to be served. You haven't stopped working since you came."

"Mama taught me to love work," I say.

"And your Venda is very good."

"I'm taking it at school."

One evening Aunt Lydia says, "I wish I had a daughter like you. Would you like to live here with me and be my daughter? I'll pay for your schooling."

It would be wonderful to be away from the smog and filth of Alexandra, the constant hunger, the endemic violence, the vicious police, the crumbling shacks, the intense peer pressure. Here I could stop worrying all the time and be myself.

"I'd like nothing more than to live here," I say, "but I'm afraid I can't."

"Why not?"

"My family is back in Alexandra," I say. "I can't leave them alone. Especially Mama. She needs me."

Aunt Lydia takes a long hard look at me.

"Your mother is a very lucky woman to have you for a daughter," she says.

"I'm very lucky to have her for a mother," I say.

After two weeks I return home feeling refreshed. People comment on my color and on the fact that I've added weight. I now understand why Papa is so miserable and frustrated in Alexandra. I would be too if I'd grown up in the Eden-like world of Venda only to end up in a ghetto. I wonder why he simply doesn't pack up and leave. I ask Mama.

"Your father talks about going back someday, but I know he doesn't really mean it because he's afraid of witches.

"He comes from a large hardworking family. His father was a very rich man with lots of cattle. He married several wives. In all, he had ten children, five boys and five girls. Rumor has it that one of his sons-in-law coveted his wealth. He was so evil that he systematically removed all obstacles to obtaining the wealth. First he bewitched your grandfather. Next, your father's oldest brother. When the other brothers realized what was happening, they all fled. Your father has not been back but once because he's afraid that his brother-in-law, who is still alive, will bewitch him."

Chapter 29

It's been almost a year since Angie was kidnapped. Florah has been begging Collin to bring her back but his stepmother has steadfastly refused. Florah fears that Angie might have been killed for muti purposes. A lot of children, especially young girls, are routinely kidnapped and taken to remote areas to be killed and their body parts used in potions.

"Collin would never do such a thing to his own daughter," Mama says. She recommends that Florah visit a sangoma to find out exactly what happened to Angie. Florah visits one, who after consulting her divination bones reassures Florah that Angie is still alive, and that they'll soon be reunited.

Not satisfied with waiting for Angie to come back, Florah seeks other means of regaining custody. A friend of hers named Rebecca suggests she report the matter at the white police station, which has departments equipped to handle domestic disputes and custody battles and can compel Collin to return Angie.

Mama begs Florah not to involve the white police, which might endanger Collin's life.

"I don't care," Florah says. "I want my Angie back."

Mama tells Collin that Florah intends to go to the white police if

Angie isn't brought back. Two weeks later Angie is returned to Florah, nearly a year after she was kidnapped and taken to Newcastle, in Natal.

Angie no longer speaks or understands Shangaan. She speaks only Zulu. She has a hard time relating to any of us, including her mother. She's grown rather quiet. Whenever her mother is able to coax her to speak, she reveals that though she was treated well overall in Newcastle, a woman she calls Auntie would beat her whenever she spoke Shangaan. In the beginning, whenever she cried for her mother, she was told that Florah was dead.

For a while following her return Angie cries a lot. I suggest to Mama that we all start speaking Zulu to make her feel at home. Mama talks to Papa, who reluctantly agrees. The move works wonders on Angie's personality. She becomes more outgoing, laughs a lot, plays with other children, and enjoys teaching her cousin Given Zulu. In turn Given teaches her Shangaan. The two soon become best friends.

After the traumatic experiences at Bovet, I never thought I'd ever enjoy attending school. But Alexandra High is the school of my dreams. Recently built as part of the redevelopment of Alexandra, it is the most beautiful I've ever seen. It has four buildings three stories high, with manicured lawns and a garden bursting with flowers and plants. In October we celebrate Spring Day.

The classrooms are tiled and have air-conditioning in the summer and heating in the winter. There's a science lab, and we even have our own athletics field where the old beer hall was gutted during the riots of 1976.

But what I like the most about Alexandra High is its principal, Miss Jones. She's a very strong woman, lives in Soweto, dresses very sharp, and drives a BMW. She's a powerful motivator and speaks impeccable English. Each morning at assembly she exhorts us to try our best to learn, despite the fact that Bantu Education is inferior to White Education. "Half a loaf is better than nothing" is one of her favorite sayings.

She runs the school with an iron fist. A lot of students consider her too tough, but she tells us that in time we'll thank her for it. I consider her every word that of an oracle. I especially admire her for standing up to anyone who tries to disrupt the peace of the school, which is like an oasis in the middle of a desert.

Everything at Alexandra High seems perfect, except for one thing. We are not allowed to choose our own courses. My dream is to be a nurse, and I had hoped to be able to study chemistry, biology, and physics, but my courses are chosen for me by the teachers, who follow the rules laid down by the Department of Bantu Education. I end up taking English, Afrikaans, Tsonga, accounting, and business economics.

Cynthia takes the same courses as I do. Other friends—Becky, Gertrude, and Latisha—are taking different ones, including home economics. From time to time they cook elaborate meals, which they serve the rest of the class. Dlayani has dropped out because of lack of funds. Other students too have dropped out for lack of funds, including Etienne, one of the most brilliant students Bovet ever had. Having lost both his parents, he's been forced to go to work.

George is now in Standard Ten. He and I get along well and he cares very much about the family. It's comforting to know that I have a big brother attending the same school, because there are gangs of dropouts who love hanging outside the school building, harassing girls. But I sometimes find George overprotective and a bit authoritarian. He loves telling me what to do and seldom does any chores in the house, preferring to play and coach tennis.

One day Miss Jones announces that the school will be going on a field trip. I didn't get to go on too many trips when I was at Bovet, for lack of money. George insists that I not go, even though the trip is free. I conjecture that it's because he's going and thinks me something of an embarrassment. I'm very disappointed but I don't complain.

A couple of hours after the buses leave, a solemn Miss Jones summons everyone to assembly. She has very tragic news. The Alexandra High students who'd gone on the field trip have been involved in a serious accident. Several students are dead and dozens have been wounded.

I'm in shock. Is George among the dead?

Miss Jones reads their names. They include Zenzi and two of my classmates in Standard Six. Petronella is among the wounded. George returns safe. I wonder if, had I gone, I'd have been among the wounded and dead.

The tragedy, however, doesn't affect the optimism of the school—especially because the annual track meet is coming up. There's fierce rivalry among students from Alexandra High, Minerva, and Realogile. Most of my friends—including Cynthia and Fikile—are star runners.

Despite their presence, Alexandra High has a reputation for coming out dead last during meets. Minerva is the premeet favorite, largely because of their undefeated star, a runner named Mandla who specializes in long distance, the most important race of the meet.

This year Miss Jones is optimistic about our chances. We have recently acquired a secret weapon, Gijima, a Xhosa student who recently arrived from the Transkei, where he ran long distances over mountains. And we also have competent athletes who've trained hard at the javelin, high jump, one hundred meters, long jump, shot put, discus, and so on.

The day of the meet the three rival teams and their supporters pack the stadium on Sixth Avenue, more than ten thousand students decked out in their school colors. I'm leading the cheering squad, along with Latisha, Becky, Gertrude, Margaret, and Petronella.

Fikile and Cynthia anchor the relay team to victory, running barefoot. But everyone is waiting for the main event: the long-distance race, which involves running twenty-two laps around the stadium.

To everyone's surprise, our school is in the lead going into the final race, barely edging out Minerva. If Mandla wins, Minerva will take first place. If Gijima wins, we'll consolidate our hold on first.

It's clear from the start that the race is between Mandla and Gijima. At the halfway point, Gijima begins pulling away. His stride is long and effortless, and his breathing is unlabored. As the distance between him and Mandla widens, Gijima runs faster. The students from Alexandra High are delirious. With three laps to go, leading by several laps, Gijima begins to perform for the audience. He stops, gets off the track, unties his shoes, looks at his panting opponents, slowly reties his shoelaces and resumes running, still in the lead. The crowd goes wild.

"Gijima! Gijima! Gijima! Gijima!"

He widens his lead. The gun sounds for the final lap. Gijima effortlessly resumes his stride and wins by nearly a lap.

As we dance on the bleachers in celebration, people start screaming. Students from Minerva, who hate to lose, are leading an attack with rocks, bottles, fists, and *keities* (slingshots).

Pandemonium breaks out. I'm struck on the head with an empty Coke bottle. A stone from nowhere hits Latisha in the back of the head. We flee as the battle intensifies.

From that day on, students from Minerva were our mortal enemies. And our feud was to grow even worse during Mzabalazo, the battle to make Alexandra ungovernable as part of a liberation struggle by the ANC and the PAC.

Chapter 30

In March of 1985, the protests against apartheid spiral. They are a continuation of the protests begun the year before against President Botha's constitutional reforms (granting representation for Coloreds and Indians in a segregated, three-chamber Parliament). A week never went by without news of police opening fire on protesters in various townships across the country. Dozens were killed and scores more detained.

"It's all-out war," George says as he reads a story in the paper about the massacre at Uitenhage, a town near Port Elizabeth where police opened fire on four thousand protesters, killing more than twenty people.

"Why is the government killing innocent people?" Mama asks.

"They're desperate," George says. "They know that the Comrades aren't going to back down until apartheid is crushed."

"Who are the Comrades?" Mama asks.

"*We* are the Comrades," George says proudly, pointing a finger at his chest. "*We* are prepared to die in order to be free."

In the days to come I was to hear the name Comrades bandied about at school. The Comrades, or the Amagabane, were radical young blacks, the storm troopers of township protest. Their aim was to smash the government's ruling structures in the townships—the police and the community councillors—to bring about a "people's revolution."

The Comrades make schools the focal point of resistance. Most of the leaders come from Minerva, which is a hotbed of student radicalism. But several come from Alexandra High, including a tall, rebellious boy named Oupa, who's always given teachers a hard time over the issue of Bantu Education. He's previously been in and out of police detention. I see Oupa from time to time in our yard at Sixteenth Avenue, where Aletta, his older sister, lives with an abusive boyfriend. And Aletta often runs to Mama for protection when her boyfriend starts beating her up during an argument.

Despite the fact that Oupa and several students from Alexandra High are among the leaders of the Comrades, the school remains relatively unaffected by the violence. Most students continue to come to school. The reason is Miss Jones. She's remained defiantly anti-Comrades. Each morning at assembly she rails against their shortsightedness and exhorts us to continue coming to school, not to heed the Comrades' call for "Liberation Before Education."

"A free South Africa will need educated leaders," she says. "Even Mandela and his fellow prisoners continue to learn while they are on Robben Island. They know they can't be true leaders without knowledge."

Whenever violence breaks out in the township, Miss Jones locks the gates to prevent it from disrupting us. I marvel at her courage, especially because Comrades have devised a ruthless method of dealing with those who defy their will. The method is called necklacing. It involves forcing a petrol-soaked tire over a victim's head and shoulders and then igniting it.

"I'm afraid that Miss Jones will be necklaced one of these days," I say to Cynthia one afternoon as we are walking back home from school after a particularly tense standoff between Miss Jones and a group of Comrades.

"They won't touch her," Cynthia says.

"Why not? Comrades aren't afraid of anyone."

"She's protected by the bands."

Many residents of the ghetto believe that certain people have a charmed life and are incapable of being killed because a sangoma has given them muti to protect them against all harm. This muti is often in the form of bands tied around the upper arms. One of my cousins was believed to have bands that protected him from harm during his life as a rapist and ruthless tsotsi.

Miss Jones indeed appears to be protected by the bands. Under her strong-willed leadership our school remains untouched by the unrest for nearly six months. But it turns out to be the calm before the storm.

One bright and hot morning Cynthia and I are in music class with about forty other students. Suddenly there is a great tumult outside, followed by screams. Our teacher stops and goes to the window to investigate. We can see a mob of Comrades pouring in the gate. They're dressed in yellow ANC T-shirts and red UDF T-shirts with slogans such as "No Peace Under Apartheid," "The People Shall Govern," "Bullets Won't Stop Us," and "Away with Bantu Education."

I recognize most of them as students from Minerva and Realogile. Comrade leaders go from classroom to classroom flushing students out into the courtyard, using water hoses. Suddenly the door to our classroom bursts open. Students start screaming as in walks Oupa, clutching a hose.

"Out! Out! Out, you sellouts!" he shouts. "Out before I flush you out."

Students scramble for the door, others jump out the windows. I jostle my way through the door, and once outside, I see that the entire school has been corralled in the courtyard. Almost everyone is soaking wet.

I look about for the teachers and for Miss Jones, but they are nowhere to be seen. I wonder if anything has happened to them. Several of the Comrades leap onto the canopied stage from which Miss Jones usually addresses assembly each morning. Oupa is among them, as is Thabo, another student leader from Alexandra High who's also been in and out of police detention.

"The time for sitting on the sidelines is over," Oupa shouts through a megaphone. "Either you join us or you're against us. We too want an education. But we don't want a slave education. We want a people's education. Bantu Education is nothing but slave education. Despite these nice facilities your minds are still being poisoned. Your brothers and sisters are dying in the streets for a better South Africa. Their blood must be avenged. Your parents toil every day for peanuts. They must have decent jobs. Most of you live in shacks with no running water or electricity. There must be decent housing for everyone. Above all we want the vote. We want to be free in the land of our ancestors. And we are prepared to die for freedom."

Oupa gives the mike to Thabo, who walks with a limp.

"You all know that I've been detained many times by the bloody Boers," he says. "Each time they tortured me. The last time they broke my kneecap. They kept me in solitary confinement. They tried to bribe me into becoming an *impimpi*"—an informer. "But they couldn't break me. I was prepared to die for the struggle. I knew that united we stand and divided we fall. So either you join us or we'll necklace the lot of you as collaborators and sellouts."

Hearing these fiery speeches, my heart thumps in my throat. I'm tossed between emotions. I agree with most of what Oupa and Thabo are saying, but still I don't want to join them. I want to graduate. I hate fighting, in part because it's against my Christian beliefs, in part because I'm afraid of getting killed like Mashudu, Florah's friend.

I wish Miss Jones were on the stage to argue her case for staying in school. Where is she? Has she already been necklaced as a collaborator?

As I'm thinking all this, a large, dark-skinned, muscular, and fierce-looking woman grabs the microphone. Her name is Theresa. Her reputation as a Comrade leader is legendary. She is decisive, fearless, and ruthless. She's always in the lead during marches, denouncing apartheid, insulting the police, exhorting the Comrades on. She never runs away in the face of tear gas and rubber bullets. She's been in detention several times.

In her deep booming voice, she says, "The time for action is now, Comrades. When we leave here we march to the firms in Marlboro. We must burn them to the ground as symbols of exploitation. Then we'll march to the police station. We must burn it down as a symbol of oppression.

"Amandla!"—power!—Theresa thrusts her clenched right fist high into the air.

"Ngawethu!"—belongs to the people!—the crowd roars. I don't say "Ngawethu." I'm too confused and scared.

"You better say it," Cynthia says, nudging me with her elbow, "or they'll necklace you."

"Amandla!" Theresa shouts again, thrusting her fist into the air.

"Ngawethu!" I join the chorus.

"Viva Comrade Nelson Mandela! Viva!" Theresa shouts.

"Viva Comrade Nelson Mandela! Viva!" the crowd roars.

"Viva Comrade Oliver Tambo! Viva!" Theresa shouts.

"Viva Comrade Oliver Tambo! Viva!" the crowd roars.

"Viva Comrade Chris Hani! Viva!" Theresa shouts.

"Viva Comrade Chris Hani! Viva!" the crowd roars.

"Viva Comrade Joe Slovo! Viva!" Theresa shouts.

"Viva Comrade Joe Slovo! Viva!" the crowd roars.

Except for Nelson Mandela's name, I haven't the faintest idea who the other ANC leaders are. But I roar their names as if they were my bosom buddies. By now a new spirit has seized the crowd. We've been whipped into a frenzy of excitement and anticipation. Even the fainthearted like myself feel imbued with new courage.

The mob begins dancing the *toyi-toyi* as they shout the Comrades' war chant. It's performed by hopping from one foot to the other with arms raised and fists clenched, while grunting, *"Hayi, hayi-hayi! Hayi, hayi-hayi! Hayi, hayi-hayi!"*

Singing and toyi-toyiing, we file out of the school yard and stream down Second Avenue, headed for the Marlboro firms. To prevent defections, the Comrades' leaders and veterans of the struggle are marching in the front and back. New recruits and the fainthearted like myself, who are likely to bolt at the slightest sign of trouble, are sandwiched in between. If any of us tries to flee we'll be beaten. I'm marching alongside Cynthia, Latisha, Becky, and Gertrude.

About two blocks from the school we come upon our first target. It's a Coca-Cola delivery truck. Our leaders order out the petrified black driver, who flees into a nearby yard. The commandeered truck is instantly looted. Bystanders from nearby yards join in the looting. I spot among them several elderly men and women with gray hair. Not having tasted a Coke in several weeks, and knowing that my niece and nephew Angie and Given love the soft drink, I timidly grab two liters. Within minutes the truck is emptied. Our leaders order that it be burned. Someone douses it with petrol and throws a match. In seconds the truck is an inferno of billowing flames and acrid black smoke.

The looting makes us forget all about the firms in Marlboro. People run home with their share of the booty. Rumors start flying that several armored vehicles called Hippos, Mello-Yellos, and Caspirs are headed our way. They are supposed to be full of soldiers and policemen.

In the panic that follows I lose my friends, so tightly clutching the two liters of Coke, I run toward home. I don't get far before I hear the sound of gunfire. I know there's no way I can reach Sixteenth Avenue in safety, without encountering an armored truck full of armed soldiers. Remembering that my cousin Jane lives on Fourteenth Avenue, I take a double-up to her house.

Luckily I find her home. She's surprised to see me.

"I was with the Comrades," I say, panting. "Do you mind if I leave these two liters of Coke? That way it'll be easier for me to run home."

"Home? Are you crazy? The streets are swarming with soldiers."

"I must get home. I have to make sure everyone is okay."

"Don't be a fool, Miriam. You'll get killed."

"I must go."

Jane lets me store the two liters in her parents' double-doored refrigerator.

"Don't go, Miriam," Jane says. "It's too dangerous out there. Hear that gunfire?"

"I'd stay, but I've got to cook and clean before my parents get back from work. Don't worry, nothing will happen to me."

I leave. The streets are deserted. People have gone inside to escape from the tear gas and the soldiers. I avoid the main road and take double-ups all the way to Sixteenth Avenue. Safely at home, I find Angie and Given barricaded inside. I utter a prayer.

I can't believe what I've done. Against my will, I've become a Comrade. I felt no compunction in looting the truck. I heartily sang the songs of defiance. But a part of me hopes that things will soon return to normal, that my friends and I will resume school, and that Miss Jones will continue to exhort us to value education, even if it is half a loaf, because without it we have no future even in a free South Africa.

Chapter 31

The *following day Cynthia, Latisha, Becky, and I go back to* school. We aren't wearing our school uniforms because we do not want to attract the attention of the police, who have been rounding up students and throwing them into kwela-kwela police trucks.

"Is it safe to go back?" I ask halfway to the school. We've hardly seen any other students and the streets are strewn with empty tear gas canisters, broken bottles, and the charred remains of burned delivery trucks.

"It is, if we aren't wearing uniforms," Cynthia says.

"What if we meet the police?"

"Then we'll run like hell."

The school is deserted, except for a couple of teachers and Miss Jones congregating in her office. They're surprised to see us.

"There's no school today," she says.

"We've come to fetch our books," I say. "We forgot them yesterday."

Miss Jones unlocks our classroom and we retrieve our books. She reassures us that school will resume in no time. She tells us to keep up with our schoolwork. "And please stay out of trouble," she urges. "The police are trigger happy."

On our way home we run into a crowd of over two thousand Comrades. Their leaders are going from house to house ferrcting out high-school-age students for yet another protest march. Those who refuse to join are threatened with beatings and necklacing. Cynthia, Becky, Latisha, and I join—albeit reluctantly.

From time to time during the march we stop to dance the toyi-toyi, raising huge clouds of dust as we pound the dirt. Several of the Comrades are holding wooden AK-47s, which they periodically thrust into the air. As we march we sing the Comrades' signature song of defiance:

> *Senzeni Na?* (What have we black people done?)
> *Senzeni Na? Senzeni Na?*
> *Amabunu a yi zinja.* (White policemen are dogs.)
> *Amabunu a yi zinja. Amabunu a yi zinja.*

I spot in the boisterous but disciplined crowd a lot of students I'd previously thought pacifists like myself.

"Margaret," I say in surprise, "what are you doing here?"

"What are *you* doing here?" Margaret asks.

"I was on my way home from school," I say.

"You went to school?"

"Yes. To get my books. And you?"

"My parents said I shouldn't go," Margaret says. "So I stayed home. Then the Comrades came and ordered me to join them."

"Do you know where we are going?"

"No. I hear people say we are going to the police station."

I'm aghast. "To the police station?"

"Yes. And I'm afraid."

I'm afraid too. What if the trigger-happy police shoot at us? I feel an urge to run away but I'm afraid of being necklaced.

After marching and chanting for nearly an hour from street to street, swelling our ranks with more reluctant teenagers, we finally reach the police station in Wynberg. A phalanx of heavily armed policemen and several Hippos barricade the paved road leading to the entrance to the police compound.

My heart is beating wildly. All I'm thinking of is the tear gas, the *sjamboks* (rawhide whips), the truncheons, and the bullets. Our leaders demand the release of all political activists. The police tell us to go home. The crowd starts taunting the police. A helicopter is hovering above us. I'm terrified that it'll start raining tear gas canisters. My terror proves unfounded. For some reason the police—most of whom are black—don't attack us. They simply stand there, shotguns raised, watching us as we dance the toyi-toyi and chant:

Oliver Tambo, speak with Botha
to release Mandela.
Mandela, remain strong.
The day of your freedom will come.

After about an hour our leaders order us to turn back. We retrace our route. Apparently our march to the police station was not to storm it. It was an act of defiance, a show of strength. The police have their Hippos, tear gas, and bullets—we have our numbers, our revolutionary songs, and our rage.

I breathe a sigh of relief but my relief is premature. Another phalanx of police is waiting for us as we round the corner into Eleventh Avenue. They waste no time lobbing tear gas into our midst. As the canisters explode, they start firing into the crowd. Pandemonium breaks out. People flee for cover. Some stumble, others run into strangers' houses, and still others don't know where to go. There are screams of terror and cries of pain everywhere.

I'm in utter shock. I can hardly think, but I have sense enough to realize that we are on Eleventh Avenue, near Cynthia's yard. My eyes burning from the tear gas, I frantically search for her house. Spotting it about three hundred yards away, I stagger toward it amid the choking tear gas and crackling sound of gunfire.

I notice through the chaos that several people are also making for the same house. Cynthia is among them, along with two of her friends and someone whose face makes my heart stop. It's my twelve-year-old sister, Linah. Everyone is clutching their throat and coughing.

Once inside, Cynthia barricades the door. Fearing that the police might be coming after us, we hide in the bedroom in the back of the house. It has a double bed, a dresser, and a chamber pot in the middle, which someone forgot to empty. Cynthia locks the door. The bedroom overlooks an alleyway and has one narrow window, which is open.

"Close it," Cynthia shouts, but as one of the girls hurries toward the open window, something comes flying in. At first I think it's a stone. It lands smack into the chamber pot and sizzles. Great puffs of acrid smoke billow out.

"Tear gas!" I scream. Within seconds the room is engulfed. I can barely see or breathe. Someone is crying, "My eyes! My eyes!" It's Linah.

I want to help her but my own eyes are burning as if someone has sprinkled them with red-hot pepper. I have an uncontrollable urge to tear off my skin. Someone is vomiting.

I notice a hand carrying the sizzling chamber pot. It's Cynthia's. The urine keeps spilling. Bodies are crashing into walls and furniture.

"Please open the door, someone," she pleads.

Find water! Find water! my mind is saying between hacking coughs. We rush out of the house. The street is deserted. The tear gas must have been lobbed in by the police from a passing Mello-Yello armored truck.

We find refuge at a neighbor's. People give us towels and pieces of rags, soaked in cold water, to daub on burning eyes and faces.

After a while we start feeling better. No one is seriously injured, but my cheeks are raw from scratching. The hardest sight to bear is of little children struggling with the effects of tear gas. They are bawling and writhing and coughing and throwing up.

Linah and I walk home using double-ups. Our yard has been teargassed too. Angie and Given are still coughing, as is Maria, who has asthma but can't afford the medication. Mama is trying her best to attend to everyone. We stuff rags into holes and crevices in the walls and windows to prevent tear gas from seeping in while we sleep. The police have the habit of blanketing the ghetto with tear gas during the night as a way of keeping people indoors.

Throughout the night I keep hearing intermittent gunfire. Toward the morning I eventually fall asleep. I have a dream. I'm in Venda, going to school, enjoying life. The air is clean, the sun is shining, people are laughing and happy. When I awake I tell Mama about the dream.

"You should've stayed in Venda, child."

"No way. And leave you and everybody alone?"

Mama smiles and gives me a hug.

"I love Venda, Mama," I say, "but I belong here, with you and everybody."

Mama and I pray. I pray to God to end the violence, to let us return to school, to end apartheid somehow, which I know is the cause of the violence. I also pray for the people of Alexandra. I now know deep in my heart that I belong with them. They are more a part of me than the people in Venda. We've shared a great deal of experiences and suffering and pain.

I also know that I belong with the Comrades. They are my sisters and brothers, even though as a Christian and a nonviolent person, I don't like many of the violent things they're doing. I'd never stone anyone, I'd never shoot anyone, and I'd certainly never necklace anyone. But deep in my heart I know they are trying to make things better, to help our community, to fight for the liberation of everyone. They simply have a different way of achieving their goal. It's a way shaped by the forces of the world in which they live. Most of us have never known anything but violence in our lives. Seeing people get killed is as normal as seeing people get married.

Despite my solidarity with the Comrades, I also believe in what Miss Jones says. Half a loaf is indeed better than no bread at all. I share her disdain for the slogan "Liberation Before Education." I believe with all my heart that a new South Africa will need educated leaders. I believe with all my heart in peace, in not hating, in not killing.

Trying to cope with this conflict, I instinctively know that whether I like it or not, I have to choose sides. I can't afford to be on the sidelines. My Christian beliefs have never been more tested. Mzabalazo is a time for anger and hate. It's a time for killing. This war is tearing apart the Alexandra community, it's pitting sister against sister and brother against brother, and it is unleashing deadly forces that maim and kill the innocent and guilty alike.

Chapter 32

T*wo days after being teargassed, I muster enough courage to go to* Jane's house and retrieve my two liters of Coke. I find them deliciously chilled.

"Do you think we'll ever go back to school?" Jane asks.

"I hope so."

"I'm afraid if we don't go back soon, people will start getting in trouble."

"What do you mean?"

"A lot of girls became pregnant the last time we stayed away from school too long."

How true. Maria became pregnant during a similarly long period of unrest, when she'd visit her boyfriend's home while his parents and my parents were away at work. And a couple of girls at Bovet became pregnant the same way.

"Miss Jones says we'll be back in school in no time," I say optimistically.

Jane shakes her head. "I doubt it. I hear people say Mzabalazo is different. They say the Comrades are determined to smash apartheid. And this time they want students to do it."

I leave Jane's worried. What will I do without school? What will happen to my dream of becoming a nurse? I begin to have doubts about the wisdom of being a Comrade, especially because I don't consider myself a fighter. I wonder if I shouldn't after all have agreed to move to Venda.

I'm still preoccupied when I round the corner on Fourteenth Avenue into Hofmeyer Street, across from a grocery store. Suddenly out of the corner of my eye I notice a Mello-Yello armored truck racing down the street. My instinct is to run, but I instantly abandon that idea—I can't outrun the police. Since I'm carrying two liters of Coke, if they stop me and ask me what I'm doing on the street, I'll simply say I've just been to the store to buy Coke.

The Mello-Yello comes to a screeching halt right next to me. Without warning, three of the black policemen leap off the truck and start whipping me with their sjamboks. For several seconds my feet fail me. Snapping out of shock, I scream at the sharp sting of the thick plastic whips flailing my back, buttocks, head, and legs.

I drop the Coke bottles and run toward the nearest yard. "Yo! Yo! Yo!" I scream at the top of my lungs. "I'm not a Comrade. I'm not a Comrade."

A high fence looms in front of me, about six feet high. I've never in my life jumped anything higher than three feet. But the sting of the whip and the fear that if they catch me I'm dead pump enough adrenaline into me that I leap. All I remember is flying through the air and landing hard on my buttocks on the other side.

As I scramble to my feet, the policemen hesitate in front of the fence and then turn back.

"Miriam," I hear someone say behind me, "you ought to be in the Olympics."

I turn and see a boy I know. He has a big grin on his face. I know full well that I could never have jumped that fence had anyone promised me a million rand.

It is not until I reach home that I realize how badly I've been whipped. The sjamboks have raised huge welts behind my legs and across my back. Some of the welts are bleeding and it's torture to remove the blouse, which is embedded in some of the gashes.

Mama is away at work.

"You should go to the clinic, Miriam," Maria says as she gingerly dabs my aching body with warm salty water, which hurts like hell.

"I've no money. Have you?"

"No. But I can try and borrow some."

"I'll be okay," I say, tears in my eyes.

I remember the glee on some of the policemen's faces as they beat me. Strangely enough, I don't feel any hatred for them. In fact I partly blame myself for what's happened. I see the thrashing as a punishment by God for looting. If I'd resisted joining the Comrades, if I hadn't looted those two liters of Coke, I wouldn't have gone to Jane's house and I wouldn't have been beaten.

I pray for forgiveness. I also pray for the policemen to stop hurting people. I also pray for schools to reopen, especially because the family has just received another letter from Johannes in America, along with pictures showing him during graduation. In the picture he's posing with Stan Smith, the former Wimbledon champion who helped arrange a tennis scholarship for him to study in America and who's been like a father to him. In the letter Johannes says that he's writing a book about growing up in Alexandra and that it will be published by Macmillan. He promises to send the family money to help us out, the first time he's done so since he left South Africa seven years earlier.

Mama is ecstatic. I'm very happy too, but also sad. I wonder if the violence will end so I can return to school, now that there will soon be enough money to buy me books and pay my school fees so I can complete matric.

I pray every night for schools to reopen. They don't. On the contrary, the violence escalates. Practically every day I'm hauled out of the house by Comrade leaders to join the marches. One time I try hiding under the bed, but Linah, who never misses a march despite her age, tells the Comrades search party where I'm hiding. I seldom sleep. I spend entire nights praying for the nightmare to end, for normalcy to return to the township. I long to go back to school. Yet deep in my heart I sense that many of us will die before it's all over.

It's early Saturday morning. As usual, I'm up cleaning while everyone is still sleeping. Maria gets up from the floor.

"How are you feeling?" I ask her. The day before, she got into an argument with her husband, Collin, and he beat her.

"Much better. My eyes no longer hurt as bad. Are they still puffy?"

I take a look. The swelling has gone down. Last night before we turned in she told me about their deteriorating relationship. She's torn. She still loves Collin, he's the father of her son, but she won't stand being abused.

"Collin has changed," I say as I prepare the stove to make a fire. "He used to be so nice."

"I know. Now he drinks. That's what changed him."

"Isn't it funny how many men become abusive when they're drunk?"

"Collin is frustrated. He recently lost his job at the dry cleaner's. He said he was laid off because he's from Alexandra and whites are very wary of hiring young men from the township for fear they might turn out to be Comrades. But I need money to buy Given food and clothes, Miriam," Maria says. "When I told Collin that, he got angry. We started shouting at each other."

"So what do you plan to do?"

"I'm off to attend a funeral. When I get back I'll ask Mama to go talk to his mother. If he refuses to stop beating me up, I'll pack and leave."

"What about Given?"

"I'll raise him by myself. I'll find a job."

I look at my sister. She's just turned nineteen and yet she looks much older. She's gained weight and is suffering from asthma. I wonder what kind of a job she'll be able to get after dropping out in Standard Five. And she's already begun drinking too.

"Why don't you return to school when schools reopen?"

"Are you kidding?" Maria says. "And be laughed at? I'd be a grandmother among children."

"Why should that matter if you're getting an education?"

"I'm not like you, Miriam. I mind very much what people say about me."

"I also mind," I say, "but I remember what Mama always says. It's not what people think about you that matters, it's what you think of yourself. If you think education is important, you should go back—especially if you plan to leave Collin. How will you be able to send Given to school without a good job?"

"I'll think about it."

After this sister-to-sister talk Maria goes to the funeral of a friend who was killed by the police. She's hardly gone half an hour when Collin stops by. He's with Florah's former boyfriend, who's also named Collin. The two have become close friends. I'm surprised to see them, especially this early in the morning. So is Mama, who has just woken up. Papa is still asleep in the bedroom.

The men exchange greetings and ask if either Florah or Maria is in.

"They're not in," Mama says.

"May we see the children?" Florah's Collin asks.

"Angie is with Florah," Mama says, "and Given is still sleeping. Come back later."

A couple of hours later Cynthia comes in distraught.

"They asked me to come and fetch you," Cynthia says to Mama amid tears.

"What happened?" Mama asks.

"Collin's dead."

"Dead?"

"Yes. He was shot in the head by a policeman. Florah's Collin was also shot. He's in critical condition. He's been taken to General Hospital."

I scream. Mama reaches out and embraces me. Curiously, despite the scream, despite the fact that my heart is breaking, no tears are flowing. I've seen so many people die and have been to so many night vigils and funerals that crying no longer seems to make much sense.

Mama immediately leaves for Eleventh Avenue. I'm in utter shock. I can't believe that the two strong young men who were so full of life just a couple of hours earlier have been shot, and that one of them is now dead.

A couple of hours later Mama comes back in tears.

"He's dead, Miriam," she says. "I saw his bloodied corpse. I even accompanied his mother and Florah's Collin's father to the police station to make a statement."

She pauses, then asks, "Where's Maria?"

"She's still not back," I reply in a leaden voice.

"My poor child," Mama says. "A widow at nineteen. What will happen to Given now?" She inhales a pinch of snuff.

"Why were they shot?" I ask.

"Nobody knows. They say the policeman came looking for Florah's Collin. He was told that he was across the street. So he goes across the street. He finds both Collins sitting together on the stoep drinking beer.

"They say the policeman asked, 'Who's Collin?' Both of them answered, then he pulled out a gun and shot them both. Maria's Collin died on the spot. Florah's Collin was shot in the neck."

Mama and I kneel down and pray for the departed soul of Maria's Collin and for the speedy recovery of Florah's Collin.

Chapter 33

We buried Maria's Collin on June 7, 1985, at the Alexandra cemetery, next to the Jukskei River. I can't stop crying. He was so young, just twenty. Who killed him? And why? What will happen to Given? And to Maria? Why are so many young men dying? Will the senseless violence ever end?

It doesn't end. The Comrades are determined to make the township ungovernable. They become even more ruthless in their dealings with suspected collaborators and impimpis. Necklacings become commonplace. Anyone fingered as an impimpi or collaborator runs the risk of being burned alive. No one is immune, not even the Comrade leaders themselves.

Theresa, the muscular, fierce-looking female Comrade leader, is necklaced on suspicion of being a police informant. In other townships the story is the same. In Duduza township, in the East Rand, a man suspected of being an informer is almost necklaced following the funeral for four young Comrades who were killed when a black member of the security forces, posing as an ANC guerrilla, gave them booby-trapped hand grenades. The suspected informer is saved from the bloodthirsty mob by the courageous intervention of Bishop Tutu.

On July 20, 1985, in response to the spiraling violence, President

P. W. Botha finally declares a state of emergency. I hear the news on the radio. It's the first time since the Sharpeville massacre of 1960 that a state of emergency has been resorted to by the government. Most civil liberties are abrogated; the police are granted sweeping powers to arrest, detain, and interrogate anyone considered a threat to the state. The United Nations condemns it and calls for limited, voluntary sanctions against South Africa.

Police launch massive midnight raids, arresting many Comrades. Those detained are tortured and come back more radicalized. Many a night I stay up wondering if the door will burst open and I'll be taken away. Within the first few days of the state of emergency over eight hundred people are detained. The Comrades respond by calling for more protests; the police respond with more firepower. I attend night vigils almost daily. Unlike in the past, the police no longer issue warnings before shooting. We are burying people every weekend. During periods of unrest in the past, we'd been allowed to bury our dead with relative dignity. Now the police issue new guidelines for funerals. No Comrade can be buried without police permission. And when permission is granted, the time for burial is stipulated and the size of the mourners is severely restricted. If we disregard the restrictions and turn out in waves, the police are there in their armored trucks. At the end of the funeral they often spray us with tear gas to disperse us, or open fire, and this leads to more night vigils and funerals.

During night vigils and funerals we often sing the ANC liberation anthem, which was composed by a Xhosa schoolteacher named Enoch Sontonga in 1897. Its words take on added meaning and poignancy given the violence of the time. I always sing the song with tears in my eyes. My heart longs for peace, for an end to the violence and the killings, and I believe that only God can make things right again.

Nkosi sikelel' i Afrika.	Lord, bless Africa.
Maluphakamis' uphondo lwayo.	Let her horn be raised.
Yizwa imithandazo yethu.	Listen to our prayers.
Nkosi, sikelela—	Lord, bless
Thina luswapho lwayo.	Us, her offspring.

Woza Moya.	Come, Spirit.
Woza Moya Oyingcwele.	Come, Holy Spirit.
Nkosi sikelela	Lord, bless
Thina lusapho lwayo.	Us, her children.
Morena boloka	God, bless
Sechaba sa heso.	Our nation.
O fedise dintwa le matswenyeho.	Do away with wars and troubles.
O se boloke, o se boloke,	Bless it, bless it,
O se boloke morena.	Bless it, Lord.
Sechaba sa heso.	Our nation.
Sechaba sa heso.	Our nation.

According to newspaper accounts, by the end of 1985 more than nine hundred people have died and 2,165 have been injured in unrest-related violence across South Africa. Thousands more have been detained without trial. It's clear that the government is determined to crush black resistance.

There are massacres everywhere. In November, nineteen people are massacred when police open fire on protesters in Mamelodi, a ghetto outside Pretoria, about twenty miles north of Alexandra. In Alexandra a more sinister force emerges to challenge the Comrades. It is the Vigilantes. These are mainly conservative Zulu hostel dwellers who can't brook the thought of being ordered around by youngsters. Armed with spears, clubs, machetes, and guns, they attack us during night vigils and at wakes.

Each time I leave home to attend a night vigil Mama prays to God that I'll come back alive. I become fatalistic. I believe that if I'm killed, then God has willed it and there's nothing I nor anyone can do about it.

Johannes is frantic about our family's safety. He writes regularly and calls Mama at her workplace to find out if we are still alive. He insists on talking in Tsonga out of fear that the phone might be tapped. Johannes tells Mama that American newspapers are full of stories about the atrocities and that protests against apartheid are growing.

He's now writing newspaper articles to inform Americans, in the wake of massive propaganda by the Pretoria regime, about what is really happening in the townships.

George, Florah, and I write him long letters, which Mama mails from the white post office. We never use the black post office in Wynberg because of rumors that letters sent there are opened by the security police and read, and that if they are found to contain suspicious information, the senders are detained. In the letters to Johannes we tell him about the killings, the death squads, the mass funerals, the necklacing of impimpis, and the constant police presence in the township. I tell him about my fears that the carnage will never end, that Linah, Diana, and I may never finish school. He exhorts us to be strong, to do our best to stay out of trouble, and to take care of Mama. Many times I wish the family were with him in America, away from all the suffering, violence, pain, and death. Sometimes I feel like I'm going mad. The only thing that helps preserve my sanity is my faith in God. I know that as long as I believe in him no harm will befall me and those I love. I derive great comfort from singing in the choir, from attending Sunday school and church, and from reading the Bible every day.

Three months after we buried Maria's Collin, Florah's Collin dies while still at General Hospital. Upon learning from doctors that he was paralyzed from the neck down by the assassin's bullet, he told Florah that he'd rather die than live the life of a cripple. Florah had begged him not to give up. With a smile he had said he'd hang on for her sake. He'd asked to see his daughter. The next day he died.

At the wake on Ninth Avenue I watch Florah—dressed in mourning, her head covered with a blanket—wailing. I know that despite her problems with Collin, despite their estrangement, she deeply loved him. I loved him too. Mama loved him too. He was so compassionate and generous, despite his faults and mistakes. Angie, who is almost four, sits unconcernedly on her father's casket. She keeps asking her mother, "Why is Daddy sleeping in a box? When will he wake up?" Florah tells her that Daddy is too tired to wake up, that the casket is taking him to a nice place called heaven, to be with God and the angels, and that someday they'll join him there and be a happy family together again.

I wonder how Angie will grow up without a father. Will she be bitter? Will she be hateful? What is this mad world I'm living in, which kills and kills and kills? And what will happen to the hundreds of fatherless and motherless children who now glut the streets of Alexandra?

I can't stop weeping. As his casket is being lowered into the ground at the Alexandra cemetery, where we buried Maria's Collin, I mumble a prayer:

Lord, please stop the killings.
Lord, please stop the killings.
Lord, please stop the killings.
Lord, please stop the killings.

By January of 1986 the unrest has abated enough for schools to reopen. Hundreds of students were arrested during the state of emergency, including many from Alexandra High. Other students have fled the country to join the ANC's military wing, called Umkhonto we Sizwe (Spear of the Nation). Among the remaining students, there's a loss of innocence.

Alexandra High assembly. A solemn-faced Miss Jones welcomes us back, but she announces that the Department of Bantu Education has decided that all students who didn't sit for final exams in December have failed. That means everyone has to repeat the same class. It's clear that the government is punishing us for our activism. There's a restless murmur across the assembly.

"What did you expect when you boycotted school?" Miss Jones asks.

Sensing trouble, she dismisses the assembly. Several Comrade leaders are in our midst, including Comrade Oupa. They confer among themselves. As we are walking to our classes, they call us back. They leap onto the stage. Neither Miss Jones nor any of the teachers attempts to stop them.

"Bantu Education is over," Comrade Oupa declares through a megaphone. "We now have People's Education. The year you spent as Comrades in the struggle hasn't been wasted. Despite what the government is saying, under the new People's Education we have a new policy. It's called Pass One, Pass All. Everyone has passed."

We're all dumbfounded.

"Does it mean we get to go to Standard Seven?" Cynthia asks.

"That's what it means," Petronella says.

"Without writing exams?"

"I guess so."

Comrade Oupa continues above the excited hubbub stirred by his dramatic announcement. He's conscious of his power and revels in it.

"Under the People's Education," Comrade Oupa says, "no one gets to repeat a class for having fought in the liberation struggle. Now go to your new classes."

There's wild cheering. The last thing I want is to repeat the same class, but in the back of my mind I wonder how in the world I'm going to understand material for Standard Seven without having completely learned the material for Standard Six.

"It's one thing for the Comrades to tell us that we've all passed," I say to Petronella, "but will Miss Jones and the teachers go along with the decision?"

"They have no choice. No one wants to get necklaced."

Indeed, neither Miss Jones nor any of the teachers questions the Pass One, Pass All policy of the Comrades. This marks the first chink in the armor of authority teachers and administrators have had in the school. I can't help comparing it to the beating of Teacher Mguni by Markos and Khatuchera.

In months to come, there is further erosion of the respect teachers previously enjoyed and of the authority they exercised over the classroom. Few teachers dare punish students, for fear of being beaten up or, worse, being necklaced. Students who in the past quaked in the presence of a teacher now boldly talk back. There are stories of teachers in other schools being beaten, knifed, or shot for assigning homework, for giving poor marks, and for whipping students.

Students are also emboldened to question their parents' authority. Some call their parents naive, fools, and cowards for not doing more to resist apartheid. At our home even Linah and Diana, who've participated in the Comrade marches and attended many a night vigil, now talk back to Papa.

I'm the lone holdout. I still see teachers as an extension of parental authority and parents as an extension of God's authority. I still take seriously the admonition "Honor thy father and thy mother, so that the days of your life may be lengthened."

Chapter 34

"*Miriam, you need to protect yourself,*" Mama says to me one sunny Saturday afternoon as we do the laundry.

"Against what?"

"Against what can happen when men are interested in you."

That was the extent of my sex education. Like most women of her generation, she considered it taboo to talk explicitly about sex to her daughters. And since Mama is older and knows best about sexual matters, I dutifully accompany her one weekday afternoon to the single women's hostel on Fourth Avenue. The place has a family planning clinic, or what masquerades as one. A lot of my friends have gone there and come back with horror stories. The staff are rude, they don't explain anything, they simply dole out defective IUDs that end up ripping the wombs of young girls or being embedded in the heads of the children they give birth to.

Florah was fitted with a defective IUD. She bled profusely throughout her entire pregnancy and there was fear she'd lose Angie. After she was born, Florah had tried conceiving again but doctors told her that she couldn't because the IUD had messed up her womb.

"I don't want an IUD," I say to Mama.

"There's something better than an IUD," Mama says.

"What's that?"

"Birth control pills."

I'm averse to taking any kind of tablets. Even when I have a splitting headache I never take any medication. "Why do I need to take birth control pills when I have no intention of becoming sexually active?"

"Accidents sometimes happen, and you want to be protected."

"How can accidents happen when I don't have a boyfriend?"

"Remember your friend Latisha?"

Latisha was my classmate at Alexandra High and a member of the church choir. No one thought she had a boyfriend, then all of a sudden she was pregnant and had to drop out of school.

The staff at the family planning center give me the birth control pills and tell me to take one each day. They don't explain anything about side effects.

I have an even stronger reason for abstaining from early experimentation with sex: AIDS. The disease has reached epidemic proportions in the ghetto, and most of its victims are women. Yet few people take it seriously. A lot of people consider themselves immune to it, calling it a white man's disease. Despite ads in the paper, on the radio and TV, and the admonitions of teachers and health care professionals, a lot of young people continue to engage in early sex—often with multiple partners. Parents seem powerless to prevent it. Many young people have sexually transmitted diseases like *drop* and herpes. Some of my friends tell stories of their boyfriends scoffing at the idea of wearing condoms or beating them up for suggesting they do.

One day a white man stricken with AIDS visits our school at the invitation of Miss Jones. He is dying and has chosen to spend the little time he has left going from school to school warning young people about the dangers of AIDS. He is as thin as a scarecrow and hollow cheeked, but his face is remarkably serene. The story he has to tell is wrenching and his warning chilling.

"Don't believe it when people tell you that AIDS is a white man's disease. Anyone can get AIDS. If you engage in sex without protection, if you use drugs, you can get AIDS. And once you get it there's no cure.

Look at me. I didn't believe I could get the disease. Now doctors say I only have a few months to live."

He proceeds to describe graphically how AIDS is transmitted and prevented. A lot of students giggle at the description of condoms, but to me the AIDS-stricken white man is like the grim reaper. I consider his every word the gospel truth and am glad I'm not sexually active. He debunks many of the myths about AIDS: It's a lie that sangomas can cure AIDS. It's a lie that only homosexuals get it. It's a lie that having sex with a virgin cures it.

I'm worried about Maria and Florah. Like so many women, they're dating men who cheat on them.

"Aren't you afraid of getting AIDS?" I ask Maria.

"I am."

"What are you doing to protect yourself?"

"Nothing."

The house of Reverend Sam Buti, a longtime anti-apartheid activist and community leader, has been firebombed. Mama and I walk past it on the way from the bank to withdraw the last of her savings so we can buy groceries. For several days she's been unable to go to work because of a stayaway imposed by the Comrades.

Mama stares in disbelief at the charred remains of what was once one of Alexandra's loveliest homes. She shakes her head. She's known Reverend Buti, a minister in the black Dutch Reformed Church, for years. She remembers the days when Alexandra was on death row, slated to be bulldozed by the authorities as a black spot to make way for hostels housing single men and women.

"Reverend Buti," she says, "along with your *oompie* Lucas, spearheaded the fight to save our community."

Oompie (Uncle) Lucas, Granny's half brother, was a businessman and noted community leader.

"Comrades consider people like Reverend Buti and Oompie Lucas collaborators with apartheid," I explain to Mama.

"What nonsense! How have they collaborated with apartheid?"

"By being members of the Alexandra Town Council."

The ATC was one of the self-governing structures the Pretoria regime had instituted in various townships as a means of pacifying Africans in the wake of protests against the granting of limited political rights to Coloreds and Indians but not to blacks. It was viewed with intense suspicion by many activists.

"I don't understand this collaboration business," Mama says, shaking her head. "And as for the Comrades, I don't like them. They prevent us from going to work. They force our children not to attend school. Tell me, what future will we have if our children are not educated? And how will I be able to feed you if I don't work?"

"The Comrades say we all have to make sacrifices."

"I've sacrificed all my life."

Mama's dislike of the Comrades is shared by many among the older generation. But they dare not make their feelings known, for fear of being beaten or necklaced. The security forces are aware of the generational split and they exploit it by blaming ANC agitators and communists for corrupting us. They appeal to tribal values by telling parents that they've failed as parents if they don't regain control over their children.

But the strategy doesn't work. People like Mama and Papa dislike the Comrades, but they adore the ANC. They remember the forties and fifties when the liberation movement had one of its largest and most active branches in Alexandra. Papa remembers the ANC's role in organizing the bus boycotts. The first were in the 1940s, shortly after Papa arrived in Alexandra from Venda, and in 1957, shortly before he began courting Mama.

"But throughout its protests," Mama says, "the ANC remained nonviolent. It never necklaced one person."

"I don't blame the Comrades, Mama," I say. "Many of us have known nothing but violence all our lives. Teachers beat us at school, parents beat us, and the police shoot us. You yourself say violence begets more violence."

Chapter 35

Shortly after the bombing of Reverend Buti's house, a youngster is shot and killed by a security guard in Wynberg. I join tens of thousands of people at his funeral at the Alexandra cemetery. As is customary, mourners wash their hands at the home of the deceased after the burial. As we are washing our hands in tubs filled with water the soldiers arrive in armored trucks. Without warning, they start firing tear gas into the massive crowd of mourners. People run in all directions, screaming, coughing, and vomiting. Several of the elderly are trampled underfoot. I find refuge in a nearby shack. I somehow manage to make my way home using double-ups.

Throughout the long day there are repeated clashes between the soldiers and the Comrades, who fight bullets and tear gas with stones, bricks, and petrol bombs. Over the next couple of weeks the war between the Comrades on the one hand and the Vigilantes and the soldiers on the other intensifies. Its fulcrum is Selborne Street. We dig ditches across the road called "tank traps" and erect barricades of burning cars to stop the armored trucks.

The soldiers respond with massive firepower. During one week police and soldiers kill nearly two dozen Comrades, most of them youngsters. The dead and bleeding strew the streets. The killings, which occurred on February 15, 1986, become known as the Alexandra massacre.

A huge mass funeral attended by hundreds of thousands of people is held at the stadium. The coffins lie in a row on a green carpet under the hot sun. They are draped in the gold, black, and green colors of the ANC and guarded by Comrades dressed in khaki uniforms. Fiery speeches are made and revolutionary songs are sung. There are clamors for revenge and for the ANC to send us guns.

Following the funeral, Comrades step up their attacks on those regarded as collaborators. Members of the ATC are forced to resign. Policemen and their families are forced to flee the township. Vigilantes and impimpis are hunted down and necklaced. While returning from visiting Florah, Angie and I see the charred and bloated body of a man accused of being a Vigilante. I shudder at the grisly sight, but Angie simply laughs and points at the man's grotesque face with its protruding teeth suggesting great agony in the fiery death. Her reaction makes me wonder what the violence is doing to young children.

Vigilantes fight back. Dressed in hooded masks called balaclavas, and armed with shotguns, machetes, and spears, they undertake what becomes known as a *hlasale,* an invasion. Using the hostels as their fortresses, they blaze a trail of destruction and carnage stretching from First Avenue to Twenty-second Avenue. Under cover of darkness, often traveling in unmarked vehicles, they move from street to street, house to house, hunting down Comrades and burning down their houses.

I attend a Comrades rally where we are told that the soldiers have given Vigilantes the green light to crush the Comrade movement, and that in some cases they are acting as their escorts.

The ensuing conflict between the Comrades and Vigilantes becomes known as "the Six Days War." Dozens of people are killed and hundreds are injured. Some wounded Comrades dare not go to the clinic for fear of being arrested. Armored trucks are rumored to be stationed outside the clinic, and troops to be patrolling the emergency ward, arresting any youngster arriving with bullet wounds.

During the war I dare not go out of the house. Fearing for his life as one of the Comrades, George goes into hiding. Several of his friends have been killed. At night we barricade the door before going to sleep. We sleep with buckets of water and damp pieces of rags nearby, our first aid kit against nightly tear gas attacks. Throughout the night there's the constant sound of gunfire.

I'm now petrified to attend wakes for Comrades. Mourners at such events have now become targets because Vigilantes and soldiers know that they will draw Comrades together in one place. At one wake, for a fourteen-year-old Comrade killed by the soldiers, which I didn't attend because I was attending a wake for another Comrade, balaclava-clad Vigilantes burst into the tent and sprayed people with bullets, killing several.

The state of emergency is lifted on March 7. I read in the newspapers that 750 people have been killed and more than eight thousand detained, two thousand of them children under sixteen. Many of the killed and detained are from Alexandra.

Despite the lifting of the state of emergency, the violence continues. The Comrades are determined to take over control of the township. They do this by largely replacing the apartheid governing structures. Street committees and yard committees are formed to run neighborhoods. The Comrades institute people's courts and set up their own police station and police force. Persons suspected of being impimpis, tsotsis, collaborators, and even witches are tried before these tribunals. Those found guilty are openly flogged, or necklaced if their crime is considered serious. Because of their fearsome reputation, the Comrades succeed in doing something the Peri-Urban Police have tried but failed. They reduce the level of crime, rape, and abuse in the township. Women have equal rights before the people's courts and can bring charges of abuse against their husbands or boyfriends.

But there are stories of Comrades engaging in extortion, Comrades settling personal scores through the people's courts, and Comrades forcing women to have sex or to become their girlfriends.

There's talk that soon we'll be returning to school to study People's Education, not Bantu Education.

"Do you think we'll ever return to school with all the violence?" Margaret asks me one afternoon. Like me, she's concerned that we'll miss yet another year of schooling.

"I don't know. The Comrades say we will as soon as they've complete control of the township."

"When will that be? I'm sick and tired of fighting, Miriam."

"I hope soon."

"You know what?"

"What?"

"I'm afraid that if we don't get back to school soon, a lot of girls will get pregnant. So many girls have Comrade boyfriends, and they are sleeping with them left and right."

One evening Gertrude and I are attending a Comrades night vigil at the Alexandra stadium. Several thousand people are listening to various speakers. While one drones on about the need to intensify the struggle, Gertrude says to me, "Miriam, a friend of my cousin's would like to meet you."

"Who's she?"

"No. It's a he."

"I'm not interested," I say firmly.

"I promise you'll like him."

"Is he a Comrade?"

Gertrude is dating a Comrade leader named Phineas, who is friends with her cousin Jacob, also a Comrade leader.

"No, he's like you. He doesn't like violence. He comes here because he has to."

"What tribe is he?"

"Zulu. He's from Natal and doesn't know too many people. He's quiet and very respectful. I promise you'll like him."

At the next Comrades meeting Gertrude introduces me to a shy-looking, soft-spoken man of about twenty-two. He has two small scars on his upper lip, a square forehead, and large round ears. I find him unattractive but decide to be polite.

"Miriam," Gertrude says. "This is my cousin's friend. His name is Sabelo."

Gertrude leaves us alone. Bored by the speeches, Sabelo and I talk. I'm glad to be talking to a man who doesn't seem threatening and who is not boastful about his prowess as a Comrade.

"Gertrude tells me you're from Zululand," I say.

"Yes."

"What brought you to Alexandra, of all places?"

"Work," he says. "My father's dead and I'm taking care of my mother and siblings."

"Did they come to Alexandra with you?"

"No. I live by myself."

"What do you do?"

"I fix cars."

"You have a car?"

"No. But my boss lets me drive one whenever I want. Would you like me to give you a ride home after the night vigil?"

I hesitate. "No, thanks. I don't mind walking."

"But it's dangerous late at night."

"My friends are here. We always walk home together."

"Remember, if you ever need a ride, let me know."

Chapter 36

As the violence spirals out of control across South Africa, it reaches even the rural areas and homelands. Willie, Mamahulu's son, flees Giyani for Alexandra. He reveals that students there have formed their own Comrade groups, which are challenging not only the homeland system but also traditional authority and practices.

"Students are fighting pitched battles with the police," he says. "In many places they have taken over entire villages. We now have people's courts. Various people accused of being witches have been tried. Some have been burned alive. Others have abandoned their practices and become Christians to escape the wrath of the Comrades."

"What about Mamahulu?" I ask.

"They didn't touch her," Willie says proudly. "No one dare. She's a powerful sangoma. Besides, her muti is always used for good."

Also from Venda come stories of violent outbreaks between students and members of the Venda security forces. Dankies, who's moved to Alexandra to find work, tells of school buildings being burned, of police firing on students, and of hundreds being detained and brutally tortured. Apparently, his mother, afraid for her life, quit being a sangoma and became a member of the Zion Christian Church.

• • •

It's about 11 P.M. I'm sitting at the kitchen table reading the Bible. There's a loud knock on the front door. My heart skips a beat. I recognize the knock. I don't want to open the door. I'm terrified, but I know I have no choice.

In front of me are four young men in casual clothes. They are the Comrades from the street committee who go door-to-door summoning the troops to attend night vigils. Markos, my former classmate, is among them.

"Let's go, Miriam," Comrade Markos says. "There's a rally tonight."

"I'm sick," I say.

"What's wrong?"

I point to my heavily bandaged right ankle. "I broke it."

"She's lying," one of the Comrades says. "I saw her early today. Her foot was fine."

"Are you faking it?" Comrade Markos demands testily. "If you are we'll necklace you."

"I'm not faking it," I say, grimacing.

"Who's that, Miriam?" Papa says from the bedroom.

"It's the Comrades," I say.

I hear the bed creaking as Papa gets up. He comes to the door in his raggedy pajamas.

"What's going on?" he asks.

"We're having a rally tonight, *ntate*"—old man—Comrade Markos says.

"And they don't believe me when I say my ankle is broken." I look pleadingly at Papa, hoping he'll have the courage to defend my lie. In the past, he's simply kept his mouth shut whenever the Comrades came by to pick me up.

Papa looks at the four Comrades, then at me. "Her ankle is broken," he says. "She broke it this afternoon. I helped bandage it."

I can't believe that Papa has just lied to save me. The Comrades study his stern face and then mine, which I'm praying isn't giving me away, for my knees are shaking.

"Get better soon, okay?" Comrade Markos says. "We need you in the struggle."

"I promise I'll be there as soon as my ankle is better."

The Comrades leave. I turn and look at Papa's short, gaunt figure.

"Thanks," I say.

"Now go to sleep," he says, then heads back to the bedroom.

Before going to sleep I kneel down and pray. Throughout the night I hear screams, the roar of Caspirs and Hippos, the sound of running feet and of gunfire.

Faking a broken ankle may have saved my life. The police opened fire on the marchers at the night vigil. George attended and was lucky to escape alive. Several of my friends, including my best friends Margaret, Petronella, and Cynthia, have disappeared. I go to Margaret's house and find her mother crying. She'd begged the Comrades not to take her daughter along.

"I've been to the morgue," she says. "My poor daughter isn't there."

"Could she have been detained?" I'd heard rumors that hundreds of those who attended the illegal night vigil had been.

"I've already been to the police station. They tell me that no one by that name is being detained. I have a feeling they killed her."

Days pass and my friends do not show up. I'm riddled with guilt. Was it right for me to fake the injury? Shouldn't I have joined my friends and died with them? After all, they didn't like the violence either. Nobody does. But it's every black person's duty to fight against apartheid.

My guilt diminishes somewhat when I take a look at Mama. She's only forty-five, yet she's gaunt and her cheeks are hollow. She leaves for the backbreaking cleaning work at five in the afternoon and isn't back till six the next morning. She barely has time to sleep before she has to leave for work again. She depends on me to clean, cook, and wash laundry. Without me she'd be overwhelmed and maybe driven insane once more. Thinking all this, I do not feel as bad about not having been at the night vigil. As a matter of fact I credit my not going to God's intervention.

The defiance of the Comrades increases with the deaths and disappearances. I'm in a crowd of about twenty thousand people who are protesting the detention of our Comrades. During the march, for the first time, the Comrades exchange gunfire with the police. Several of the Comrades now have AK-47s. Rumor has it that the ANC has begun supplying the Comrades with guns.

The streets are dangerous to travel at night. Vigilantes and security forces are constantly on the prowl. I rely on Sabelo to give me rides home. I divide my time between home and the streets. At home I try to keep Diana, Angie, and Given out of trouble. Angie and Given find the marches fun and have the habit of following the crowds. I'm afraid they'll get killed, especially because the police no longer discriminate between older and younger kids. I'm glad that Linah, who adored the Comrades and was always sneaking out of the house to join them at night vigils and rallies, has been sent to Venda by Mama to attend school there.

Since the disappearance of my friends, I've been visiting their homes to inquire if there is any news. One afternoon I stop by Margaret's and find people wailing. I knock at the door and to my relief and joy, I find that everyone is crying tears of joy. Margaret is back. So are Dlayani, Petronella, Gertrude, Cynthia, and my other friends who'd been detained.

I can't believe how thin Margaret looks, and how pale. Over the next couple of days she relates a story that horrifies me and makes my blood boil. The night she was arrested, the police had fired at the marchers who were headed for the police station in defiance of the state of emergency.

"They fired real bullets," Margaret explained. We were having a lunch of peanut-buttered bread and orange Kool-Aid. "People started dropping down like flies. Cynthia, Gertrude, Petronella, Dlayani, and I ran into a nearby house, along with twenty or thirty other people. Unfortunately, the police saw us and ordered us out at gunpoint. As they loaded us into the kwela-kwela, they kicked and cursed us."

Margaret stops to sip her Kool-Aid. Her hands are shaking. I reach out and hold her right arm reassuringly.

"They drove us to John Vorster," Margaret continued. John Vorster was a notorious detention and interrogation center in downtown Johannesburg. "There they locked us up in cells overnight. There were so many of us, including children as young as ten. Most of us were crying. We'd never been arrested before. Some people were asking for their parents."

"They'll get what's due them someday."

"I'm not a hater, Miriam," Margaret says with a sigh, "but what *amabunu*"—white policemen—"did to us has made me hate. If I had a gun I'd kill the lot of them.

"The next day they took me to a special room. It had one chair and a table. No windows. They strapped me to the chair. There were four or five of them. They were very scary looking."

"Were they hairy?" I ask.

"How do you know?"

"When I was little, hairy white policemen used to break into our house during pass raids. To this day I'm scared of hairy white men."

"They were hairy, all right, and big, like rugby players. They had red faces, thick necks, and spoke in guttural Afrikaans. There was a black policeman with them. Large and very black. Looked like a Venda. He's the one who strapped me to the chair. One of the white men hovered in front of me and said, 'If you tell us what we want to know, we'll let you go. If you don't, we're going to kill you.' "

Margaret paused and swallowed.

"I said to them, 'I'll tell you everything I know.' They replied, 'Good.' They then asked me if I was a Comrade."

"What did you say?"

"I said no. I said I was a student at Alexandra High. I said I hated the Comrades. They asked me why. I said because they were preventing us from going to school. They laughed. One of them then asked me what I was doing at the rally if I wasn't a Comrade. I told them that I was at home getting ready for bed when the Comrades came and got me. The policemen said I was lying because I'd given the same answer as other students. They said I'd soon tell the truth. They asked me who were the leaders of the rallies and the marches. I replied that I didn't know. That's when they began shocking me."

"Shocking you?"

"Yes. They'd hooked electrical wires to my arms and legs. As soon as they pressed the switch I started shaking. It was as if someone was stabbing me with a thousand needles. I screamed and kept on screaming until they stopped. I almost lost consciousness. Then they unstrapped me and took me back to the cell. They interrogated other students. After they were done with them, they began again at the beginning."

"Began again?"

"Yes. They shocked us four times a day for ten days."

"The bastards," I say, shaking my head. I can't imagine such barbarity. At that moment I hated the police with all my heart.

"Did they give you anything to eat?" I ask. "You look so thin."

"The food they gave us was filth," Margaret said. "I had to force myself to eat. Also, I couldn't sleep. The harsh light in the cell was kept on all the time. People kept screaming throughout the night as they were being tortured. Our cell was wet. And from time to time they'd spray us with tear gas just for the fun of it."

"Why did they let you go?"

"I guess they finally realized that we were telling the truth when we said we didn't know who the leaders of the Comrades were," Margaret says. "When they let us go, they promised that if they ever caught us at a rally again, they'd kill us. But I don't care anymore. They can kill me if they want to."

She surprises me by saying, "You know what? I wish nothing better than to be able to go back to school."

"Me too."

"Do you think we'll ever go back?"

"I don't know. It's almost June. We've lost half a year."

"I feel so old, you know. Yet I'm only seventeen."

"I know the feeling."

"They tell me you have a boyfriend," Margaret says suddenly.

I blush. "He's just a friend."

Margaret smiles knowingly. "What's his name?"

"Sabelo."

"He's Zulu?"

"Yes. He's very nice. And boys don't bother me at night vigils because of him. He also gives me rides home from time to time."

"Have you done it?"

"Done what?"
"You know what I mean."
"No. I told you, he's just a friend."
Margaret laughs.
"Can I meet him?"
"Sure."

Chapter 37

Sabelo receives a stamp of approval from Margaret. Still, I'm always very careful around him. Several times he's invited me to meet the family he's staying with and I've refused. I've also refused his invitations to drive me to Soweto and to the city in one of the many cars he has access to as a mechanic. I don't want him to start getting the impression that we're dating, because I'm afraid that will lead to his pressuring me for sex.

But I do enjoy Sabelo's company. He's sensitive and nonthreatening. During night vigils, particularly when speeches by Comrade leaders get very boring, he and I talk a lot about our families, about the importance of family members taking care of one another, and about the importance of education. He wishes he'd finished school, but like so many black students he had to support his family. He is very encouraging of my plans to become a nurse.

I keep my friendship with him a secret from my family. I'm afraid of how Mama and Papa will react. Sabelo is anxious to meet my family, but I'm reluctant to introduce him.

"I don't want them to get the wrong impression—that you and I are dating. My mother wants me to finish school."

He laughs. "The reason I want to meet them is because I want to reassure them that I'm different from other men. I enjoy your friendship. I want nothing more."

Being around a man I like makes me start thinking about sex, especially since I've stopped taking the birth control pills from the women's hostel after they started making my breasts big and sore.

As long as we don't sleep together, I say to myself, there's no danger.

On June 12 the spiraling violence forces the government to reimpose the state of emergency. The second state of emergency is more draconian than the first. Journalists are banned from covering violence in the townships. All reports of violence are to be issued by the Bureau for Information. Anyone who promotes illegal strikes, boycotts, and banned organizations like the ANC and UDF is threatened with prosecution for treason. Night vigils are banned.

The Comrades defy the ban. At a night vigil the army arrives and sprays us with tear gas and then open fire.

"This way, Miriam," Sabelo cries as I search for cover. He grabs my hand and jostles his way through the stampeding crowd. The streets leading to the stadium are barricaded by Hippos and Caspirs. Fortunately Sabelo has parked his black Plymouth away from the stadium and we grope our way through dark alleyways to reach it.

"Please take me home," I say, trembling as he starts the car.

"There's no way," he says. "There are soldiers everywhere."

"Where are we going, then?"

"To my place. I know a shortcut. We'll be safe there. I'll take you home after the shooting stops."

The streets are blanketed with tear gas. Somehow we manage to reach the yard on Seventeenth Avenue where he rents a two-room shack in the back.

"I'm going home," I say as soon as we're inside the shack. It's sparsely furnished but neat. "My parents will be wondering where I am."

"Do you hear that gunfire?" he says. "Do you want to walk home in that? I promise I'll take you home as soon as the shooting stops."

"I'm tired," I say, yawning.

"You can lie down in my bed in the other room."

"Where will you sleep?"

"On the sofa."

I lie down on the bed with my clothes on, but the sound of gunfire keeps me awake. I hear Sabelo in the other room. I'm even beginning to like him for his gentlemanly behavior. I feel completely safe.

I must have dozed off, for suddenly I'm awakened in the middle of the night by the sound of a door opening.

"Who's that?" I ask.

"It's me," Sabelo says.

"Has the firing stopped?" I ask.

"It has."

"Can you take me home now?" I ask, getting up.

"No," Sabelo says.

I tried to fight him but he was too strong. He pinned me down on the bed and forced himself on me. He wouldn't even stop when I said it hurt. Why did I believe that Sabelo would be different from the men who can't take no for an answer? I pray that I'm not pregnant. I feel terrible shame.

After the brutal crackdown, a sort of calm is restored. There's word that schools will reopen for the second quarter of the year, but I have little enthusiasm for going back. I'm wrestling with the guilt of being raped. I haven't told anyone, not Mama nor any of my friends. I'm afraid what people will think of me. I blame myself for what happened. Part of me considers it a punishment from God for participating in Mzabalazo. I'm prepared to suffer alone in silence.

One afternoon a week before schools are scheduled to reopen, Gertrude visits me at home. She's almost in tears.

"Miriam, please help me. I don't know what to do."

"What's the matter?"

"I'm pregnant."

"Are you sure?"

"I'm sure. I've missed my period two times. And my stomach is starting to get big."

"Oh my God! How did it happen?" My heart is racing. I wonder if I'm pregnant too since I've missed my period.

"Phineas and I have been sleeping together."

"How many times?"

"A couple of times."

I have a sigh of relief. Sabelo and I slept together only once. I can't possibly be pregnant.

"Do your parents know?" I ask.

"No. I'm terrified to tell them. My father will kill me."

"So what do you plan to do?"

"I'm going to abort."

"Kill the baby?" I cry in astonishment.

"Yes."

"How?"

"Using laxatives. I can't afford to be pregnant. School starts soon and my parents expect me to go."

"Aborting with laxatives can kill you, you know? They've killed several girls already."

"What else can I do? I don't have money to buy abortion muti."

"Keep the baby. Tell your parents. Explain to them that it was a mistake. Promise them that you'll go to school after you have the baby. They'll understand."

Gertrude tells her parents, but they are furious. Her mother goes to Phineas's parents, but Phineas adamantly denies paternity.

"I was deeply hurt when I heard that," Gertrude says to me one afternoon. I'm at her place. She's bedridden with morning sickness. "He's the father. No doubt about that. He's the only man I've ever slept with. I now wish I'd had protection. Are you using any?"

The question takes me aback. "Why should I?"

"Aren't you dating Sabelo?"

"Me, dating that creep—who told you such a lie?"

Gertrude manages a weak smile. "He told Phineas that you two slept together."

"The bastard," I say. "He forced himself on me."

"That's how it happened with me and Phineas the first time. Did you have protection when he forced himself on you?"

"No."

"I thought you were taking birth control pills."

"I stopped taking them months ago."

"Why?"

"They made my breasts too big, and I didn't like that. Boys were always coming on to me. But I can't possibly be pregnant. He did it only once."

"It doesn't matter how many times he did it," Gertrude says. "I know of a lot of girls who are pregnant from having done it only once."

Chapter 38

I *don't believe Gertrude. I go ahead with preparations to return to* school. The thought of having to return to school after being away for almost a year feels strange. I never touched a schoolbook during Mzabalazo. I had no inclination. I wonder if I'll have to repeat Standard Six because I didn't sit for exams. But no one else sat for exams. I still have lingering doubts that schools will reopen as promised.

Those doubts are soon dispelled. One sign of a return to normalcy in the township is the restoration of the black policemen and the ATC councillors to power following the detention of the Comrade leaders. The army's occupation of Alexandra continues to insure that Mzabalazo doesn't resume. Roadblocks on strategic roads remain in place to monitor traffic in and out of the township so as to prevent the infiltration of ANC guerrillas and activists from other townships. Soldiers take over the stadium where we used to hold rallies and night vigils. Word has it that when it is handed over, only soccer will be allowed there, no mass assemblies or funerals.

"Have you heard the good news, Jackson?" Mama says excitedly at the dinner table. "They plan to rebuild Alexandra. There will be electricity, sewers, new houses, streetlights, flats, playgrounds, and new schools."

"I'll believe it when I see it," Papa says. "The government always talks about rebuilding Alexandra after every riot."

"This time they mean it," Mama says. "People everywhere are talking about it. They say ninety million rand will be spent. Ninety million, can you believe that? Alexandra will be just like Sandton."

Sandton, a whites-only suburb of Johannesburg, was one of the richest in the world.

"That will be the day," Papa scoffs. "Alexandra is a slum because the government refuses to spend money on black people. And it will remain a slum."

"Isn't it true, Miriam," Mama says, looking at me, "that the government is going to spend ninety million rand to rebuild Alexandra?"

"That's what the papers say," I say absentmindedly from the chair by the stove, where I'm sitting with my dinner plate, which is untouched.

"I can't wait for the children to return to school," Mama says brightly. "Being away from school has meant nothing but trouble. I'm told that a lot of girls got pregnant during Mzabalazo."

"If there's any school to return to," Papa says. "The Comrades have burned all of them down."

"Did they, Miriam?"

"No," I say. "They just vandalized them. They're being fixed."

"I don't know why Miriam has to return to school," Papa says. "She's old enough to get married."

"She wants to be a nurse," Mama says. "Don't you, Miriam?"

Suddenly I start crying. "I don't feel well," I say. "I think I'll go for a walk."

I get up and leave.

I rendezvous with Sabelo under the streetlight at the corner of Seventeenth Avenue. Since he raped me, we've been seeing each other clandestinely. I feel that I'm damaged goods, that I might as well stick with the man who violated me. Also, since the rape, he's been very understanding. He's apologized, and promised to take care of me if I ever become pregnant. Though I know I don't love him, the last thing I want is to give birth to an illegitimate child.

"Did you tell them?" Sabelo asks.

"No."

"Why not?"

"I still don't believe I'm pregnant."

He laughs. "Why don't you? Everything points to that."

Blushing, I say, "Because we did it only once."

He laughs even harder. "Poor Miriam," he says. "Don't you know that you can get pregnant from only making love once? You yourself said you didn't use any protection."

I look beyond him at the dim shacks in the background. If I'm pregnant my future is ruined.

Alexandra High reopens. The school is half empty, with lots of students still in detention. Many others have fled the country or been killed. Some have simply disappeared without trace. There's little enthusiasm for learning.

I can't concentrate. What should I do, should it turn out I'm indeed pregnant? I dare not consider the possibility. It means dropping out of school. It means abandoning my dream of becoming a nurse. It means breaking Mama's heart.

I can't afford a pregnancy test kit but I miss my second period. I continue to be in denial. My breasts aren't sore and I don't have morning sickness, symptoms my friends who became pregnant constantly complain about. Three months go by. I attend school as if everything's fine. Then one morning I feel my stomach. It's bigger and tighter. I've gained weight. I can't fit into any of my dresses. Throughout the day I feel nauseous. There's no denying it anymore. I am pregnant. I break down and cry. My future is ruined. I feel like killing myself.

I'm shocked to find out that Cynthia and Petronella too are pregnant. Cynthia tells me the news during lunch break. Like Gertrude, she wants to abort using laxatives so she can finish school. I dissuade her, reminding her of the dangers.

"I'm pregnant too," I say.

Cynthia gives me an incredulous stare. "You—pregnant!"

I nod.

"I didn't even know you had a boyfriend."

I tell Cynthia all about Sabelo and the night he forced himself on me.

"What will you do if you're pregnant?" she asks.

"I plan to have the baby," I say.

"And school?"

"I'll drop out. And after I raise the baby I'll come back and finish."

"A lot of girls say that but they never go back to school," Cynthia says. "They say it's too humiliating."

"I know. But I'm determined to come back."

"I'm so scared, Miriam," Cynthia says.

"About what?"

"I don't know anything about having babies."

"I don't either. So we'll teach each other."

Chapter 39

"Miriam," *Mama says one afternoon, "are you pregnant?"*

"No," I say quickly. "Why do you say that?"

"You look *fresh*"—rosy cheeked.

"I guess it's because we're finally eating right, now that you're working," I say evasively.

I know I can't continue to hide the fact that I'm pregnant. Soon I'll start to show. I finally agree to have Sabelo tell my parents. I purposefully leave home when Sabelo tells them. He comes out shaking his head.

"Your father threatened to kill me."

"What did you tell them?"

"I told them that it was a mistake and that I take full responsibility."

"Does it mean you're going to pay lobola for me?"

"I plan to as soon as I've spoken to my parents."

At home, Mama has a defeated, powerless look. She's on the verge of tears. It's almost as if someone has died. Papa is so incensed he can hardly find the words to express his rage. He looks at me as if he'd like to throttle me to death.

"I'm sorry," I say.

He makes no reply but gets up and goes outside.

"How could you do this to yourself, Miriam?" Mama says simply.

"I'm sorry," I say, fighting back tears. "It was an accident."

I can live with Papa being mad at me, but I can't live with having disappointed Mama's expectations.

"What a costly accident," Mama says with a deep sigh. "Do you know that you may have ruined your future? I had such high hopes for you, my child. I really did. I love all my children, but you were the apple of my eye. You did so much to make me proud. You loved the Lord, you loved school, and you are a hard worker. The last thing anyone thought you'd do was get pregnant."

"I'm sorry, Mama," is all I can say.

"Sabelo took advantage of my naïveté. I trusted him."

I tell her I'm determined to go back to school after I have the baby.

"Maria promised me the same thing, yet she never went back. Now she's expecting a second baby. Is that what you're going to do too, have one baby after another?"

"No, Mama. I promise I'll go back. I know it'll be hard, but I'm determined to do it."

"Will Sabelo let you?"

"If he won't I'll leave him. I'm determined to finish school."

Mama gives me a big hug. "I'm glad to hear you say that, my child. I'll help you take care of the baby. And I'll save whatever I'm making to ensure that there's enough money to pay for your schooling when you do go back."

"No, Mama," I say. "I'll pay for my own schooling."

"How?"

"I'm planning to go look for a job."

I find a job near the fiberglass factory where Florah worked during her pregnancy with Angie. Latisha helps me find the job, which used to be held by her sister. Latisha is pregnant for the second time, after suffering a miscarriage. We are the only two workers in a large building, which is owned by an Italian. The building has two large machines that produce plastic containers and combs.

The workplace is crude. There are no chairs. We sit on round rusted metal tins while working. Our dangerous job is to trim excess plastic off juice bottles as they come out hot from the machine at a breakneck speed. We start work at six in the morning and end at five, with only a half-hour break for lunch.

The building is very hot and badly ventilated. We wear no face masks or gloves, and the fumes from the machine are often overpowering and my hands are raw from handling hot plastic. My back is always aching from bending over. For our pain we are paid seventy-five rand ($22) a week.

"I wish I were back at school," I say to Latisha one day during our lunch break.

"Me too," she says.

"I plan to go back as soon as my baby is weaned."

"I want to go back too, but I'm having a tough time at home."

"What's wrong?"

"My mother is beating me," Latisha says.

I've noticed the bruises on her arms and neck.

"She's angry with me for having become pregnant again by Buti. She hates Buti's mother."

"Do you love Buti?"

"I think I do. Yet he can be very difficult sometimes, but he's the only man I've known, and he's the father of my baby."

"Do you think he'll marry you?"

"He says he wants to, but his parents won't let him."

"Why?"

"His mother doesn't like me. She says he could have done better. She accuses me of being after his money because he's working. And yet I'm the one supporting him because since Mzabalazo he's been drinking a lot."

"I don't understand why you're supporting a man," I say. "He should be the one supporting you, especially because you're pregnant."

"My mother wants me to give her my wages. When I refuse she beats me. Then I run to Buti's home. But he also wants money from me. I don't know what to do."

Tears prick the corners of my eyes. Latisha is one of the sweetest and kindest persons I know. She loves the Lord and singing; she is faithful and hardworking. But as with so many women I know, the relatives of their husbands or boyfriends often determine their matrimonial fate.

"Why don't you find a place of your own?" I suggest. "You have what it takes to stand on your own two feet. You don't need a good-for-nothing man."

"Buti has threatened to beat me if I leave him. You know, I often wish my father were alive. He's the only person who's ever loved me."

I recall how kind and gentle Latisha's father had been and how gruesomely he had died.

He was an underdeacon and then a priest at Mama's church. He was a rarity among men. He'd done everything his wife asked him without complaint, leading people to think that she'd bewitched him into effeminacy. One day, in a fit of madness induced by heavy drinking, Latisha's mother had accused him of philandering. She'd then doused him with paraffin and set him on fire. After his death, the demented woman had turned her wrath on poor Latisha, who was as sweet natured and pacific as her father. She'd repeatedly beat her, often with a thick hosepipe, even during her first pregnancy, which ended in a miscarriage. What kept Latisha sane was her unwavering faith in God, her love for singing in the choir, and our friendship. We are each other's biggest supporters.

Latisha reaches over and hugs me. "Don't worry about me, Miriam. I'll survive."

One Monday I stop by her home on Eleventh Avenue to pick her up to go to work. I find her outside the shack she shares with Buti, weeping. Her meager belongings are strewn across the yard.

"What's the matter?" I ask, noticing her swollen eyes and disheveled clothes.

"Buti beat me."

"What for?" I say angrily.

"I did as you suggested," Latisha says. "I refused to give him my wages. I told him that I was planning to use it to buy myself new underwear and maternity clothes. He got mad and started beating me up. And you know what?"

"What?"

"His mother and grandmother cheered him on. They ordered him to throw me out."

I help Latisha gather her clothes. "Let me take you home. You need some rest. I'll go to work alone. I'll tell the Italian that you're ill."

"It won't work. He'll fire me. And I need the job, especially now."

I accompany Latisha to her mother's place, where she leaves her belongings. Latisha joins me and we walk the long and tiring distance to work. During lunch Latisha finally breaks down and cries.

"Life is so hard, Miriam," she says. "Sometimes I feel like giving up."

"Don't give up," I say. "You can make it. Save your money and as soon as the baby's born, go back to school. You're a good student. Get your matric and you'll find a good job."

"You're lucky because you have a mother who supports you," Latisha says. "I don't. I'm all alone. But I'll try."

Latisha is right. I'm very lucky to have Mama's support. That's why I plan not to disappoint her again. I have saved enough to take care of my baby's needs, to buy books and a uniform, and to pay school fees, rather than burden Mama with the responsibility of supporting me and my baby.

Chapter 40

I*'m devastated. The money that I'd painstakingly saved in the* piggy bank for nearly a year is gone. Someone found my hideout in the wardrobe and stole my entire savings while I was at work. I have a feeling I know who did it.

"Why did you steal my money?" I confront George when he returns home from playing tennis in the evening.

He blushes, then avoids eye contact.

"I'm sorry, sister," he says in a contrite voice, "but I needed money badly."

"For what?"

"To pay school fees and buy books. I'm graduating this year, remember. And I've been hunting for jobs for months without any luck. Whites aren't hiring young men from Alexandra. They think we're all Comrade troublemakers."

"Why didn't you simply ask? You know I'd have helped you out."

"I'm sorry," George says. "I'll pay you back as soon as I have a job."

I don't know if George is telling the truth, but I give him the benefit of the doubt. Yet I'm deeply hurt. I must have had close to one hundred rand in the piggy bank. And I'll need the money to pay the clinic and the nurses. I'm halfway through my pregnancy and I haven't a penny to my name.

Sabelo has promised to give me some money, but I can't rely on him, in case he changes his mind, as men often do after the baby is born. I just have to start saving all over again.

I'm very concerned about the health of my baby. I watch what I eat, I make sure I get enough rest despite working long hours, and I visit the clinic nearly every week. Two and a half months before I'm due, at a checkup I'm given one hundred tablets, to take three times a day.

"What are they for?" I ask the nurse.

She glares at me. The room is crowded with patients. The nurse is harried.

"Every time you come here you ask questions," the nurse says. "Do you think I have time just for you? You aren't the only patient, you know."

I'm not angry with the nurse. I'm angry with myself. I should understand that the nurse is overworked. It's just that I have an aversion to taking tablets. I want to know what it is I'm ingesting.

I begin taking the tablets as instructed, even without knowing what they're for. The tablets make me nauseous. I also feel very weak. Some days I don't feel like getting up. I'm afraid to lose my job, because I haven't saved enough to take care of my baby. I stop taking the tablets. I feel better. I continue working.

Latisha has a stillbirth. Her in-laws are glad. It means that there won't be a baby to tie her to Buti. Latisha is distraught. She'd really wanted the baby.

"I don't know what's wrong with me," Latisha says. "I must be bewitched."

"It's not your fault," I say. "You're under a great deal of stress. Also, you are being beaten black and blue."

"Maybe it's just as well," Latisha says with a sigh. "Now I can return to school without having to worry about who would take care of my baby. Especially because no one would have wanted it except me."

Latisha returns to school in January of 1987. She continues her relationship with Buti, who's become more abusive and beats her regularly. She seemingly can't muster the courage to leave him. She is very supportive of me as I enter the last stages of my pregnancy and my fears of childbirth increase. I've gained about forty pounds and I'm easily exhausted, yet I refuse to slow down. I've thrown away the strange tablets from the clinic. Each time the nurses ask if I'm taking them, I lie and say yes.

Two white men visit our home, a rare sight. Neighbors peek out through windows and stand outside doors to view the phenomenon. I regard the white men with intense suspicion, especially the tall brown-haired one with the thick Afrikaner accent. He reminds me of some of the police officers who used to terrorize me during pass raids. But my suspicion decreases after they introduce themselves. The Afrikaner is Gary Beukes, a Johannesburg businessman for whom Florah is now working as a secretary. The other is an American named Lyston Peebles, who's brought the family important news about Johannes and a package from him.

Lyston explains that Johannes has moved from New York City to High Point in North Carolina, and that *Kaffir Boy* has just been published. As Lyston is speaking, I catch Gary's eyes roving about our shack. He seems bewildered by its small size and poverty-stricken appearance.

Lyston says that he was deeply moved by *Kaffir Boy,* especially by the story of Mama's courage in the face of adversity and her indomitable Christian faith.

"I'm a Christian too," Lyston says, and adds that he's in Alexandra to see for himself the horrible conditions depicted in the book. He's director of a foundation that plans to help black South Africans improve their lives.

Gary confesses that he's never been to Alexandra, even though he lived barely ten miles away and has a friend in the township. He expresses shock at the squalor of the township and promises to inform his fellow church members about the conditions in the ghetto, in the hope that they might do something to change things. Gary strikes me as genuine and caring. I wonder if there are more Afrikaners like him.

The package Lyston has brought from America is a lovely wall clock in the shape of a swan. He also gives us pictures of Johannes, and some letters. Papa's eyes light up when Lyston hands over the money Johannes had promised to send the family.

"Your son hopes you can visit him in America someday," Lyston says.

"Tell him I pray every night for the miracle to happen," Mama says.

Gary and Lyston leave. The family opens the letter. In it Johannes recommends to my parents that they save the bulk of the money and use it only for school needs and emergencies. He's also given each member of the family a hundred rand to use for themselves. Papa rejects the hundred rand. I don't understand it because the amount is ten times what he used to make a week.

"I'm not a child," Papa says. "I need double that."

"What do you need it for, Mr. Mathabane?" Mama asks good-humoredly.

"It's my business what I need it for," Papa says. "Don't forget Johannes is my son."

Mama laughs. "He's your son now that he's working and making good money, is that it? Do you remember how you used to refuse to pay for his schooling or buy him books? Do you remember how you excoriated me for letting him go to America? Have you forgotten all that?"

"Stop lecturing me, woman," Papa says, "and give me the money."

Mama relents and gives Papa two hundred rand. I use my hundred rand to finally open the long-dreamed-of account at First National Bank. Mama asks George to accompany her to the bank so she too can open an account in which to save the remaining sixteen hundred rand.

With part of the money Mama installs a phone.

"No more begging neighbors to let us use their phone," Maria says.

"And Johannes can call us anytime," Mama says.

"What about TV?" asks George.

"What about it?" Mama asks.

"It's high time we got one," George says.

"Do we really need a TV?" Mama asks.

"We do, Grandma," Angie says.

"And there are wonderful shows to watch," Given chimes in.

"Okay," Mama says. "I'll buy one on layaway."

"But we have no electricity yet," says Diana.

"We'll use a generator like the Sitholes," Florah says.

The Sitholes are our neighbors. They own the only TV in the neighborhood. Angie and Given are constantly begging Mama for twenty-five cents with which to pay admission in order to watch their favorite American show, *Mr. T. and Tina,* which is dubbed in Zulu.

"I can't afford a generator now," Mama says.

"We'll use a battery," George says.

Everyone is delighted except Papa. He's been sitting quietly, listening to the whole conversation. Finally he speaks. "Did Johannes send you the money to waste it on frivolous things like TVs?"

"Every decent family has one," Florah replies.

"All it does is make noise," Papa says. "I don't want it in my house."

"Why don't you indulge the children, Jackson?" Mama says in a soothing tone. "Do you want them to waste money paying the Sitholes to watch TV?"

Papa is adamant. "I don't want a TV inside this house. And that's final. If I find a TV inside my house I'll smash it."

"You know what, Jackson?" Mama says. "I've been married to you long enough to know that you're against my buying the TV because you see that as a challenge to your authority. If the suggestion had come from you it would be fine. But no, it came from a woman so you have to oppose it."

"You don't know what you're talking about," Papa growls.

"I do," Mama says, like a subject petitioning a king. "I'm begging you, Jackson, as head of this household, to please allow the children to have a TV. It will keep them home, for one."

Mama buys a twenty-seven-inch black-and-white TV set. Papa doesn't carry out his threat to break it, but he insists on regulating when it can be viewed.

Chapter 41

One day Mama returns from work and says to me, "Miriam, you won't believe what I saw today at the store."

Very pregnant, I turn with difficulty on the bed and ask, "What did you see?"

"I saw the most wonderful dining room table. It's all glass, brand-new and dirt cheap. Do you think I should buy it?"

"If you think we need one."

"I was very embarrassed when Lyston and Gary visited us and we had nowhere to serve them tea. And on the phone the other day Johannes said that because of his book, we'll be receiving important visitors from America from time to time. We must have a place to serve them tea. We can't embarrass him."

"You're right, Mama," Maria says. "A lot of people are wondering why, if Johannes is in America, we still live in a shack."

"We'll get a decent house someday," Mama says. "First things first."

The next day, a Saturday, I accompany Mama to the First National Bank branch in Bramley. The branch is crowded with women clutching their savings books. We wait in the queue and a young, prettily dressed black woman with a friendly smile helps us.

"I'd like to withdraw two hundred rand from my savings account, please," Mama says.

"Certainly," the teller says as Mama hands her the booklet.

The teller checks the balance. She flips rapidly through the booklet. "How much did you say you wanted, Mrs. Mathabane?"

"Two hundred rand, please."

"I'm sorry, but there isn't enough money in the account."

Mama and I are stunned. Mama asks, "Did you say there isn't enough money?"

"Yes. There's only four rand and ninety-nine cents."

"Four rand and ninety-nine cents," Mama says with wide eyes. "That's impossible. I've saved almost two thousand rand."

The teller checks the balance again.

"You had nineteen hundred and ninety-eight rand, Mrs. Mathabane, but most of it has been withdrawn."

"Withdrawn?"

"Yes."

"By whom?"

"By you, Mrs. Mathabane."

Mama shakes her doek-covered head. "I never withdrew any money. Each time I come here it's to make a deposit."

The teller shows us the booklet.

"You've made ten withdrawals so far," the teller says, "and they were made on these dates."

She shows us the dates. There's no mistake about it.

"But I've never been to the bank to make a withdrawal," Mama insists.

"The withdrawals weren't made at the bank," the teller says. "They were made at various teller machines, using your bank card."

"What bank card?"

The teller describes to Mama what a bank card is. Mama is adamant that she's never gone to a teller machine to use a bank card because she doesn't have one.

"But we gave you one the day you opened the account, Mrs. Mathabane," the teller says politely. "It says so right here."

I immediately guess what happened. I feel like crying. Finally it dawns on Mama.

"Oh, my God!" she lets out a cry. She stares at me. "Oh, my God! I remember now. George wanted me to get the card. I told him I didn't need it because I planned to save, not to constantly withdraw money. He must have gone ahead and gotten it anyway. I remember he asked me to sign some paper."

Back home, Mama confronts George. "How could you do this to me, my son?"

"I needed the money, Mama," George says in the same contrite voice he used after he'd emptied my piggy bank, "and I knew that if I asked you for the money you wouldn't give it to me."

"You needed it for what?"

"I'm about to matriculate and will soon be looking for jobs," George says. "I need to look my best when I go for interviews. So I bought several suits, ties, and a pair of shoes."

"I thought you said the white people you played tennis with gave you those things."

George smiles nervously. "I lied."

"You know what hurts me, son?" Mama says. "It's not that you used the money to buy clothes you say you need. It's because you stole the money. Stealing is a violation of God's commandment."

"I'll pay it back as soon as I start working."

When Papa gets wind of the stolen money, he's livid.

"How dare you steal money from your poor mother?"

"I didn't steal it," George says. "I took it because money is the root of so much evil in this house. Ever since Johannes sent Mama the money, you've been hounding her for it. You've even threatened to beat her up if she didn't give it to you. At least now there won't be any more reason to quarrel."

"You bloody thief!"

"Who are you to call me a thief?" He's not afraid of Papa. "What about you? You're constantly taking food money to go buy beer and gamble. Isn't that thieving?"

Papa has no answer, except to say, "I'll kill you one of these days."

"I'll kill you first before you kill me," George shouts back.

• • •

Several days after George's bank robbery, Florah returns from work very excited.

"We're going to America," she cries. "We're going to America."

"What are you talking about?" Mama asks.

"I say we're going to America."

"Stop fooling, child," Mama says. "What do you mean, we're going to America?"

"Johannes called me at work this afternoon," Florah says. "He says he wants the family to visit him in America."

Everyone is stunned. Visit America! See Johannes for the first time in almost ten years!

"When?" I ask.

"In a couple of weeks," Florah says.

"Are you sure he wants *all* of us to visit?" Mama asks.

"Yes," Florah says with a smile, "including Granny."

"How can he afford it?"

"He's a very rich man, I told you," George says.

"He's not a rich man," Florah says. "He's being helped by a famous American woman named Oprah Winfrey. She'll be paying for our tickets."

"You mean the glamorous talk-show host?" Maria asks.

"Yes. She read *Kaffir Boy* and was deeply moved."

"God bless Mrs. Oprah Winfrey," Mama says.

"When do we leave?" George asks.

"As soon as we have passports and visas," Florah says. "Gary promised to help. He'll be coming over to talk to us about it."

"Will we be able to go?" I ask. "I'm expecting any day. So is Maria."

"I don't know," Florah says. "I'll ask Gary."

"I don't think pregnant women are allowed on planes," Mama says. "What if you go into labor?"

"Mama's right," George says.

I feel utterly wretched. I've never regretted more having become pregnant. But I try to put the best face forward.

"I'll stay," I say. "I don't want to embarrass Johannes anyway by showing up pregnant and unmarried. Especially when he'll be with Oprah Winfrey."

"I'll stay too," Maria says, but there are tears in her eyes.

The door suddenly opens. In walks Papa. He's drunk.

"There's wonderful news from Johannes, Mr. Mathabane," Mama says exuberantly.

"Did he send more money?"

"No," Mama says. "He wants us to come to America."

"I'm not going," Papa says. "Give me my food."

All eyes turn and stare at Papa. I go over to the stove and remove his dinner from the oven. I set the warm pap and *vleis* (meat) in front of him at the kitchen table.

"Why don't you want to go see your son?" Mama asks. "You haven't seen him in almost ten years."

"He's not my son. If he were my son he'd send me money instead of giving it to white people."

"What are you talking about?" Mama says.

"Where does this Gary come from?" Papa says. "When did white people start helping black people? He's in it for the money, I tell you."

"What a preposterous idea," Mama says. "Gary is a Christian. Florah works for him. He's simply helping us. Do you know how difficult it is to get a passport if you're black? Have you forgotten the runaround they gave you after you lost your passbook and had to apply for a new one? They kept telling you to bring this and that paper, this and that certificate."

"I'm not going to America, and that's final," Papa says.

Chapter 42

On the morning of May 3 I awake with a terrible backache. I don't make much of it. I ascribe it to sleeping on the hard cement floor. As I go about making breakfast I suddenly feel warm liquid gushing between my legs.

"Mama! Mama! The baby is coming out!"

Mama runs out of the bedroom. "What's the matter?" she asks.

"The baby is about to come out."

Mama smiles. "Don't panic. You just broke water. We must get you to the clinic."

Mama rushes outside and gets a *kombi* (minivan) to take me. I'm so afraid that I long for someone to be with me when I deliver. But the clinic has a policy of not allowing anyone to be with the mother during delivery except for the nurse.

I arrive there shortly after 7 A.M. The place is already teeming with patients. Despite the fact that I'm already experiencing contractions, I have to fill out papers for about an hour before being admitted. I'm placed inside a medium-sized room with five other expectant mothers, all older women.

The women are howling and screaming with each contraction as they writhe on the narrow cots. There is one nurse—no doctor—for the six of us. I can tell that her nerves are frazzled and that she's been working overtime, by the way she barks at the women.

"Stop screaming! Why did you get pregnant if you can't bear the pain of labor!"

The nurse looks at me as I clench my teeth through a contraction.

"Look at Miriam," she says. "She's younger than the lot of you and she hasn't let out a sound. Aren't you ashamed?"

I want to holler at the top of my lungs because the pain is so unbearable. But I remember a common saying of Mama's, which was reinforced during my confinement as a khomba: part of being a strong woman is being able to bear pain. Also, I realize that screaming would only earn me the wrath of the overworked nurse.

The contractions come and go at regular intervals. I take deep breaths as Mama told me to do. I'm hungry but the nurse has told us that we can't have anything to eat during labor. I'm thirsty but I'm afraid to even ask for water. The five other women continue to scream and holler.

"Push! Push!" the nurse barks.

The face of one of the women is a mask of agony. Her baby is a breech. But there's no doctor. The nurse helps her as best she can. Finally the baby is born, feetfirst. The baby of another woman doesn't cry when it's slapped on the buttocks. It's stillborn. Its mother cries uncontrollably as she's wheeled out to make room for another expectant mother.

My baby is very large. I rip as he finally makes his grand entrance. The umbilical cord is tied around his neck. He's all blue. He doesn't cry when the nurse slaps him on the buttocks. There are tears in my eyes. I'm afraid he's dead. The nurse slaps him once more. He lets out an infantile scream. I cry with joy.

It's a boy.

"Do you have a name for him?"

"Sibusiso," I say. A Gift from God.

I long to hold Sibusiso in my arms but the nurse says I can't. She's in a panic. She's trying to stitch me but can't. I'm badly ripped and bleeding heavily. Apparently the tablets I'd been given but stopped taking when they made me sick were meant to treat anemia. There's no doctor available. I get loaded into an ambulance and transported to Tembisa Hospital, about thirty minutes away.

Tembisa is more overcrowded than Alexandra. We arrive shortly after 1 P.M. I'm dizzy from hunger and exhausted from the labor. There's no food to give me because lunch is already over. Fortunately one of the five women sharing a room with me didn't finish her lunch. She has an orange and a banana left over. I finally have my first bite of food in nearly fifteen hours.

There are few doctors, and all are attending to emergency cases. It's almost five before I'm finally seen and stitched. As I lie there, waiting for permission to go see my son, I finally realize why apartheid is so evil.

White hospitals go begging for patients; white women deliver their babies under the most hygienic and comfortable conditions. According to an aunt who works as a charwoman at a white hospital, white women are even allowed private rooms during labor, which they share with their spouses. We black women are penned like animals. No one cares if we live or die, or if our babies live or die.

I'm released the next day even though I'm still racked with pain and am not fully recovered. The bed is needed for someone else. On the way home I vow that I'll never have another baby under such conditions. I'm more determined than ever to go back to school and study to be a nurse. I see more clearly now the need for compassionate nurses, for nurses who, despite being stressed and overworked, will still remember that their patients are human beings, not garbage.

For two weeks I'm confined inside the house. It's taboo for Sibusiso to be seen by his father and by strangers until the end of the confinement period, when a christening party is held. I name the baby Mark after my brother Johannes, who now goes by that name in America. He adopted it after the 1976 riots in order to elude the authorities who were hunting down students who'd taken part in the student rebellion. I give my baby the name because after learning I was pregnant, my brother had encouraged me to go back to school and had promised to pay for my schooling. It was my way of thanking him.

Sabelo comes to see his son. He is thrilled to be a father. He gives me thirty rand for diapers and other baby needs. He promises me more.

"I'll work hard to support you and the baby," he says.

I smile. Maybe I've misjudged him.

"Is there reason for me to hope?" he asks.

"Hope for what?"

"That you and I will get married."

"I'm still young," I say.

"You're eighteen and I'm twenty-two," he says. "There are people younger than us who are married."

"Gary says you can come with us to America," Florah says one afternoon. "I talked to him and he says that you can travel with a three-week-old baby."

I can't believe my ears. I'll get to go to America after all.

"What about me?" Maria asks.

"Gary says you too can come," Florah says, "but you'll both have to get passports in a hurry."

The next day Maria and I take the bus to downtown Johannesburg. We walk to the passport office on Harrison Street. An unsmiling, brusque white woman with a thick Afrikaner accent interrogates us.

What do we want passports for?

"To go to America."

She looks at us incredulous.

"To do what?"

"To visit our brother."

"What's his name?"

"Johannes Mathabane."

The woman gets up and disappears behind a door.

"If Gary were with us," Maria whispers, "we'd be receiving better treatment."

The white woman returns. "What did you say your brother's name was?"

"Johannes Mathabane."

The woman disappears again. Maria whispers to me, "You fool. You made them very suspicious."

"What do you mean?"

"Remember that when Johannes applied for a passport he used the name Mark."

"Oh, my God!" I exclaim. I'd forgotten. And he'd applied for it at this very same office. They'd have denied him one and thrown him in jail had it not been for the intervention of his white friends.

Were they going to deny us the passports because of our association with Johannes, who'd been speaking out against apartheid and had written a book exposing its inhumanity?

The white woman returns.

"You didn't bring all the papers," she says, then gives us a list of what else we have to provide: birth certificates, a copy of Mama's permit, affidavits from the school. Two days later we bring everything the white woman has requested. Again she disappears behind a door, then comes back out.

"We need more papers," she says.

"What papers?" Maria asks.

"We need a letter from your brother in America showing that he's inviting you over there. We also need your parents' rent receipts."

I look at Maria in astonishment. When Gary applied for passports for the family, they didn't ask him for all these documents. Maria and I dig up whatever receipts Mama has saved. We make an expensive call to Johannes in America.

"I'm not surprised," he says. "They're trying to prevent you from coming. They don't like the fact that I wrote *Kaffir Boy*. And since they can't reach me because I'm in America, they're punishing you."

Johannes faxes us the letter. Finally they agree to process our applications. The white woman assures us that we'll have our passports before the family leaves for America.

Chapter 43

W*hile waiting for the passports, I deal with the challenges of* caring for an infant. It's hard sleeping with him on the floor, squeezed between half a dozen bodies. I shield him with my body for fear that someone will roll over on him. I constantly wake up in the middle of the night to change dirty cloth diapers and to breast-feed him. He has quite an appetite. And once every week I take him to the clinic for immunization shots and checkups.

The wait in long queues in the hot sun tries my patience. I wake up early, at about five or six, in order to be among the first on line, but it doesn't always turn out so. On some days I'm not seen, because the newborn section closes around noon. Then I have to return the next day. Other women simply stop coming altogether, and their children are not immunized. I'm determined not to miss an immunization shot, despite the hassle. I'm familiar with the many diseases that afflict newborns in the township and that have led to Alexandra having one of the highest infant mortality rates in the country. Also, Florah has told me that Sibusiso can't travel to America if he's not properly immunized.

On those days when I'm lucky to make it to the immunization and checkup room, I dread the experience. The nurse responsible for newborns has a dreadful reputation. Her name is Sister Mary. She's been with the clinic for decades.

One day I'm in a room crowded with over a dozen other young mothers. I can tell from the fearful looks on their faces as they wait for their babies to be weighed and checked that the last person they want to be in the presence of is Sister Mary. I soon understand why. She arrives late from another section of the clinic and immediately begins the inspection.

She grabs the first infant by the shoulders and faces us. The infant is underweight and quite malnourished. Its ribs are showing and the belly is a bit distended.

"Do you call this a baby!" Sister Mary barks at the mother, waving the baby like a rag doll in front of the woman. "Why do you have babies if you can't take care of them? This baby needs food."

Sister Mary hands the bawling baby back to its mother. She grabs another, who looks sickly and has a drooping head.

"Did you bring this baby in for immunizations like I told you to?"

The mother looks sheepish. "I didn't."

"Speak up so all can hear what an irresponsible mother you are!"

"I didn't," the woman says a bit louder.

"Why?"

"I forgot."

"And your chart says you're pregnant again. Now tell me why in the world you'd want another baby if you can't take care of this one?"

Suddenly Sister Mary grabs Mark. I'm quaking, wondering what she'll find wrong with him.

"Look at this fat boy!" Sister Mary cries. "Look at its cheeks! They are nice and round. This is a healthy baby. At this clinic we want all babies to look like this."

I heave a sigh of relief.

"The reason this baby is healthy is because it has a caring mother. A good mother. And here at the clinic we want all of you to be caring mothers."

Half the women in our group are judged good and caring mothers. As we leave, several women who've been judged bad mothers vow that they won't be back for such humiliation again.

"But Sister Mary wants the best for our children," I say.

"Yes, but she doesn't know what kind of lives we lead back home," one woman says. "We're constantly working."

"And our husbands don't want to give us money to buy formula," says another.

"And we have other children to take care of," says a third woman.

"Also, many of us can't read," says a fourth.

Maria and I are devastated. We've been to the passport place but the Afrikaner woman says that ours won't be ready on time. The family is leaving for America in two days. Oprah has wired the money to Gary's account and he's already purchased the tickets.

When Papa realizes that the trip to America is indeed a reality, he changes his mind. He tells Mama that he wants to go after all. Mama tells Gary but he replies, "It's too late, Jackson. You had your chance. You should have applied for a passport the first time."

Gary invites everyone in the extended family for a farewell party at his house near the Johannesburg zoo. Granny, Aunt Bushy, Uncle Cheeks, Granny's former husband, who is blind, Fikile, and Uncle Piet are there. Papa is still mad and refuses to come.

We stuff ourselves at an elaborate meal. Gary offers those of us who can swim the use of his pool. Only Angie, Given, Linah, and Diana have learned to swim in the Jukskei River. But they are too shy to swim in a white swimming pool.

Afterward Mrs. Beukes gathers everyone on the porch for a pep talk. No one in the family has ever flown in an airplane before, and Granny is terrified. Especially because one of her friends has told her that people vomit their entrails when the plane takes off, and that planes habitually run out of petrol and drop out of the sky, killing everyone aboard.

Mrs. Beukes reassures everyone that planes are actually safer than cars. She reminds everyone to be exemplary in their behavior, especially in front of Oprah Winfrey, who is well known and popular in South Africa. Mrs. Beukes gives everyone a crash course on etiquette, so "everyone can be a good ambassador for South Africa." There are lessons on how to make introductions in English, how to sit at the table, and how to use knives and forks. She also warns everyone that in America elevators, flushing toilets, and electricity are commonplace.

All the talk about America makes me want to cry. I'm convinced that I'd be going if I had not had a baby.

When we get home, while everyone packs and laughs, I sit in the corner fighting back tears. The next day Gary comes in two cars to take them to Jan Smuts Airport. There's room for us all, but Maria and I decline to go. Both of us are depressed. Papa also doesn't go.

Maria and I stand outside and wave good-bye. After the cars disappear around the corner, I go back inside and cry.

The house is quiet and lonely. I miss Diana, Linah, George, Florah, and especially Mama. Even Papa is depressed. He sits outside in the sun all day watching the sky. Every time he sees a plane zoom past he points and says, "There's the plane from America with your mama and everyone."

The family calls from New York City. The flight was long but exhilarating. No one slept a wink on the plane. It flew over the length of Africa and stopped in London before continuing across the Atlantic Ocean to New York City. There were TV cameras filming the reunion—the first one in almost ten years—in the crowded JFK terminal.

Johannes introduced them to Gail, his girlfriend, who was as nice as in the photos he's sent home. He also introduced them to Oprah. She was wonderful, glamorous, and very kind. She had everyone ride into Manhattan in stretch limousines. The Sheraton New York Hotel & Towers on Fifty-third Street, where everyone was staying, was one of the most beautiful and expensive hotels in the world.

Helen Beukes's lessons on etiquette come in handy. They are eating like kings and queens. Oprah is very rich. She has a tall, handsome boyfriend named Stedman Graham, who Florah thinks is absolutely gorgeous. Oprah has Beverly, her personal assistant, take everyone to Alexander's department store, where they buy all kinds of clothes. Everyone will be flying to Chicago to appear on the Oprah Winfrey show, which will be broadcast all over America.

The phone call lasts nearly two hours. Never mind, Oprah is paying for it. How they wish Maria and I were with them so we could see the great New York City, all the bright lights, Broadway, blacks living in freedom. Toward the end of the marathon phone call, during which I speak to nearly everyone, including Gail, Mama comes on and says, "I miss you and Maria terribly."

"I miss you too, Mama," I say, fighting back tears.

"Do you have everything?"

"We're running low on groceries," I say.

"Don't worry," Mama says. "On the way to the airport Gary stopped by Seventeenth Avenue and introduced us to his friend Linda Twala. Do you know him?"

"I've heard of him," I say.

"He'll be coming over any day to give you some money," Mama says. "Johannes has already talked to him about it. What do you want us to bring you back from America?" Mama asks.

"I badly need a pram," I say. "Sibusiso is a very big baby. Carrying him on my back all the time is killing me. I could also use some clothes. I only have a couple of dresses."

"I'll talk to Johannes about it," Mama says. "And is your father there?"

"No. He's out drinking. He was very down after you left. He missed you so much that he'd sit outside staring at the sky. And whenever a plane flew past, he'd point and say it was the plane from America bringing you back."

"Aauww sham," Mama says. How sad. "My dear husband misses me. Tell him I miss him too."

Chapter 44

A *week after the family leaves for America, Maria is rushed to the* clinic. After eight hours of labor she delivers a premature baby boy. His father, a Mosotho mechanic, names him Tsepo (Trust). Maria gives him the name Lionel, after her favorite American singer, Lionel Ritchie.

We are running low on money, having used part of it to pay for the kombi and the clinic. Neither of us is working because we are nursing. Nor is Papa working. He's ill with what doctors at the clinic call a bad cold. He coughs a lot, complains of pain in his chest and leg, and his lower lip has swollen to twice its normal size. Yet he hasn't given up drinking, despite our imploring him to.

One Friday morning a large black man with a bushy beard and a ready smile stops by the house. He finds Papa sitting outside watching the sky.

"Do you know who I am?" the bearded man asks in Zulu.

"Yes," Papa says, "you're Mr. Linda Twala."

The man takes a seat next to Papa. "What's happened to us black people?"

"What do you mean?"

"Why does it take a white man to introduce us to one another when we live in the same community? I heard about your family from Gary Beukes. He's a friend of mine. He stopped by on his way to the airport and introduced me to your wife and kids, who were leaving for America. Have you heard from them yet?"

Papa looks at me.

"They called a couple of days ago from New York City," I say.

"Why didn't you go?" Linda asks Papa.

Papa lowers his head and says, "I wasn't feeling too well."

"You don't look too well," Linda says. "What happened to your lip?"

"I don't know. It started swelling up a couple of weeks ago."

"Have you been to the clinic?"

"I don't have money."

"I'll give you some," Linda says. He then turns to Maria and me. "And you two, why didn't you go to America?"

"They wouldn't issue us passports," I say.

"Well," Linda says, "I've come to tell you that should you need anything—anything at all—don't hesitate to call me, okay? You know where I live, don't you?"

"Yes."

Linda reaches into his wallet and removes a bundle of bills. He gives Papa one hundred rand and Maria and me fifty each.

"You should go to the clinic and have them take care of that lip," Linda says to Papa. "And you two make sure those babies are well fed."

Linda then gives me two hundred rand.

"This is for groceries," he says. "If you need more, just phone me."

"We will," I say.

Two days later, Papa's one hundred rand is gone. He spent all the money at the shebeen. He staggers home drunk. Maria is on the bed breast-feeding Tsepo.

"I want money," Papa growls.

"What money?" Maria says.

"The money Linda gave you."

"He said it's for groceries."

"I need some of it, you hear?"

"You can have twenty rand of my money," I say quickly, reaching for my purse. I'm anxious to diffuse the situation. Maria is about to say something but stops. Papa takes the twenty rand and returns to the shebeen.

"You fool," Maria says. "You shouldn't have given him the money."

"I wanted to get him to stop harassing you."

"He won't stop," Maria says. "You'll see, he'll be back demanding more money."

"What should I do when he comes back?"

"Don't give him any more," Maria says. "If you do, we'll starve. And who knows when Mama and everybody are coming back? Maybe they'll find America so nice they'll decide to stay there."

"Hold on to the money, then. At least you're not afraid of him. I am."

Maria takes the two hundred rand and stashes it underneath the mattress. Sure enough, an hour or so later, Papa returns.

"I want more money," he says, looking at me.

"I don't have it."

"What do you mean, you don't have it?" Papa snaps. "I saw Linda giving you two hundred rand."

"Maria has it."

Papa turns to Maria. "Give me the money."

"I don't have it."

"You have the money," he says to Maria. "Give it to me."

"Linda said the money is for groceries, not for liquor."

"Give it to me or I'll beat you."

"I don't have any money," Maria says, rising from the bed. As she does she stops suckling Tsepo and he starts crying.

Papa, fuming, goes to the bedroom. Seconds later he emerges grasping a leather sjambok. I start inching toward the door.

"Now give me the money," he says, brandishing the sjambok at Maria.

"I told you I don't have it," she says defiantly.

Papa strikes Maria. Instinctively she reaches out to grab the sjambok to prevent it from hitting Tsepo. I start screaming. Maria and Papa grapple for the sjambok, but Maria has only one hand free because the other is holding Tsepo to prevent him from falling off the bed to the cement floor.

"Give me the baby, Maria!" I shout, reaching for Tsepo, who's bawling and dangling precariously from Maria's arm.

With Sibusiso and Tsepo in my arms, I run to our neighbor, screaming, "Help! Help!"

Mrs. Sithole rushes to our house.

"Shame on you, Jackson," she says, standing by the door. "What kind of a man are you to beat your own daughter? A nursing mother at that!"

Papa lets go of Maria, who then runs outside.

"She needs to be taught a lesson. She disrespects me."

"I don't disrespect him," Maria says, taking Tsepo back. "He wants food money so he can go drink it. Linda gave him one hundred rand two days ago and it's gone."

"Don't give him any more money," Mrs. Sithole says firmly. "As a matter of fact I'll call Linda."

Mrs. Sithole does call Linda and he comes over and he and Papa spend time inside the house talking. Linda says to Maria and me, "I've talked to him. He won't bother you again. Can you come to my place tomorrow? I'm having a big festival for the oldies."

The next day Linda sends a kombi to come pick us up. Papa too comes along. He's now completely changed. He's even neatly dressed in a suit. I wonder what Linda said to him following the fight with Maria over money. We arrive at the Phutadichaba Qoqizizwe (Gathering of Nations) Community Center on Seventeenth Avenue and find the place packed. There are two long queues winding down the street.

"Who are these people?" Maria asks the driver.

"One queue is for the elderly," the driver says. "The other is for the orphans. Linda gives both groups a meal each day. He started feeding orphans back in nineteen sixty-seven. Today he's giving out blankets for the winter. That's why there are so many people. A lot of these people sleep in abandoned buildings, cars and buses, and in shacks with no heat."

"He gives everything out for free?" Papa asks, incredulous.

"Yes."

"He must be a rich man," Papa says.

"He's not a rich man," the driver says. "Everything is donated."

"Does he get paid?" I ask.

"No. He does it for free," the driver says. "He cares about the people of Alexandra. And since Mzabalazo there's been a lot of destitute people."

We are ushered into a hall that is already packed with the elderly. There's a choir on the stage, singing. It's made up of members from the Alexandra High School Christian Movement. I recognize several of the singers and wave to them.

A cow has been slaughtered for the occasion. Several black three-legged pots are brimming with pap. There's plenty of vegetables, cake, and cool drinks. Tears come to my eyes when I notice how grateful everyone is for the food. I realize that without Linda many of these people would starve.

Most of the elderly are well into their eighties and nineties. Several are over one hundred years old. They're all neatly dressed. In the past they'd have been taken care of by the extended family. But since Mzabalazo, many breadwinners have been killed, detained, or have fled the country, and unemployment in Alexandra is about 50 percent.

"We have with us today Jackson Mathabane and his two daughters," Linda says from the stage. People are fanning themselves with pieces of newspaper and a variety of hats. "Some of you may have heard that several members of the Mathabane family are in America. They've gone over there to see Jackson Mathabane's son Johannes. Many of you may know about him."

I'm surprised to see a lot of heads around the hall nodding. It's been so long since my brother went to America, I thought people might have forgotten about him.

"He's now a famous man in America," Linda says, "and he's written a book about growing up in Alexandra. So a lot of people around the world know about us. Isn't that nice?"

There are smiles and murmurs of approval.

"Now, while members of the Mathabane family are in America,"

Linda says, "I want all of you to embrace Jackson and his two daughters. We are one family, remember. We must help each other."

I now understand why Linda is so beloved in Alexandra. I remember that during Mzabalazo, his house was firebombed by the police for his activism. Why would anyone want to harm a human being who so loves the people of Alexandra that he's willing to risk his own life to help the poor, the needy, the orphaned, and the neglected?

Maria and I are so moved by the work that Linda does that we spend most of our days at the Phutadichaba Center, helping out. We feed the elderly, wash dishes, and clean up. Through these visits I come to learn a lot about Alexandra from talking to the elderly, who have so many stories to tell and whose minds are still sharp. Many of them have lived in the township since it was founded, in 1912. It got its name from Alexandra Papenfus, the wife of the owner of the farm who registered it as a township for resale as residential plots. He had hoped to attract white residents, but few wanted to be so far away from the city. As a result, Papenfus had applied for permission to have Alexandra converted into a "native" township. Luckily for the residents of Alexandra, the conversion took place before passage of the 1913 Native Land Act, which prohibited blacks from owning land anywhere in "white" South Africa.

Some of the elderly remember how proud their parents were to be among the few landowners in "white" South Africa. They also remembered the various battles that were fought to retain that ownership, and to preserve the community at a time when the Johannesburg city council wanted no responsibility for its upkeep. Without funds for basic services, Alexandra gradually degenerated into a slum and became known as "Nobody's Baby" and "Lost City."

Alexandra was home to one of the largest ANC branches in the country and provided the organization, which was also founded in 1912, with most of its leadership, including a young lawyer named Nelson Mandela, who rented a room in the back of a yard on Seventh Avenue.

Many of the elderly had participated in the various protests to save the township from being razed after it was designated a black spot because of its squalor and crime. Alexandra was terrorized by notorious gangs with names such as the Spoilers, Msomis, Zorro's Fighting Legions, the Black Koreans, the Mau-Maus, the Berlins, the Stone Breakers, and the Young Americans. The Okapi switchblade was the preferred weapon for many gang members, who loved wearing American-style outfits: colorful double-breasted suits, broad-brimmed hats rakishly angled over the eyes, shiny black shoes, and gaudy ties. Members of these gangs squeezed workers for protection money. They also operated sophisticated rackets that extorted "cost of living increases" from shebeen queens, taxi drivers, grocers, butchers, and various other Alexandra entrepreneurs.

Listening to all these stories makes me realize the importance of caring for the elderly. It makes me thankful that I still have Granny around, who when I was growing up would baby-sit me whenever Mama went off looking for work, and entertain me with stories, songs, and dances. I feel saddened that when TV came, her stories, songs, and dances were dismissed as boring by Angie, Given, and their friends, who preferred to watch shows like *Mr. T. and Tina* and the Ninja Turtles.

I wonder what stories Granny will have to tell about America, the land of Mr. T. and Ninja Turtles, when she and the family return home.

One day a friend calls me and asks if I heard the news.

"What news?"

"Your family in America has just appeared on the Oprah Winfrey show."

"Really?"

"*Ja.* My relatives in America called and said they saw them. Your mother, Granny, Linah, Diana, George, and Johannes. Johannes was being interviewed about *Kaffir Boy.*"

That evening I get a call from Chicago confirming the story. The family is staying at yet another fancy hotel, special guests of Oprah. Linah and Diana can't stop talking about how wonderful it was to be on TV. After the phone call, Maria and I are a bit down.

"I wish I were in America with them," Maria says.

"Me too."

Chapter 45

Linda's kombi arrives to take us to Jan Smuts Airport to welcome Mama and everyone. The sky is threatening rain. They've been gone nearly three months, but it seems like they've been gone a year. Those packed inside Linda's kombi include Maria, Papa, Fikile, Aunt Bushy, Uncle Cheeks, Angie, and Given. Mama is the first to emerge through the gate. She is pushing one of the most beautiful prams I've ever seen. Following close behind her are Granny and Florah. They are wheeling huge, stuffed suitcases.

I hug and kiss everybody.

"Where are Linah, George, and Diana?" I ask.

"They stayed behind in America," Mama says.

I'm stunned. "Why?"

"Your brother Johannes insisted they stay."

Before Mama can elaborate she is already swamped by the rest of the family, who give her hugs and kisses. Papa stands sullenly in one corner.

On the way home he says not a word. I can tell he's mad.

"Where are my children?" is the first question he asks Mama as soon as Linda and everyone else is gone.

"I left them behind in America," Mama says.

"Why?"

"To go to school."

"What bloody school? Aren't there any schools here?"

"Schools in America are much better, Jackson," Mama says.

"Why didn't you consult with me?"

"I'm sorry," Mama says, "but there was no time. I had to make the decision then and there. But I assure you they are in good hands. Johannes and his wife will take good care of them."

"His wife?"

"Yes. He got married in August to Gail," Mama says. "We were at the wedding. It was very beautiful. I wish you all were there."

"I want my children back, you hear me?" Papa says, wagging a finger at Mama. He stalks out of the house.

I understand why Papa is mad. Diana was his favorite. But I also understand why Mama made the decision to leave her, Linah, and George in America to go to school, without consulting Papa. He would never have allowed it.

My heart aches at the thought that, had Maria and I not had babies and had we gone to America, we too might have remained there to go to school. Children there, according to letters from Johannes, have school buses, they eat free lunches, they have libraries and computers, they aren't packed more than fifty to a classroom, they aren't beaten for not wearing uniforms, not having the proper books, not paying their school fees on time.

Maybe if I finish matric, like George, Johannes will invite me over so I can go to university there.

"I'm planning to go register for Standard Seven, Mama," I say the day after New Year's 1988. In a couple of weeks the school year will be starting.

"Good," Mama says.

"But before I do, I wanted to know if you'll be able to take care of Sibusiso for me."

"Of course I'll take care of my grandchild."

"I'll come back during lunch and nurse him. And if we have study hour, I'll come back in the afternoon to nurse him before returning back."

"Do you have any money to register with?"

"Yes. I saved the money Johannes gave me."

I can't stop shaking. There's a long queue of students as Miss Jones registers them in class. I wonder if she knows that the reason I missed a year of school is that I was pregnant. If she does, I'm in trouble. Students with babies are registered last, and often, when enrollment is beyond the school's capacity, they end up not being allowed to register. The reasoning is that students with babies are more likely to drop out during the school year due to problems with sick babies or abusive boyfriends. When they do drop out, it means a valuable slot that could have gone to a "more deserving" student who is not pregnant is lost.

"Where were you this past year, Miriam?" Miss Jones asks me when it's my turn.

"I was away, Miss Jones," I say, trying hard to stop my voice from trembling.

"We missed you," Miss Jones says. "What was wrong?"

Does she know? Should I go ahead and tell her the lie I've come up with to explain my absence? I hate lying, but this time I feel I must. My future depends on it.

"I was away in the homeland, Miss Jones," I say.

"Were you attending school there?"

"No. During Mzabalazo I developed swikwembu. My parents sent me there to see if I could twasa."

Miss Jones raises her eyebrows. "Are you a sangoma now?"

"Yes."

"Well, now I know who to call upon when I'm sick and white doctors can't cure me," Miss Jones says with a smile. I hold my breath as she registers my name on the list of those accepted for Standard Seven.

A lot has changed in school during the year that I've been away. There are fewer students and they are more subdued. Even the teachers seem to have given up hope. A lot of them now drink. But they still do their best to teach.

The most difficult adjustment to make is that of being a mother and attending school at the same time. During lunch I have to excuse myself from friends and run all the way home to feed Sibusiso. My participation in extracurricular activities is also curtailed. Not only do I have to feed Sibusiso, but I have to be home in time for Mama to go to work. After feeding Sibusiso I have to clean and then cook. But still I find time to sing in the choir and to attend church every Sunday.

Whenever Miss Jones talks at assembly about the importance of young girls abstaining from sex, I now know what she means. I pity the girls who make fun of her and call her a prude. I wish I could tell them how right Miss Jones is and how difficult it is to be a mother and attend school full time.

Letters from Linah, Diana, and George in America fuel my determination to matriculate. They describe the challenges of adjusting to life in America: having to speak English all the time; getting used to different food, like hamburgers; their first time seeing and touching snow; getting used to strange accents; the shock of attending integrated schools. They describe attending schools with facilities I can only dream about: computer labs, gyms, tennis courts, cafeterias, libraries, and school buses. They shock me when they tell me that they had to take placement tests that revealed that Bantu Education is so inferior that all of them had to go back several grades. George, who had matriculated and would normally be going to university, was back in tenth grade. Linah and Diana were back in seventh and eighth, respectively.

"But it's all worth it," George says on the phone. "Even if they'd said I should begin in first grade, I'd have done so. The education system over here is first-class. And teachers never beat you."

Every day I dream of someday attending school in America. And I don't care if I have to start in first grade.

I long to talk to Miss Jones about my problems. But I'm afraid to talk to her because it would mean admitting that I have a child and that I'd lied during registration.

I draw encouragement from a student in Standard Ten. Her name is Rachel and she has a two-year-old son. She's failed Standard Ten twice and yet she keeps coming back. She's determined to matriculate so she can apply for a job as a bank teller. I tell myself that should I fail at the end of the year, I'll go back and repeat Standard Seven until I pass.

I study every day, hand in my homework on time, and deny myself many things my classmates enjoy: going to parties and movies, playing, going shopping. The only recreation I have is singing in the choir and attending church. Occasionally I accompany Sabelo to a soccer game.

The hardest time as a student mother is when Sibusiso is sick. It means being absent from school and missing lessons, which are never made up. It's hard for me to catch up. Mama helps as best she can, but she too is overwhelmed because Papa is unemployed, drinks, and is still sick.

Final exams are in three weeks. Sibusiso is very sick. I have to stay home to nurse him. I'm afraid I'll fail. I can't afford to fail, for repeating Standard Seven means coming up with money to pay school fees and buy books all over again.

I pray that Sibusiso will get well enough so I can at least sit for exams. Cynthia helps by coming over and sharing her notes with me and giving me assignments. Sabelo is also helpful. He sets aside a portion of his wages to give me to take care of the baby. I finally take Sibusiso to the clinic, they give him an injection, and he gets well.

I sit for final exams. Two weeks later I get the results. I've come out number seven of forty students. I have passed and am going to Standard Eight, and in two years, if all goes well, I'll be matriculating. I'm overjoyed.

Chapter 46

Linda's kombi has been stolen. I'm sad because the kombi is vital to the work Linda does at Phutadichaba Center. Many of the elderly have arthritis and other ailments and can't walk to the center for their meals, so Linda has someone drive around the township picking them up. After the meal the elderly are then driven back to their shacks and homes. Without the kombi many of the elderly will miss out on their most important meal of the day.

Linda visits our home one afternoon. He asks Mama to talk to Johannes to see if anyone in America can help his center, which is desperately in need of funding. The center receives nothing from the government. Johannes promises to help. He asks Linda to send him information about Phutadichaba so he can make flyers to hand out to his various audiences. Since publication of *Kaffir Boy* Johannes has been traveling around America telling his life story to students, community groups, and others interested in South Africa and in fighting against the injustices of apartheid. In their letters Linah and Diana tell me about the trips and about the many times they've been on TV with him, and how they've become celebrities at their school because of Johannes's book, which is popular with students and teachers.

At times Johannes seems unlike any member of the Mathabane

family. I'm amazed at how he's been able to succeed in America when he comes from so poor a place as Alexandra and is the son of illiterate parents.

I talk to Mama about it.

"Education can accomplish miracles, my child," she says. "That's why I sacrificed so much to see to it that your brother became educated. I knew that someday he'd be able to help the rest of you. But it wasn't easy. I remember the hard time people used to give him for loving books and speaking English a lot. They accused him of trying to be white."

"Students still say the same things today."

"But your brother never cared what others said about him. He had a goal and he was determined to achieve it. He had a great deal of self-discipline, determination, and willpower."

"I wonder if I have those qualities. It's hard sometimes not to listen to what others say about me."

"I know it is," Mama says. "Every day people say all kinds of things about me because of my love for the Lord and because I'm determined to learn how to read and write. I simply shrug it off because I know I'm right and they're wrong."

"I wish I were that confident. Sometimes I'm so full of doubts."

"All people have doubts, my child," Mama says. "But those who eventually succeed overcome those doubts. They keep trying and trying and trying. In life you never fail as long as you've tried your best."

Mama never went to school and yet she understands more about life and about the importance of education than anyone I know. And her love of learning is insatiable. She has a greater desire to learn than I or any of my siblings. And despite the frustrations and difficulties of learning to read when one is old, she keeps plodding on.

Her resolve inspires even Maria, who through a friend has found a job at a Kentucky Fried Chicken in downtown Johannesburg.

One evening Maria says to me, "You know, I'm thinking of going back to school. I'm tired of frying chickens."

"Wonderful," I say, then quickly check my enthusiasm. Does Maria mean that at twenty-two she's going back to Standard Four, to be in the same class with fifteen-year-olds?

Maria must have read my mind, for she says, "I'm too old to attend school full time. Besides, I need to keep working to support my children. But I'd like to go to night school."

I'm very happy that Maria has decided to go back to school. She loves sewing and says that her ambition is to enroll in sewing school so she can learn how to design African outfits. When Johannes hears that Maria has gone back to school and that she wants to be a designer, he promises to pay for her schooling.

One day I visit Gertrude. She has a baby boy and is married to a man from Mozambique who doesn't mind raising another man's child as some men do. Gertrude, too, is thinking of returning to school. I give Gertrude some advice. I tell her about the difficulties, but am also very encouraging.

"So when do you think you'll be going back?" I ask one day.

"I won't be going back," Gertrude says.

"But I thought all along you were planning to."

"My husband is against the idea. Also, he doesn't want me to be friends with you anymore."

"Why?"

"He says that you're a bad influence on me," Gertrude says, "when you say I should go back to school. He's against it. He thinks if I go back I'll leave him. Also, he says you told him that I'm still seeing Phineas."

"What?"

"He says you told him that I not only still see him but also give him my husband's money."

"That's a lie."

"I know. He's trying to drive a wedge between us."

There's a pause. I realize what I must do. Gertrude is a dear friend, but I don't want to jeopardize her marriage to a man who rescued her from humiliation and is taking good care of her, as far as men go. I say to her, "I'll stop coming to visit you."

"Don't do that," she says.

"It's the best thing," I say. "I don't want your husband to leave you on my account."

Gertrude abandons her dream of returning to school in order to keep her husband. Our friendship continues, but not as intimately as before.

One day Johannes calls to tell us that an organization called Habitat for Humanity has decided to start building low-income houses in South Africa and that Alexandra has been chosen as the place where the first houses will be built. He spoke to representatives of Habitat for Humanity and they promised that our house will be among the first to be built.

Everyone is stunned and excited. The dream of finally living in a real house, a house with electricity, indoor plumbing, and a flushing toilet, sounds too good to be true.

"Since returning from America I've had a persistent dream that we were living in a beautiful house," Mama says. "Priest Mathebula says that the dream will come true. Nothing is beyond the power of the God of Israel."

Johannes sends us a packet of information about HFH. Reading the information, I'm intrigued by the concept of HFH. The program is designed to help families earning less than one thousand rand to become homeowners. Families contribute 25 percent of their income and five hundred working hours to the project of building other HFH houses. No interest is charged. The money is used to purchase land from the Alexandra Town Council and to pay for building materials and whatever specialized services might be needed during the building. The families are expected to work on building their own home, assisted by volunteers. Our house will cost about thirty thousand rand, compared to the price of between forty-five thousand and fifty-five thousand rand for houses built by conventional developers.

Papa is delighted. An exceptional carpenter and builder, he's looking forward to finally being able to use his skills to build his own house. HFH representatives—Helen Friedman, an American, and Dorothy Steele, a South African—work with the family in assessing our needs and means. Both are caring, patient, and committed Christians. Along with David Ditson, director of HFH in Alexandra, they coordinate the building of our house.

Papa wants to be involved in everything. He demands to see the plans and cost estimates. Over the next couple of months he works around the clock with a multiracial crew of about 140 people, laying foundations at three Habitat sites—one on Twelfth Avenue, the second on Seventeenth Avenue, and the third on Sixth Avenue. Our house is being built at the Twelfth Avenue site, along with four others. Mama and various women work alongside the men. They mix concrete, lay bricks, and haul wheelbarrows full of cement.

"I don't like the fact that our house is made of *mampharacement*"—cement blocks—Papa complains. "Why didn't they use real brick?"

"Real brick is expensive," Mama says.

"And they made it too small."

"Too small?" Mama says. "You call three bedrooms, a living room, a kitchen, a bathroom too small?"

"For twelve people it is."

"What are you saying? There are twelve people in this two-room shack. The Habitat house will have three bedrooms. You and I will take one. Florah will have one. Maria and Miriam will share the third. And Angie, Given, and Tsepo will sleep in the living room. That's more room than most people have. And don't forget, we won't have an open sewer running past our new house."

The stench from the open sewer flowing past our house on Sixteenth Avenue is one reason I can't wait to move. Since Mzabalazo there hasn't been any regular bucket pickup in the township. In our yard, sewage from the overflowing latrines, used by over thirty families, flows past our shack. Its reek seeps in through cracks in the door and windows, making it impossible to sleep at night. Sibusiso and Tsepo on more than one occasion have had to be reprimanded for playing around the open sewer.

As the building of the Habitat houses progresses, it's clear that Papa knows a lot about construction. People come up to him with questions about everything from setting the foundation to laying bricks to roofing.

Impressed, Dorothy says to Papa, "Jackson, why don't you go to building school and get certification?"

"I'm too old to attend school."

"It'll only take a month. With certification you'll be able to earn more money."

"I'm too old."

Despite Papa's refusal to get certification, I'm happy to see him be recognized and appreciated for his skills. It's obvious that he loves construction. He's among the first to arrive each day at the various sites and among the last to leave, despite the fact that his cough has worsened and his swollen lower lip still bothers him. He's relaxed and confident, and often jokes with the crew.

One day while he's nailing the roof to our house he accidentally drives a nail clean through his right hand. He doesn't let out a sound. Instead he calmly pulls out the nail and continues working. Only when Mama insists that he needs to have the wound bandaged does he do so.

Papa's involvement in the Habitat project brings unexpected changes in his personality. He no longer goes to the shebeen and he no longer gambles. He and Mama spend a great deal of time together talking about the house, about whether to have tiles or carpet, about what size *geezer* to install for heating hot water.

One Sunday morning Papa does something I thought he'd never do. He tells Mama that he wants to accompany us to church.

Mama thinks he's joking. "You really want to come to church with us?" Mama asks.

"Yes," Papa says.

"Why?"

"Stop asking me too many questions, woman, otherwise I'll change my mind."

At church everyone is astounded to see Papa. He's introduced by Priest Mathebula, who says, "Our brother has finally come home."

Priest Mathebula proceeds to relate the parable of the prodigal son. He ends by saying that Mama deserves all the credit because every time she came to give her report, she always asked the priest for a prayer to God to help her husband see the light and stop walking in darkness. I've never seen Mama happier as she proudly watches Papa take his seat with the other husbands, on the right side of the church, and she sits with the wives on the left. Priest Mathebula asks God to bless the construction of the Mathabane house, and their children in America.

As our house is nearing completion, disaster strikes. During the night someone comes and steals all the windows and doors.

"The Habitat people say they can't complete our house," Mama says.

"What can we do?" Florah asks. "I called Johannes this morning and told him the bad news. He says that he and Gail are financially strapped. It'll be a while before they can send us the money."

"And the Habitat people can't wait," Mama says. "They say they'll have to abandon our project and finish building the other four houses. When they're done, they'll come back and finish ours, provided we have the doors and windows by then."

"I wonder who stole them," I say.

"Anyone could have," Florah says. "Unemployment in Alexandra is over fifty percent. People are desperate."

Chapter 47

The completion of our house is delayed four months. Papa moves into the unfinished, windowless and doorless house to prevent further thefts. There are stories of people stealing bricks and roofs at construction sites and using the material to build shacks, which have begun proliferating across the township.

In February President Botha suffers a stroke and is replaced as leader of the ruling National Party by F. W. de Klerk. Few blacks consider the change in leadership significant, particularly after de Klerk rules out black majority rule even as he promises to continue the reforms begun by Botha.

During the same month an earthshaking event occurs among the black leadership. Winnie Mandela, wife of the legendary Nelson Mandela and a revered leader in her own right, is denounced by the United Democratic Front. I read the story in the paper. Winnie, who is very popular with Comrades in Alexandra, is accused of having abused the trust of the nation's black community. She and her "bodyguards," called the Mandela United Football Club, are implicated in the death of a youth named Stompie Sepei. Most people don't believe the story, myself among them, mainly because to us Winnie is the single most powerful voice of the black liberation struggle. We call her Mother of the

Nation. She's earned that title because of her defiance over the years in the face of relentless persecution including banishment to a bleak black township in Brandfort in the Orange Free State.

"Are the charges against Winnie really true?" I ask George.

"I'm afraid they are true," George says.

"I don't believe it," I say, shaking my head. "The police must have framed her."

"I thought so too, until I heard from friends who live in Soweto about her reign of terror."

"What reign of terror?"

"The so-called Mandela United Football Club was nothing but a bunch of thugs. They terrorized residents with impunity, believing that their connection with the Mandela name put them above the law."

"But how could she terrorize people who revere her?" I ask.

"It baffles me too, especially because she's such a great leader. But I guess even great leaders make mistakes."

Finally Johannes is able to send us money to buy new doors and windows. Two weeks before Christmas of 1989, amid great fanfare, the family's dream comes true and we move into the new house. Priest Mathebula and select members of the church come for a prayer service. They ask the God of Israel to bless the house and bring peace and prosperity to its dwellers.

Mama uses some of her wages to buy a refrigerator on layaway, and Johannes sends us money for a geezer. Angie, Tsepo, and Given can't get enough of the flushing toilet, and Papa has to chastise them about wasting water. And in the morning it feels wonderful to be able to take a hot shower or a bath before going to school, instead of washing in the rusted bathtub. One of the benefits of the move to Twelfth Avenue is not having an open sewer near our house. At night I sleep soundly and I wake up refreshed.

Granny, who is now living with Fikile, Uncle Piet, his wife, and four children, moves into our two-room shack on Sixteenth Avenue, and Florah and Sipho, her new boyfriend, move into Granny's one-room shack on Seventeenth Avenue. Nothing is wasted. Not even shacks.

• • •

Nineteen eighty-nine closes with a historic meeting in Cape Town between de Klerk and Nelson Mandela, who is still in jail. The meeting raises hopes that the legendary ANC member, who went to jail in 1964 for fighting for freedom and democracy, five years before I was born, will soon be freed. People wonder if Mandela's release will bring an end to the violence and to apartheid.

Papa continues to have problems with his cough. He goes to the clinic and to Baragwanath Hospital. At both overcrowded and understaffed places he's told that he's suffering from the remnants of a cold. As for the pain in his leg, they attribute it to old age.

"The bloody doctors don't know a thing about medicine," Papa says. "I may be sixty-nine years old, but I'm not an old man. There's something wrong with me."

Papa then asks for some money so he can go see a local sangoma. The sangoma gives him enemas and some herbs, which seem to help.

Late one night shortly after the family moved to Twelfth Avenue, I'm awakened from a deep sleep by faint noises in the kitchen. The door to the bedroom I share with Maria is slightly open. I peer down the hallway in the inky blackness but see nothing. I think I'm dreaming, but the noises persist. I stare at the fluorescent alarm clock. It's almost 3 A.M. Crawling on all fours, I go to the opposite side of the bedroom, where Maria is sleeping.

"Wake up!" I whisper, shaking her.

"What's the matter?" she asks drowsily.

"I think there's someone in the house."

"Where?"

"In the kitchen."

Maria listens.

"I don't hear anything," she says.

"I tell you I heard noises," I say.

"It must be your imagination," Maria says. "I bolted the door before we went to sleep."

With that Maria goes back to sleep. I crawl back to my bed and also go to sleep. I'm the first to get up at dawn to get Angie and Given ready for school. When I walk into the kitchen a shocking scene awaits me. I find the cabinets flung open and empty. Everything inside—pots, pans, groceries—is gone. In the living room the scene is the same. The clock is gone, along with the dining room table Mama had purchased with borrowed money after George wiped her savings account clean.

Mama gets back from work. "I'm relieved no one was hurt," she says.

Johannes sends us money to buy burglar-proof bars, which Papa installs.

Sibusiso is sick again. I stay away from school for a couple of days to nurse him back to health. On the morning of February 2, 1990, while giving him a dose of medicine in the living room, I'm startled by a speech on TV. Bald-headed president F. W. de Klerk is at a podium in the large chamber of the Parliament in Cape Town, addressing a stunned audience. Speaking slowly and deliberately, with a thick Afrikaans accent, he announces the lifting of the ban on the ANC, the PAC (Pan African Congress), and the SACP (South African Communist Party). Thirty-three other organizations that had fought against apartheid—including the UDF, COSAS (Congress of South African Students), and AZAPO (Azanian People's Organization), all three of which are active in Alexandra—are also legalized. I catch my breath when I hear President de Klerk announce that his government has decided to release Nelson Mandela unconditionally.

Shortly after the speech, I hear noises outside. The street is clogged with honking cars. Young men are dancing the toyi-toyi and women in the yards are ululating and dogs are barking at everyone in celebration of the momentous news.

Florah calls from work to say that people are celebrating there too. Johannes calls from America where he and the family are also celebrating. On the SABC news that afternoon Archbishop Tutu says that the announcement took his breath away, and leaders of the opposition praise de Klerk's courage. De Klerk is praised by world leaders, including American president George Bush and British prime minister Margaret Thatcher.

But a lot of whites are shell-shocked. Leaders of the neo-Nazi AWB

(Afrikaner Resistance Movement) are enraged. They call de Klerk a traitor and vow to fight to the bitter end to preserve white power.

For days after de Klerk's stunning announcement, people speculate that the end of apartheid is close at hand. At school there's talk that we'll soon have integrated schools, and even one person, one vote. Students who'd participated in Mzabalazo feel vindicated. Even my parents welcome the news.

"Child," Mama says, "I never thought I'd live to see the day when Nelson Mandela would be a free man."

Mama goes on to relate that she was nursing Florah when Mandela was sentenced to life imprisonment on Robben Island in 1964. She didn't understand much about politics at the time, but she knew that Mandela was a brave man and that he must have been fighting for something important to have earned the wrath of the government.

Nine days after de Klerk's speech to Parliament, the entire extended family is gathered in the living room. All eyes are glued to the TV. The day before, de Klerk had told the nation and the world that he'd be releasing Mandela the next day, February 11.

"I can't believe it's happening," Aunt Bushy says as we watch the thousands of black and white spectators gathered outside the gates of Victor Verster prison in Cape Town. There are thousands of journalists from all over the world recording the historic occasion. It is summer in South Africa, and the day is warm and sunny.

"It is happening," Florah says with bated breath. "De Klerk is serious. It's a new day in South Africa."

Uncle Cheeks says, "I grew up idolizing Mandela. I remember after he formed MK (Umkhonto we Sizwe) and went underground they called him the Black Pimpernel because the police couldn't catch him. I even considered joining MK because of him."

"How was he caught?" I ask.

"He was betrayed by an impimpi," Uncle Cheeks says. "But the man couldn't be broken. That's a true leader for you."

"We were never taught about Mandela at school," I say. "I didn't start hearing his name until Mzabalazo."

"There's a reason why," Uncle Cheeks says. "Bantu Education didn't want you to know about the people's true leaders."

"If you'd asked me I'd have told you about Mandela," Papa says. My siblings and I look at him in surprise.

"Did you know him?" George asks.

"Yes. He used to live in Alexandra. On Seventh Avenue."

"Right across from the street where my husband has a store," says Aunt Bushy.

"And I marched with him," Papa says.

"You did?" Florah asks.

"Yes. During the bus boycott of nineteen forty-three."

I'm surprised by how many of the older generation have vivid memories of Mandela. Even Granny remembers him. I realize that even though he was sent to Robben Island five years before I was born, his memory couldn't be erased from the minds of the people. I wonder what he'll look like at seventy-one years of age. I've never seen a photograph of him because the government has forbidden any from being published.

Finally, shortly before 4 P.M., a motorcade fills the screen and makes its way toward the prison gate.

"Mandela and Winnie are in the lead car," one commentator says.

Just before the gate the motorcade stops. Winnie Mandela emerges followed by a tall and gray-haired man with a regal bearing, who is wearing a business suit and tie. The two begin walking toward the cheering and screaming throng gathered outside the gate.

"That's Mandela," Uncle Cheeks cries.

When the tall, gray-haired man thrusts his right fist in the air in the amandla salute, I know it's him. People yell and scream and cry and hug. Granny dances a jig in celebration. "He's free at last! He's free at last!" she cries.

Chapter 48

"The news is that Mandela is coming to Alexandra."

For almost a week people talk about nothing else. I hear stories about Mandela's years in Alexandra everywhere I go. We are very proud that our much-maligned township was once home to so great a leader.

I can't believe that I'll finally be able to catch a glimpse of the legend. The day of his visit Maria and I join hundreds of thousands of people thronging the Alexandra stadium. We try to jostle our way to the stage, but it's impossible. We only catch a glimpse of him from afar, but his rich, resonant voice is carried by loudspeakers.

Mandela's release brings renewed optimism about the future. In speech after speech he sounds a conciliatory note. He reassures whites that they have a role to play in South Africa's future. He reaches out to the ANC's bitterest rival, the Inkatha Freedom Party, which is led by Chief Mangosuthu Gatsha Buthelezi. Buthelezi had once been a stalwart ANC member. He fell out of favor with the more radical elements within the organization when he opposed the 1976 uprising, the armed struggle, and the use of sanctions to pressure Pretoria to end apartheid. In Alexandra most residents, who are ANC supporters, hate Inkatha followers.

The overture to Inkatha is seen as the last hope to heal the Alexandra community by ending the bloodletting between Comrades and Inkatha followers. But not many Comrades want peace; they want Inkatha driven out of the township. But they respect Mandela and go along.

The hope for peace infects students. I do very well in midterm exams and look forward to finals at the end of the year. I'm confident I'll pass and be promoted to Standard Nine. Johannes writes and tells me that if I complete matric, he'll arrange for me to come to America to study nursing. I'm beside myself with joy; finally I have a specific goal to achieve.

As has happened so often in the past, violence erupts to spoil everything. The euphoria that attended Mandela's release proves short-lived. Every day I hear on the news reports of clashes between ANC supporters and the police, and ANC supporters and Inkatha members, particularly in Natal. Even after the state of emergency is lifted on June 10, the violence continues.

In Alexandra the long-simmering tensions between residents, most of whom are ANC supporters, and hostel dwellers, most of whom support Inkatha, lead to the most serious bloodletting since Mzabalazo. Residents demand that the hostels be demolished, but the authorities refuse.

Schools are again closed as pitched battles are fought in the streets between ANC and Inkatha supporters. I spend the days locked inside the house because bands of Zulu warriors—*impis*—armed with spears, machetes, knobkerries, and AK-47s, roam the street at will, hunting down and killing ANC supporters. Again there are rumors that they are doing so with the blessing of the security forces, that in several instances the police have been seen escorting impis on their rampage.

One day while sitting in the living room watching TV with Angie, Given, and Mama, I hear screams outside. We run to the window to investigate. Down the street we see a Comrade being chased by an Inkatha member wielding a spear. "Help! Help!" the Comrade screams as he stumbles. The Inkatha member attempts to stab him with the spear but misses as the Comrade rolls to one side. He gets up and continues running.

The Inkatha member continues the pursuit, which takes him farther and farther away from his colleagues, who are chasing other Comrades in the opposite direction. Suddenly, the shacks alongside the street pour out men who've heard the Comrade scream. The men are armed with bricks and knives. One of them hurls a brick at the Inkatha member. It strikes him in the back. He staggers but doesn't fall. Another brick catches him behind the head and knocks him down.

In an instant, the mob from the shacks descends on the Inkatha member like a pack of hungry wolves.

"Bulala i nja!"—kill the dog!—people scream as they stone and stab the Inkatha member. The bleeding Inkatha member, his clothes torn and his face bloodied, manages to crawl toward our house. Just before he reaches the gate I see a bearded man from one of the shacks pick up a huge rock, raise it high in the air, and then bring it crashing down the head of the prone Inkatha member.

I turn my head in horror. I hear Angie and Given, whose faces are glued to the window, laughing. I open my eyes and realize that they're laughing because the skull of the Inkatha member has been crushed open, exposing his brains.

"Go back inside." I shoo them away from the window.

I look at the Inkatha member. He's stone dead.

For days I have nightmares over the grisly sight. But more grisly sights follow. Inkatha retaliates for the killing of their member. During several days of violence they rampage through an entire neighborhood near the clinic. They firebomb houses and kill suspected ANC supporters and families. When the carnage is finally over, the neighborhood has been turned into a wasteland. Dozens are dead, scores wounded, and hundreds displaced. The streets are strewn with the carcasses of burnt vehicles. The houses are eerily silent. It's as if a bomb has been dropped on the area, which people rename Beirut.

Beirut becomes a deadly no-man's-land. A pregnant woman is disemboweled on her way to the clinic. One day Papa tells Mama that he's going to walk through Beirut to the clinic to get a refill of medication for his persistent cough and the pain in his right leg.

"Inkatha will kill you," Mama says.

"They won't," he says. "I'm not a Comrade."

"They don't care."

Papa, ever stubborn, leaves. Several hours pass and he hasn't come back. The family is worried. Finally, toward evening, he returns with his medication.

"I told you they wouldn't touch me," he says.

"You were lucky," Mama says.

"I wasn't lucky," Papa says. "I'm a warrior. No Zulu stripling dare fight a Venda warrior."

A worried Mama goes to Priest Mathebula to report the incident.

"Don't worry, Mrs. Mathabane. Now that your husband is a member of the Twelve Apostles Church of God, he's protected by the Almighty."

"But Inkatha rules Beirut, Priest Mathebula," Mama says.

"God is more powerful than Inkatha, sister," Priest Mathebula says. "And any servant of God who walks through there will be untouched."

A couple of weeks later Papa again decides to tempt fate by walking through Beirut on the way to the clinic. This time he never reaches the clinic.

"What happened?" Mama asks a clearly shaken Papa after he returns home without the medication.

"They grabbed me just as I emerged from the double-up," Papa says. "There were ten or twelve of them. They were armed with machetes, guns, and spears. They asked me what I was doing in their territory. I told them that I was on my way to the clinic. They didn't believe me. They thought I was a spy."

Mama laughs. I can't help but smile. Papa, who is sitting on the black leather sofa near the TV as he's relating the story of his narrow escape, pulls out a handkerchief and wipes his sweaty brow.

"They marched me to the hostel," Papa continues. "I kept protesting my innocence but they wouldn't listen. They told me that if I didn't tell them the truth they were going to kill me."

"I warned you not to go, Jackson," Mama says, "but you wouldn't listen."

"Stop interrupting Papa, Mama," Florah says. "Let him tell us what happened."

"Once I was inside the hostel, they took me to a room where their *induna*, their chief, was sitting at a table," Papa says. "He was a heavyset man with a fierce-looking face. He had a gun in his hand. He asked why they'd brought me. They said that I was a spy. The induna turns to me and asks, 'Are you a spy?' I vehemently denied that I was a spy. The induna was quiet for a while, then I noticed that he was looking at my right hand. 'Where did you get that watch?' he asked, pointing at the golden watch you brought me from America. I told him that my son in America had given it to me. He asked to see it. I took it off and gave it to him. He again asked if I was a spy. Again I said no. He ordered his men to release me."

"What happened to the watch?" Mama asks.

"I left it with him," Papa says.

"I can't believe that you, a Venda warrior, would let a Zulu stripling take your watch," Mama says facetiously.

"I was unarmed," Papa says. "If I'd had my spear, I'd have resisted. I'd have challenged him to a duel."

We all laugh.

One day Priest Mathebula's wife stops by to see Mama.

"You know, sister, you were right," she says.

"Right about what?"

"About Inkatha."

"What happened?"

"Priest Mathebula was recently mugged by Inkatha."

"Where?"

"On his way to the clinic."

"Is he okay?"

"He's fine," Mrs. Mathebula says with a smile. "He's just three rand poorer. Your husband and mine are the same. They don't like to take advice from women. After you came to see him I told him that you were right to express concern about your husband walking through Beirut. I then asked him to stop walking through Beirut on the way to the clinic as he used to do."

"He too walked through Beirut?"

"Yes. But he rejected my suggestion. He said that women are unduly afraid. He said that no one dare mug a priest of the living God. But Inkatha doesn't care about priests. Just before he reached the clinic, near the big water tower, they stopped him and robbed him of the three rand he had on him to pay for his treatment. I told him he was lucky to escape with his life."

Mama and Priest Mathebula's wife had a good laugh at the expense of their stubborn husbands.

Chapter 49

After being mugged by Inkatha, Papa stops going to the clinic for his medication. But his pain and cough don't go away. He has me write letters to Johannes in America telling him about his medical problems. A month later, Johannes calls and says that he'd like Papa to come with Mama to America so he can be checked by specialists.

Papa immediately responds and says he wants to go, that he'd like to visit America to see his children, whom he misses terribly. In the past Johannes has not existed for Papa. Attending church has definitely changed him. After only a year of attending, he's been made an under-deacon.

Linda, who has helped us in many ways, arranges to accompany Papa to the passport place in order to avoid the runaround Maria and I were given when we applied. Papa gets a passport in less than three weeks. The next day Linda accompanies him to the U.S. Consulate in Johannesburg, where he's issued a visa with no problem.

The day before my parents are to leave for America, Priest Mathebula brings a letter from the church wishing them a pleasant journey.

"Don't stay over there, now," Priest Mathebula says. "The church needs you over here."

"We'll come back," Mama says.

I look at Papa and notice how gaunt he's grown. I wonder what's ailing him. I hope that American doctors will be able to properly diagnose his illness, the way they diagnosed Mama's type-A diabetes after doctors in South Africa's black hospitals failed to.

Linda provides the family with a kombi and a driver to take us to Jan Smuts Airport. Maria, Florah, and I cry when we part from our parents and see them board a British Airways jumbo jet bound for New York via London.

As Christmas 1990 approaches, a fierce battle is raging between ANC supporters and Inkatha supporters. The papers and TV news report massacres just about every week, mostly in KwaZulu-Natal and the East Rand. Mandela is quoted in the press as saying that he believes a "sinister third force" is responsible for much of the violence, which is aimed at derailing black majority rule.

In Alexandra third force death squads are blamed for a massacre of Comrades during a night vigil. Despite the violence, schools stay open and teachers tell us that there will be exams at the end of the year.

I seldom venture from home alone at night. Women are being raped in record numbers.

One night Sabelo invites me and Fikile to a party for one of his friends. I don't want to go, but Fikile, who loves partying, urges me to go. At the party I'm miserable. I hate the loud music, the lewd dancing, and the smell of alcohol. An hour into the party, I ask Sabelo to take me home. Fikile comes along. Just as we are emerging from a double-up on Fifteenth Avenue, six armed men burst out of the shadows of an abandoned building and aim AK-47s at us.

"Move and you're dead," shouts one of the men.

The men grab Fikile and me and start dragging us toward the abandoned building. Sabelo attempts to come to our rescue but one of the men prods him back with the muzzle of the AK-47.

"Please, brothers," Sabelo says. "Let them go."

"Shut up!" one of the men bellows.

Aware that we're about to be raped, I'm shaking like a leaf. Without thinking, I begin muttering a prayer as I'm being dragged toward the abandoned building.

"Jesus Christ! Please help me!"

"Shut up!" my captor screams.

I don't shut up. I continue muttering a prayer. Suddenly Fikile wrenches herself loose from the grip of the man dragging her. A sprinter, she's gone before the men can react. As she's racing down the dimly lighted street, she screams, "Rape! Rape! Rape!"

"Please let her go, brothers," Sabelo pleads. "She's my wife."

"Tell her to shut up!" one of the men says.

"She won't shut up," Sabelo says. "She's possessed. She's a Jesus freak."

I don't know whether it is Fikile's screaming or my uncontrollable prayers or Sabelo's entreaties that convince the men to let me go. I don't even see where they went. They simply disappear back into the shadows.

A couple of weeks later, on a Sunday before exams, I'm at home with Fikile. I'm studying for the big three: English, vernacular, and Afrikaans. If I fail any of them, I fail the entire exam and have to repeat Standard Nine. Fikile is looking after Angie, Given, and Sibusiso. They are in the living room watching TV and I'm at the kitchen table.

Suddenly the door bursts open and in walks Sabelo. He's drunk. It's the first time I've seen him drunk, even though I know he drinks.

"I want you to come with me," he says.

"Where?"

"To a party."

"I'm busy."

"Busy with what?"

"I'm studying. I have exams tomorrow."

"You'll study when we come back."

"What about the kids?" I say. "I'm baby-sitting. Florah and Maria are away."

"Fikile will take care of them."

"She has to leave before it gets dark," I say. "You know how rough the streets are."

Suddenly Sabelo snatches my hand and starts dragging me outside.

"What are you doing?" I protest, trying to wrench loose.

"I said come with me to a party," he says drunkenly.

"I told you I'm studying for exams," I say, "and you know I don't like parties."

Sabelo continues to drag me down the street. I start screaming. People come out of their houses to watch but no one comes to the rescue. People seldom intervene when a man is abusing his wife or girlfriend, for fear of being killed.

Sabelo drags me eight blocks to his friend's place on Fourth Avenue. We find his friend not home. He turns and then drags me in the opposite direction, to the home of another of his friends, on Sixteenth Avenue.

"Why are you doing this?" I ask him.

"Have you been spreading lies about me?"

"What lies?"

"Why did you tell Mrs. Xele that I'm seeing other women?"

Mrs. Xele is the wife of the man Sabelo works for. A very kind, childless woman who adores Sibusiso, Mrs. Xele was the first to warn me that Sabelo might be having an affair. But I refused to believe it, because I didn't think him capable of cheating on me.

"Have you been seeing other women?" I say boldly.

"Of course not," Sabelo replies.

"Then why are you worried?"

Sabelo says nothing. We find his friend home with a woman. The minute Sabelo sees the woman, his face turns pale.

"Why did you bring her here?" Sabelo demands of his friend.

"She was looking for you."

"Is that your little girlfriend?" the woman asks Sabelo sarcastically, pointing at me. She's older than I, about thirty-five, and fancily dressed.

Sabelo doesn't answer. Yet he has "guilty" written all over his face. He knows the woman. I'm convinced it's his girlfriend.

Enraged, I slap him across the face.

"Did you drag me all this way to humiliate me?"

"You fucking bitch," Sabelo says furiously. Before I know it, his right fist smashes into my face. "You take me for granted, I see. I'll teach you a lesson."

I've never been beaten so badly in my life. Sabelo punches and kicks me. I scream and try to run away. I fall down and he stomps on me.

"Stop it, Sabelo," I hear his friend beg him. I can hardly see. Both my eyes are swollen shut.

But Sabelo doesn't stop. Somehow I manage to escape. I run through the maze of shacks, with him in pursuit. Realizing that I can't outrun him, I seek refuge inside a nearby shack, outside of which several women are sitting. I bolt the door.

Sabelo comes and starts banging on the door. "Open up! You fucking bitch! Open up!"

"Go away, you asshole!" I curse him back. "I never want to see your ugly face again."

"Can someone open the damn door?" I hear Sabelo saying to the people sitting outside. "That's my wife in there."

I hear a female voice say, "There's no way to open it from the outside. She's bolted it."

For almost an hour Sabelo keeps banging on the door and shouting for me to come out. I refuse. Finally there's silence. I look about the crowded shack. It's almost midnight.

"He's gone now," I hear the woman say. "You can come out."

I tentatively open the door. Facing me is a tall thin woman and her sister and neighbors.

"Thank you very much," I say.

"My God," the woman exclaims. "Look at your face. Did the bastard do that to you?"

"Yes."

"Where do you live?"

"Twelfth Avenue. But my granny lives about a block from here. I'll go to her place."

"You should report the bloody bastard to the police," the woman says.

"I'll be okay," I say as I head toward the double-up that will take me to the street where Granny lives.

Chapter 50

T*he double-up is between rows of tightly packed shacks. In the* middle flows an open sewer. Just as I round the corner I feel a cold hand grab the back of my dress.

I freeze.

"Don't scream," I hear Sabelo say.

I brace myself for more blows.

"I won't hurt you," he says. "I just want to talk to you."

He leads me to a streetlight. Suddenly he flinches, noticing that my eyes are almost swollen shut from his punches and that I'm bleeding from a cut on my upper lip.

"Oh, my God," he cries. "I didn't mean it. I swear, Miriam. I didn't mean it. You made me mad."

"It's okay," I say, anxious to leave his detestable presence. "Let me go."

"To Twelfth Avenue by yourself at this time of the night?" he says.

"No. To my granny's."

Suddenly a terrified look crosses his long face.

"I'm not going to let you go to your granny's looking like that."

"Let me go, please. I have school tomorrow. I have to take final exams."

"You're crazy. I can't let your granny see you like that. I'll find some ice. Oh, my God! I'm sorry. I'm really sorry."

"It's okay. Just let me go."

"You're starting again," he snaps. "I don't want to hit you. Now let's go find some ice."

Afraid of being hit again, I agree to go with him to his shack. He gets some ice and applies it to my swollen mouth and eyes. All the time he keeps saying he's sorry.

"You know I can't let you go anywhere looking like that," he says. "Wait until the morning. The swelling will be down by then."

"But I have exams," I plead.

"You'll take them."

I refuse to sleep in his bed. Instead I sleep on the sofa, curled up. My body is aching all over from being kicked and I have a splitting headache. He locks the door and pockets the key to prevent me from escaping. I'm awakened at dawn by a loud knocking at the door.

"Open up, Sabelo! Open up!" It's his girlfriend. "I know you have that bitch from Twelfth Avenue in there with you. Open up!"

"Go out and talk to your girlfriend," I say bitterly.

Sabelo hesitates.

"Go out!" I repeat, then burst into tears.

He goes out. He's gone for about five minutes. He comes back.

"I can't let you go to school," he says.

"What!" I cry, standing up, despite my head feeling like lead.

"You heard me," he says. "I can't let you go to school looking like that."

"But I have final exams," I protest. "If I don't take them I'll fail."

"They'll let you take them another time," he says.

"They won't."

"I can't let you go," he says. He grabs the key, locks the door, and leaves. I bang on the door but no one comes to let me out. The shack has no windows. I throw myself on the sofa and start weeping. I know it's all over. I'm going to fail. I'm going to have to repeat Standard Eight. I've wasted an entire year. My hatred of Sabelo knows no bounds. I vow that I'm going to leave him.

Sabelo, knowing that my parents are away in America, keeps me locked up in his shack half the day. At about 1 P.M. he releases me and I go home. When Florah sees my face she asks what happened. I burst into tears. Sobbing, I tell her what happened. She's so furious she goes over to Sabelo and shouts at him, calling him a low-down dog who doesn't deserve a woman like me.

I'm most concerned about Sibusiso. When he asks me what's happened I hide the truth from him. I don't want him to grow up hating his father. I tell myself that even though I hate Sabelo, he should have a normal relationship with his son.

For several days after the beating I can't stop crying. I'm devastated. I feel like killing myself. Having to repeat Standard Eight has thrown a wrench into my dream of matriculating and going to America. I don't know what to tell Johannes when he calls and asks how I did on the final exam. He's expecting me to graduate in a year, and here I am having to repeat Standard Eight. What excuse will I give him for failing? Will he think I'm dumb and change his mind about bringing me to America?

Johannes calls a week after the beating. I'm afraid to come to the phone. Florah answers. I hear her screaming as she listens to Johannes. Then she bursts into tears.

"What's the matter?" Maria and I ask simultaneously.

"Johannes says Papa has cancer," she says, sobbing.

The announcement is like a bolt of lightning. I feel numb. I know one thing about cancer, having done a research paper on the disease. It can kill. Florah talks to Johannes for a while and then hangs up.

"How bad is it?" I ask.

"It started in his prostate and has spread. It's in his leg and lungs. The cough he kept complaining about for months was cancer."

I weep but no tears come out. I'm numb with pain.

"Is he going to live?"

"Johannes says he had an operation yesterday," Florah says. "The doctor removed his prostate and testicles. He says it should help prolong his life some."

• • •

Papa and Mama come back two weeks before Christmas. Papa looks surprisingly healthy. He no longer complains of the pain in his leg, but he has a hard time dealing with the fact that both his testicles have been removed. He also has trouble dealing with hot flushes. But in typical Papa spirit, he wants no pity. He's determined to live the remainder of his life his way. He goes to church every Sunday. He converts the stoep into a spazza and sits in the sun all day selling tomatoes, onions, candy, cooked chicken feet, Popsicles, and cool drinks to passersby and neighborhood children.

He keeps a picture of himself and Johannes prominently displayed in his bedroom. He's proud of telling people that he's flown on an airplane and that he's seen the great America. When asked for his impression of the country, he calls it "boring." There isn't the least indication that he's slowly dying. Johannes had asked him to remain in America for further treatment but he refused, saying that he wanted to return to his house.

I tell Mama that Sabelo beat me and made me fail the final exam. It's one of the few times I've seen Mama angry. She threatens to call the police on Sabelo but I ask her not to.

"Let him be."

"What an evil heart he has," Mama says, "locking you in his shack and making you miss your exams."

"Maybe it was meant to be," I say. "Now I know that he and I don't belong together."

"The year will soon be over, child," Mama says. "Before you know it you'll be in Standard Nine."

"I'm worried that if Johannes hears that I've failed, he'll change his mind and not invite me to come to America to go study nursing."

"You mean he shouldn't be told?"

"Yes."

I'm not the only one in my family who's battered. During the Christmas holidays Maria accompanies her taxi-driving husband to Venda. During an argument over a woman he beats her and breaks her right arm. She vows to leave him, even though she's pregnant with his child.

• • •

I'm full of shame as I register for Standard Eight in January of 1991. Miss Jones is surprised, and when she asks me how I failed I tell her that I was sick during exams. Repeating Standard Eight is the hardest thing I've ever done. Cynthia has passed and gone to Standard Nine. For the first time since we both started Sub-A at Bovet, we're separated. What's most galling is that I'd mastered the material for Standard Eight. I'm confident I could have passed if I'd been allowed to take the exam. But the rules say there's no second chance to take exams; if you fail you have to repeat the same class. So essentially I'll be sitting around for a year in order to take finals. Now I understand why a lot of students who fail don't return to school to repeat. But I'm determined to matriculate.

Violence again disrupts schooling. Alexandra is in a state of war. ANC supporters are killing Inkatha supporters and Inkatha supporters are killing ANC supporters. Death squads, rumored to be operated by the South African police, are blamed for fomenting the violence. Caught in between are the residents of Alexandra, especially students.

During one week in March sixty-one people are killed. Shortly thereafter Vigilantes from the hostels target schools, which they consider breeding grounds for Comrades. One day word reaches our school that Inkatha impis are marching from school to school hacking and shooting students to death. Teachers tell us to go home. I run home and find Maria in a panic. Angie and Given haven't returned. Both of us race toward Bovet. The streets are filled with running and screaming students from other schools. None of them are from Bovet.

When we reach Bovet we see students pouring out of the school yard screaming. We frantically search for Angie and Given. Luckily we spot them heading our way. We grab them and run back home, where we lock the doors.

There is no schooling for a couple of weeks. I stay home glued to the TV. South Africa is a battlefield. There are massacres and revenge killings every day and everywhere. Mandela blames de Klerk, and de Klerk blames Mandela. Evidence mounts that the police and security force death squads are fomenting so-called black-on-black violence, especially between the ANC and Inkatha.

In Alexandra the third force is particularly active. Guns are everywhere and people don't know where they're coming from. The third force is implicated in massacres of mourners, Comrades, and ANC activists. Necklacings become routine as Comrades retaliate. There are rumors of police spies everywhere. Phineas, Gertrude's boyfriend, is accused of being an impimpi and is necklaced.

Once more I lean on my faith in God. I read the Bible several times a day. I pray for the violence to abate and schools to reopen. I want to matriculate. I want to go to America and be away from all the violence.

There is no end in sight to the violence. But schools do reopen. At the end of the year I sit for exams. Miraculously, I pass. Christmas comes but there is little celebration across the country. We mark another "black Christmas." Thousands have died and the killings go on.

One of the few bright spots is that the government, the ANC, and over a dozen other groups have hammered out a historic document known as CODESA, the Convention for a Democratic South Africa. The document commits all groups involved to "bring about an undivided South Africa with one nation sharing a common citizenship, patriotism and loyalty, pursuing amidst our diversity freedom, equality and security for all, irrespective of race, color, sex or creed; a country free from apartheid or any other form of discrimination or domination."

Chapter 51

In February of 1992 Florah and Angie go to America. Johannes and Gail have just published a book called *Love in Black and White.* They have two little children, Bianca Ellen, named after Granny, and Nathan Philip, named after Gail's grandpa. They want Florah to take care of Bianca and Nathan while they go on a nationwide promotion tour. Linah and Diana are off to boarding school, and George is off to college.

As I read the letters from America, I can't believe how much the environment in America has benefited my siblings. Many of their peers in Alexandra are dropouts, drunkards, victims of abuse, killers, or dead. On the other hand Linah and Diana are highly accomplished. Now both speak better English than some of my teachers in Standard Ten, yet they left barely able to speak the language. Though they'd never played tennis or basketball before coming to America, they are now stars on their high school tennis and basketball teams. And each has won a prestigious scholarship. Diana is headed for Westtown School in Pennsylvania, and Linah for St. Mark's School in Massachusetts, and George has a full academic scholarship to Guilford College in North Carolina.

They send me brochures of their schools and some of the textbooks they're using. The textbooks are far superior to my own. I can't believe the courses they'll be taking: literature, foreign languages, calculus, world history. They write essays, do research papers, and are taught to think for themselves. (On the other hand, Bantu Education emphasizes memorization.) Whenever I speak to them on the phone I feel somehow inferior because of my broken English. I also feel envious. I wish I hadn't been pregnant and had gone to America with them.

But I do not wallow in my unhappiness. Their success fuels my determination to matriculate so I can join them in America. Johannes's offer still stands, even after Mama told him that I had had to repeat Standard Eight because of Sabelo. Another reason I want badly to go to America is to be away from Sabelo. I know I can never be free from him while I live in South Africa. Because he's a man and able to intimidate me, I know he'll always force me to remain in the relationship, when I've already made up my mind to end it but I'm afraid to tell him. And if the examples of my friends are any indication, I know that if I stay in the relationship I'll end up having one child after another and will eventually be forced to abandon my dream of becoming a nurse.

I live only for that dream. I know that if I have a career of my own, I won't be dependent on any man. I'll be able to provide for Sibusiso, who is now five years old. I'm concerned about the effects on him of growing up in a world full of violence and abuse. I've gone to great lengths to shield him from the worst aspects of ghetto life. He is very sensitive and cries easily. He is not as hardened as many of the children I see around me. Some as young as ten carry guns and kill without remorse. Others grow up without any respect for women. They beat them, they rape them, they kill them, all mainly because the world in which they live teaches them these bad things.

I want my son to grow up differently. Maybe if I make it to America he will.

Florah returns from America without Angie. She finds us having taken in her husband's entire family—his mother and her five children—after they had to flee their house because of Inkatha attacks. There are now almost twenty people living in a house meant for no more than five people. The overcrowdedness creates strains. Papa, who is very orderly and likes his privacy, can't cope with the chaos.

"They've been here too long," he says to Mama. "Can't they find a place of their own?"

"There are no empty shacks in Alexandra," Mama says. "People who were driven out of their homes are still living in shelters."

The shelters Mama is referring to are overcrowded beyond belief. In one church building there are over a hundred families. And a new problem has arisen. Waves of Mozambican refugees, fleeing poverty in their homeland and seeing the new South Africa as a paradise, have begun streaming into the ghetto. Shacks are mushrooming everywhere. When we moved to Twelfth Avenue a little over two years ago, the yard across from us was an open field where Angie, Given, Tsepo, and their friends often played. Now the open field is covered with shacks. Our dream house now overlooks a row of portable toilets. And in front of our house is an open sewer because the portable toilets overflow and residents of the shacks dump dirty water in the street.

Sipho's family leaves and moves into Florah's one-room shack on Seventeenth Avenue. That creates strains in Florah's marriage. She complains of the awkwardness of having to sleep in the same room as her mother-in-law. But there's nothing she can do. In less than five years the population of the one-square-mile ghetto has mushroomed from a little over two hundred thousand to over four hundred thousand. Unemployment is still over 50 percent. Crime has risen. Guns keep pouring in, along with all sorts of drugs: cocaine, heroin, Mandrax, and crack. With the abolition of the Alexandra Town Council and the Peri-Urban Police, there is no law and order. The violence continues. I try my best to concentrate on my studies, mindful that my dream of going to university in America hinges on my matriculating. Several friends and I form a study group. We spend three to four hours after school quizzing one another. Miss Jones gives us copies of previous matric exams and we go through those. Whenever we don't understand something we ask one of the teachers, who are ever eager to help.

"I wish more students were doing what you're doing," Miss Jones says one day. "Then they'd increase their chances of matriculating."

Many students simply don't want to sacrifice time for playing and partying to study, especially on Fridays. Whenever they see my friends and me returning from school late, they crack jokes about our being bookworms.

Along with belonging to the study group, I read all the books Linah and Diana have sent me from America. I watch the news regularly. I do everything to insure that I'm prepared for the toughest exam of my life, which will not take into account the fact that my years at Alexandra High have been beset by one problem after another. Those who design matric exams don't care that I've had to deal with frequent school boycotts and teachers' strikes. They don't care that the Pass One, Pass All demand by Comrades during Mzabalazo promoted me to Standard Seven when I hadn't yet mastered Standard Six material. They don't care that there's drug abuse in the schools and a shortage of teaching materials. And they certainly don't care that I'm stressed out from caring for a son, dealing with an abusive boyfriend, and doing chores at home.

In the back of my mind I have the nagging feeling that I'll fail. I'm well aware of last year's disastrous matriculation results. Only 36.4 percent of black students nationwide who took the exam passed. This compared to 97 percent for whites, 95 percent for Indians, and 79 percent for Coloreds.

There are rumors that the matric results this year will be worse than last year's. During the first week of January 1993, as the country eagerly awaits publication of the results, I'm a nervous wreck. I can't eat or sleep. I have a strange foreboding that I've failed.

"Don't be so hard on yourself," Florah says. "Wait until the results are published."

"I know I failed."

"You're such a pessimist. You did your best, didn't you?"

"But it may not have been enough."

One afternoon Sarah, George's former girlfriend, who is now working, comes to our home all excited.

"Have you seen a copy of today's *Star*?"

"No. I haven't been buying the newspaper lately. I'm scared of what I'll find inside."

"You fool," Sarah says. "So you don't know that you're among the few students from Alexandra High who passed."

I'm struck dumb. "Don't joke about such things, Sarah," I say.

"Why do you think I'm joking?"

"How could I have passed?"

"Because you worked hard, that's how. I read the results twice. No mistake. Your name was among those who passed. I was so happy I started dancing in the street. People thought I was crazy."

I read the results in the *Star.* Not only did I pass but all my study partners—Petronella, Joyce, Julia, Simon, and Ophelia—have passed. As I scan the list I'm struck by the fact that all the smart students who thought they didn't need to study failed. On the other hand, those of us who are average students and studied had passed.

Strangely enough, I don't feel any elation at having passed. I feel only a sense of relief. I let out a deep sigh, in part because I'm still in shock. I can't believe that I've made it, after all I've been through, all I've suffered. The miracle finally sinks in when people start coming up to me full of congratulations. Mama is besides herself with joy.

"I told you you'd make it, child," she says. "God never abandons his children in times of need."

Mama is right. I made it against all odds because God didn't abandon me in my time of need.

Johannes calls from America.

"How did the exams go?"

"I passed."

Johannes screams with joy. "Are you ready to come to America?" he asks. "And I want you to bring Sibusiso with you."

My heart is thumping in my throat. I can't believe my ears. Tears come to my eyes.

"Thank you very much," I say. "When will I be coming over?"

"This spring. I'm planning to write a book about Mama, Granny, and Florah. Gail will be coming over to interview them for me."

"She'll be coming over?"

"*Ja.* She wants badly to come because she's never visited South Africa."

While waiting for word about Gail's arrival, I make preparations to enroll Sibusiso at Bovet. As I was seventeen years ago, he is apprehensive.

He doesn't want to leave my presence, but I do my best to reassure him. I tell him about the importance of an education. I buy him a brand-new uniform, including a tie, shoes, and socks. I trim his fingernails and comb his hair. I give him lunch money.

For the first couple of weeks he is thrilled about school, especially because he is classmates with Maria's Tsepo. He loves hebelungu. He loves his mistress, who says that he's a very smart student. And he always rushes home to show me the *right* on his slate.

"I'm very proud of you," I tell him.

One day something happens to jar me. He comes home crying.

"What happened?" I ask.

For a while he's unable to say anything. Finally he manages to stammer, "The mistress beat me."

Suddenly memories of my own traumatic experiences in Sub-A come flooding back. I feel like crying. I give him a hug and ask, "Where did the mistress beat you?"

"Here," he says, pointing to his tiny hand.

"Why did she beat you?"

"She says I was naughty."

"Were you naughty?"

Sibusiso doesn't say anything. He simply looks down.

"If you are naughty the mistress will beat you from time to time."

"Why?" Sibusiso asks. "You've never beaten me for being naughty. You always talk to me."

"School is different. The mistress will beat you if you are naughty."

"Why?"

"Because she wants you to learn," is the only reply I can give to this question, even when I know that beating doesn't always result in learning. I remember how Fikile was transformed from a brilliant pupil to a delinquent because she was constantly whipped. I also remember how terrified I became of school because of a fear of being whipped.

"Do they beat schoolchildren in America, Mama?" Sibusiso surprises me by asking. I've already told him that there's a possibility he'll be attending school in America.

"No, my child," I say. "Your aunts Linah and Diana say they were never beaten at any of the schools they attended."

Chapter 52

I *can't believe Gail is on her way to South Africa. Johannes called* to say she'll be arriving the morning of April 6 from New York City and we should be at Jan Smuts Airport to meet her. Because of all the violence, she'll be staying at an apartment complex in Rosebank.

"We should do everything to protect her during her visit," Mama says. "And one thing she shouldn't be allowed to do is to drive around alone."

"Especially in Alexandra," I say.

"What about staying alone at the apartment?" Florah asks. "Wouldn't it be a good idea for one or a couple of us to stay with her?"

"Let's ask her tomorrow when we meet her at the airport."

The next morning Linda's kombi, which is to take Florah, Fikile, Mama, and me to Jan Smuts Airport, is delayed because it has to make several stops around the township picking up the elderly for their meal. We arrive at Jan Smuts forty-five minutes late. There is no Gail. Everyone is in a panic.

"Where could she be?" Mama asks.

"I hope she didn't try taking a kombi to Alexandra by herself," Fikile says apprehensively.

Mama and I have horrified looks on our faces. "She wouldn't do such a thing," I say.

"You don't know Gail, Mama," Florah says. "I spent time with her in America. She's a very independent woman. She used to be a journalist and isn't afraid to go to dangerous places alone."

"I hope she didn't get into the wrong taxi," I say as we are racing back to Alexandra.

There is a deadly war raging between taxi owners loyal to Inkatha and those loyal to the ANC. People are killed for boarding the wrong taxi. Besides, Gail is white. And since the violence escalated, there is now an ominous slogan among the Comrades: "One Settler, One Bullet." The slogan is born partly out of the frustrated feelings that all whites are complicit in apartheid and that many support the government's crackdown. Comrades therefore regard as heroes any one of their members who kills a settler, a white person. As a result few whites dare set foot in Alexandra or any other ghetto.

"She shouldn't have come here at this time," Florah says.

"Don't worry," Mama says. "She'll be fine."

"What if she's been kidnapped?" Fikile says. "What if she's dead?"

"Don't say such things," Mama says.

Mama leads us in a prayer for Gail's safety. When we arrive home Maria tells us that Gail just called. She's fine. She waited for us at the airport, but when we didn't show up on time, she hailed a taxi driven by a black man and headed for the apartment complex where she is staying in Rosebank.

"She's very brave," I say, impressed. "Her first day in South Africa and she's not afraid to ride in a taxi driven by a black man."

"I agree," Florah says. "Few white people would do that."

"She's foolish, that's all," Papa says. "She could have been killed. I want you to take good care of her while she's here, you hear?"

I'm surprised by Papa's concern for Gail. Mama tells me that it's because Gail always fussed over Papa during his visit to America, especially when he was recovering from the operation to remove his cancerous prostate.

Florah calls Gail. She's all excited about visiting South Africa for the first time and is eager to see all of us and to give us the boxes of old clothes and presents she's brought over. But Mama says we should let her rest first from the long flight. Gail agrees when Florah asks if she should come and spend the night with her.

The next day Fikile, Granny, Mama, and I board a kombi to Rosebank. Before we leave Papa reminds us to ask Gail for money.

I'm very impressed with Gail. She is tall, athletic, confident, and very warm. She's not in the least self-conscious around black people. She hugs and kisses us with ease. She talks funny but I can understand a great deal of what she says. She's very inquisitive, and her first impressions of South Africa are revealing. She recounts them as we are bustling about the kitchen preparing lunch before she starts interviewing Granny, Mama, and Florah for the new book Johannes is writing, called *African Women: Three Generations.*

"I'm amazed by how many black people are constantly cleaning things and wearing uniforms," she says. "This morning when I went to the grocery store there were at least three black employees per aisle, one sweeping, one mopping, and one stocking food."

"Black labor is cheap and unemployment is very high," Florah says. "Whites can afford to hire as many servants as they want."

"And yesterday, shortly after I arrived," Gail says, "I went for a walk around the Rosebank mall. I was hungry and thought of stopping by a restaurant for a bite. The two restaurants I went into had no blacks dining. Only whites. The blacks were standing all around in uniforms, waiting to be called upon. So I went instead to the grocery store and bought several things to cook."

"There's no more apartheid in restaurants," Florah says, "but a lot of blacks can't afford to eat there because they earn so little."

"I've never dined in a restaurant in my life," I say.

The conversation about South Africa continues through lunch, at the end of which Mama asks Gail if she'd like to go to church with her in Tembisa on Easter Sunday.

"I don't think it'll be a good idea, Mama," I say, mindful of what Johannes has said about keeping Gail out of the townships as much as possible, until the violence subsides.

"Can you come to our church in Alexandra, then?" Mama asks.

"As soon as the situation calms down," Gail says.

After lunch Gail conducts the interviews with Granny and Mama, and I translate for her. She tapes the interviews, in which they speak in Shangaan. They keep laughing heartily as they relate events in their hard lives, and Gail expresses frustration that she knows only a few words of Shangaan. Already fluent in German and Russian, she promises to learn Shangaan so she can communicate with us. I find this very revealing, because few whites bother to learn any of the black languages.

I spend a lot of time with Gail at the apartment complex in Rosebank, helping translate as she interviews Granny and Mama about their lives. When Florah is present she translates and I simply listen. One day the conversation turns to Fikile. Mama and Granny are worried about her future. She's now twenty-one and has no job. She dropped out of Standard Eight and has begun drinking. Mama and Granny are afraid street life will ruin her.

"Why doesn't she go to secretarial school like Florah did?" Gail asks.

Florah thinks it's a good idea but Mama and Granny don't.

"She's been bewitched," Granny says. "She needs to be taken out of the country. I'm told there are no witches in America."

Florah translates. I can tell that Gail is amazed to meet people who believe in witches. But she's sensitive enough not to burst out laughing as some white people do.

"Johannes and I are a bit overwhelmed at the moment," Gail says. "We are currently supporting three of the Mathabane children in America, and we send monthly allowances to the family here in South Africa. On top of that we have two children of our own."

"I understand," Mama says.

"But I'll talk to Johannes about it."

On the way home, Mama says, "Gail is a very special human being."

"Why do you say that?" Florah asks.

"She's so understanding and caring. Ever since she married your brother she hasn't had him to herself. She's gone along with Johannes helping the family. Johannes is doing what is expected of him because he's the oldest child. He is supposed to take care of his family. But Gail is from a different culture. When she married your brother she expected to live alone with him and their children. She didn't expect to be taking care of an entire family. It's unfair. It hurts me to think of it. That's why I pray every day for God to bless her."

"I don't think you should have brought up the issue of Fikile, Mama," Florah says.

"Aunt Bushy and Granny begged me to," Mama says. "They're concerned about Fikile."

As I'm listening to all this talk, I'm thinking, Is it fair for me to further burden Gail by going to America with Sibusiso? When will she ever have a life of her own?

Gail and the extended family are at the Johannesburg zoo. It's a beautiful sunny day with blue skies. As we walk about to various cages containing gorillas, zebras, giraffes, buffaloes, crocodiles, and lions, people continually stare at us. They must be wondering what in the world a white woman is doing in the company of eighteen Africans. There's Mama, Granny, Florah, Aunt Bushy and her two daughters, Fikile and Nkensani, Uncle Piet, his wife and their two children, Florah and Angie, Maria and her three children, and Sibusiso and myself.

Everyone is colorfully dressed in their Sunday best. Several people have sweaters on despite the warm weather.

Gail buys everyone ice cream. Florah, who as we've been walking around has had her arm linked with Gail's, proudly informs the black ice cream vendor that Gail is her *skwiza,* her sister-in-law.

The ice cream vendor smiles and shakes Gail's hand. "If you're their skwiza you have nothing to fear. The PAC won't necklace you."

It's been nearly a week since Gail arrived in South Africa and she has yet to visit Alexandra. The situation in the township is very tense. There have been clashes between Comrades and Vigilantes, and several people have been killed. All over South Africa the situation is tense as the bloodletting continues. This despite calls for peace by Mandela, de Klerk, and Buthelezi.

• • •

One morning Aunt Bushy stops by and asks if I can accompany her to Gail's apartment complex.

"Shouldn't we wait to go with everybody this afternoon?" I ask.

"I want to talk to her without everyone being there," Aunt Bushy says.

We find Gail has rented a car. It's an old beat-up Volkswagen, one of the few inexpensive cars she could find to rent because insurance is so high due to carjackings. Gail tells us she felt strange driving such a car through the rich white northern suburbs, where many a home has four-car garages and the road is littered with BMWs, Rolls-Royces, Alfa Romeos, Lamborghinis, and other expensive cars.

"White people here live much better than most white people in America," she says.

"It's because of apartheid," Aunt Bushy says. "I've been working since nineteen seventy-two serving tea to white people. You know how much they pay me?"

"How much?"

"One hundred and fifty rand a month."

"A hundred and fifty rand a month?" Gail exclaims.

"Yes. That's not enough to live on. And I have no benefits."

The conversation soon turns to Fikile.

"I want her to have a different life," Aunt Bushy says. "That's why I came to beg you to take her with you to America. I'm afraid if she stays here she'll die."

"What do you mean?"

"She's a naughty girl," Aunt Bushy says. "She sleeps around a lot. I'm afraid she'll get AIDS or end up being killed over men. Can you please take her with you?"

I notice the tears welling in Gail's eyes.

"Another reason I want her to go is because I'm afraid she's starting to have a bad influence on Nkensani," Aunt Bushy says. "Nkensani likes school. She's a very good student. But she sees what her older sister is doing."

"I'll talk to Johannes about her," Gail says.

"Thank you very, very much," Aunt Bushy says. "And I'm sorry to burden you and Johannes with my problems. It's just that I don't know what else to do as a mother. I've tried beating her up but it hasn't worked. I think she's been bewitched. I'm confident that if she goes to America she'll change. She's a very smart girl."

Chapter 53

I'm torn. I don't know if it's right for the family to burden Gail and Johannes with our problems. Is it selfish of me to want to go to America with Sibusiso, given the fact that Gail and Johannes already have enough problems and responsibilities on their hands? And will I like America? How well will I do in American schools? Now that I've matriculated, shouldn't I stay and get a job and provide for my son?

These questions torment me each time I'm with Gail and I hear family members asking her for this and for that. Everyone wants something from Gail. Papa wants money from her, and he's mad that she hasn't given him any. Maria wants Gail to take Given with her to America because she's afraid that at eleven years of age Given has begun to fall in with the wrong crowd, boys who steal, smoke, drink, and kill. Florah wants Gail to take Angie with her because she's afraid that at twelve years of age Angie will be sexually abused or become pregnant. Uncle Piet also wants Gail to take one of his children with her to America.

Gail is anxious to visit Alexandra so she can see what is making everyone want to leave.

"Are things really that bad?" she asks Florah one evening after dinner.

"They are horrible," Florah says. "Worse than when Johannes was here."

"Worse than in *Kaffir Boy*?" Gail asks, incredulous.

"You'll see when you visit one of these days."

On April 10 Gail finally visits Alexandra. As we drive through the narrow streets she is overwhelmed by the number of shacks and by the extent of the poverty, the filth, and the overcrowdedness. It being a Saturday, the streets are teeming with people.

"How many people live here?" she asks.

"The exact number isn't known," Florah says. "Some people say it's now close to a million."

"In one square mile?"

"Yes. You should see where the Mozambicans live," Florah says. "It's nothing but a sea of shacks."

We drive along the Jukskei River, whose banks are plastered with shacks, many of them leaning precariously over the bluff as if about to tumble into the dirty, stinking water.

People stare at us as we drive. But Gail is safe with us because we live in the ghetto and people know us.

We arrive at Twelfth Avenue. As Gail climbs out of the car and enters our house, people stand on stoeps and verandas to stare and whisper. I'm glad things have calmed down a bit, because if they hadn't, Gail would be in serious trouble as a white person venturing into the ghetto, whether or not we know her.

The house is crowded with relatives. Papa acts cool toward Gail because she won't give him more money. She's already given him a hundred rand. He also wants Johannes to send him another watch to replace the one he was robbed of by Inkatha Vigilantes.

We spend the afternoon talking and then Gail joins us for a dinner of pap and vleis. As we are eating, we hear noises outside. Florah goes out to investigate and returns with an ashen face.

"Chris Hani has been assassinated," she says, breathless.

There's a collective gasp from everyone. We turn on the TV. It is true.

Chris Hani, the secretary general of the South African Communist Party and the most popular black leader after Nelson Mandela, was gunned down by a white neo-Nazi in front of his teenage daughter, Nomakwezi, as the two were getting out of their car in the driveway of their house in Dawn Park, a predominantly white suburb.

Everyone is in shock and scared. This could mean war. Chris Hani was the idol of the Comrades. And the fact that a white person killed him means that all whites are targets for retaliation. And Gail is in Alexandra, a Chris Hani stronghold.

"We must get her out of here quickly," Mama says.

"How?" Florah asks. "If we got out now and they see her they'll necklace her."

"Let's wait until it's dark," Mama says. "Then we'll smuggle her out."

Several tense hours follow. We lock the door and draw the curtains. People speak in low tones. From time to time someone goes outside to gauge the mood in the streets. It's very tense. Black people are very angry; they are clamoring for revenge. There are cries of "One Settler, One Bullet." There are reports that in other townships vehicles driven by whites have been stoned and burned. In Cape Town several people have been killed. Whites are said to be fleeing the country in droves, and those that remain have armed themselves to the teeth.

Mandela goes on TV and appeals for calm.

"Comrades won't listen to him," Florah says, turning off the TV. "Chris Hani was their leader."

"I wonder what will happen now," Gail says.

"There will be war," Florah says.

"I think I should go back," Gail says. "It's dark enough."

"You can't drive by yourself," Florah says. "Let's wait for Sipho to get here. He'll drive you."

Sipho arrives. We cover Gail with a blanket and smuggle her out of the house. She crouches under the backseat of her beat-up Volkswagen. Sipho drives slowly out of the yard and the car disappears around the corner. The family prays that she makes it safe out of Alexandra.

About an hour later Gail calls to say she arrived at her apartment complex safely. Everyone is relieved. She asks us not to mention the close call to Johannes because he'll be very worried.

In the aftermath of Chris Hani's assassination I spend most of the time at the apartment complex with Gail, helping translate for her. When Florah gets back from work she also helps. All the women in the family are determined to make *African Women: Three Generations* a success because we know that the reason Johannes is able to help all of us is the books he writes.

One morning Gail says, "I spoke to Johannes last night about who we can afford to bring over. At this point we can only afford to bring you and Sibusiso. The total airfare is going to be about five thousand dollars. I'd like to bring Fikile, Angie, Given, everybody. But the truth of the matter is that we can't. In fact, we'll be borrowing the money to pay for your ticket and Sibusiso's."

I'm stunned by this revelation. I thought they had the money. I didn't realize that they planned to go into debt for my sake. I feel somehow selfish. Why am I imposing on people who are doing so much to help everybody?

"I don't want to be a burden to you and Johannes," I say. "You don't have to borrow money to bring me and Sibusiso over. I passed matric and can find a job. And maybe someday when I've saved enough I'll pay my own way."

"No, no," Gail says vehemently. "You deserve the opportunity. We want to help you. You stayed in school despite the odds, unlike the others. Johannes wants you to go to university and become a nurse."

Again Aunt Bushy, Mama, and Granny beg Gail to take Fikile along. Gail, ever understanding and patient, tells everybody that she'll talk to Johannes about it again. She does, but Johannes says there's no money to pay Fikile's airfare at this point.

"But he says I should apply for a passport for her so she can come later," Gail says.

Gail takes me, Sibusiso, and Fikile to the passport office in downtown Johannesburg. I expect all kinds of problems from the Afrikaner woman behind the counter. To my surprise, she's extremely polite. She doesn't demand this and that paper. She gives us the passports without a murmur.

"You know, Gail," I say as we are leaving, "had we come here alone she wouldn't have given us the passports."

"I know," Gail says. "I read Johannes's book about the difficulty of black people getting papers."

The U.S. Consulate issues us visas with no problem.

The violence abates some after Chris Hani is buried and Mandela makes yet another appeal for calm and restraint. Gail visits Alexandra several more times unmolested, in part because she is the guest of Linda Twala, one of the most respected community leaders. One time she visits the Phutadichaba Community Center, where Linda proudly introduces her to the elderly as their *makoti,* daughter-in-law. Gail helps serve meals and it's heartwarming to see her completely embraced as one of our own because she has married Johannes.

On another occasion Gail accompanies us to the Alexandra stadium for a huge celebration organized by Linda to welcome back the exiles. Thousands of people attend. There are revolutionary songs, speeches, and even marching bands. The exiles, many of them former ANC and PAC guerrilla fighters, are dressed in their neat brown military uniforms and black berets. Among the returnees are Comrades who fled during Mzabalazo and students who fled the country during the 1976 student rebellion.

I can hardly believe that in three days my son and I will be leaving for America to start a new life. Gail asks me to begin packing and says that she'll be making arrangements to buy the tickets. I pray that nothing goes wrong at the last minute. Gail calls from her apartment to say she can't get through to the travel agency to book our tickets. Phone lines are jammed. Whites are fleeing the country because Mandela, frustrated by what he calls de Klerk's treachery and racism, has threatened to call for a resumption of the armed struggle by the ANC.

"Does that mean we won't be leaving?" I ask.

"I don't know," Gail says. "I'll drive there tomorrow morning. I only hope that there are still cheap tickets left."

Gail calls to say that she has the tickets. Not only that, but she was able to borrow enough on her credit card to also purchase a ticket for Fikile.

"Ask her to get packed," Gail says.

"She's not home."

"Where is she?"

"She didn't come back last night."

"Do you know where she went to?"

"She could be at her friend's in Soweto or with one of her boyfriends."

"Oh, my God," Gail cries. "What am I going to do with the ticket? It's nonrefundable."

"I'll inform Aunt Bushy," I say. "She might know how to track her down."

Half an hour later Gail calls.

"You won't believe what happened," she says, all excited. "I ran into Fikile."

"Where?"

"In Sandton City, where I'd gone to pick up the tickets. I told her the news. She was so happy she jumped up and down in the middle of the mall and hugged me."

"Where is she?"

"She is on her way home. I told her to get packed and to go to Alexandra High and get her school transcripts. Both of you also need to bring your immunization records along."

The only reason I told Sabelo I'm leaving is that I want him to say good-bye to his son. He asked if he could come with us to the airport.

"I don't think it'll be a good idea. You can come and say good-bye here at home."

"I want to give Sibusiso some money for the journey," he says. "And I can't go to the bank now because it's closed."

"Okay," I say.

The next day Sabelo joins the family on the ride to the airport. As always, Linda generously drives us there in his kombi. Many tears are shed as we say good-bye. Sabelo takes Sibusiso aside and the two talk for some time. Though I know that my relationship with Sabelo is about to end, I know that his relationship with his son is important and should continue.

They announce the boarding of our flight to New York.

Sabelo asks if he can speak to me in private.

"Take care of yourself," he says, "and please write."

I say nothing.

"I know I've been a brute in the past," he says, "but I'm prepared to change."

I feel like telling him off, like reminding him of his girlfriends, including the one who became pregnant by him and had a miscarriage, and the one who just had his baby. But I don't say a thing. It's not worth it. I feel no bitterness. I feel sorry for him. He thought that by raping me he could ruin my life. But he failed. God didn't let him.

Sabelo reaches into his pocket and pulls out a wad of rand.

"I promised I'd give you five hundred rand for Sibusiso," he says, "but I've changed my mind."

I stare at him in amazement. "What made you change your mind?" I ask.

"They told me your brother in America is a very rich man," he says.

For a moment I think he's joking. But no, he's serious. He thinks that Johannes, who had to borrow money to pay for his son to come to America to have a chance at a better future, is a rich man. Then and there I realize that I wasn't wrong in deciding that the two of us had no future together. All I say to him is, "Take care of yourself. And I'll ask Sibusiso to write."

Our plane is now boarding. I pick up my son. Together with Fikile and Gail we make our way to the departure gate. As we are walking, I wonder what awaits me in America. Whatever awaits me, I cannot imagine it to be worse than the hell I'm leaving behind. And whatever it takes, I'm determined to achieve my dream of becoming a nurse. All I ask from America is the opportunity to do so.

About the Author

Mark Mathabane is a best-selling author and lecturer whose book *Kaffir Boy* raised national consciousness about the horrors of apartheid in South Africa. He has been a White House Fellow during the Clinton Administration and continues to write books and articles about education, race relations, social justice, and human rights abuses around the world. He lives in North Carolina with his extended family and welcomes readers to his Web site: mathabane.com.